I0136165

Swords of
ILLUMINATION

DAVID C. OLCOTT

Samurai ☯ *Success*

MVM

Copyright © 2023 David C. Olcott

SWORDS OF ILLUMINATION

All rights reserved. No part of this publication may be reproduced, distributed, or transmitted in any form or by any means, including photocopying, recording, or other electronic or mechanical methods, without the prior written permission of the publisher, except in the case of brief quotations embodied in critical reviews and certain other noncommercial uses permitted by copyright law.

For permission requests, write to the publisher, addressed "Attention: Permissions Coordinator" carol@markvictorhansenlibrary.com

Quantity sales special discounts are available on quantity purchases by corporations, associations, and others. For details, contact the publisher at carol@markvictorhansenlibrary.com

Orders by U.S. trade bookstores and wholesalers. Email: carol@markvictorhansenlibrary.com

Cover Design & Illustrations - J. Collin Phillips
Book Layout - DBree, StoneBear Design

Manufactured and printed in the United States of America distributed globally by markvictorhansenlibrary.com

MVHL

New York | Los Angeles | London | Sydney

ISBN: 979-8-88581-103-3 Hardback
ISBN: 979-8-88581-104-0 Paperback
ISBN: 979-8-88581-105-7 eBook
Library of Congress Control Number: 2023912022

Acknowledgement and Gratitudes

I would like to profoundly thank Paul Lirette for his counsel and friendship over the years, for without it, this book would never have been completed. I would like to thank my beautiful wife, Dr. Lorena Lavarne, for her magnificent demonstration of love. The love she has shown to me, our son Josh, and everyone who has ever encountered her is truly remarkable.

I would like to thank all the authors of the countless books I have read that have moved me with their words and thoughts.

Without their keen insights into people, this world, and the universe, I would have been lost.

And most of all, I want to thank the Angels that have come into my life, who have completely forgotten who they are, so that I could experience who I am. And the Angels that have allowed me to have forgotten who I really am and loved me anyway.

Contents

Prologue		3
Chapter 1	Wrong Turn	8
Chapter 2	Out of Tune	17
Chapter 3	Battle of Hamasuka	24
Chapter 4	Where Wisdom Lies	37
Chapter 5	School of Aspen	57
Chapter 6	Sword of Identity	72
Chapter 7	Sword of Mission and Purpose Part I	87
Chapter 8	Sword of Mission and Purpose Part II	103
Chapter 9	Sword of Roles Part I	121
Chapter 10	Sword of Roles Part II	137
Chapter 11	Sword of Roles Part III	156
Chapter 12	Sword of Outcomes Part I	178
Chapter 13	Sword of Outcomes Part II	194
Chapter 14	Sword of Values Part I	220
Chapter 15	Sword of Values Part II	239
Chapter 16	Sword of Decisions Part I	264
Chapter 17	Sword of Decisions Part II	283
Chapter 18	Sword of Decisions Part III	303
Chapter 19	Right Turn	327
Epilogue		334
About the Author		337

PROLOGUE

I want to take this moment and thank you for choosing to read this book.

There may be many reasons why you have chosen to read this book and all of them are deeply appreciated. One reason that I hope attracted you to Swords of Illumination was curiosity, since that was the overriding motivation for my writing it.

For as far back in my life that I can remember, I have been blessed (or cursed depending on perspective) with an insatiable sense of curiosity. At first, it was an obsession on how things worked. Automobiles, business, wealth. As I got older, my curiosity shifted from how things work to how people worked. I am fascinated about how we interact with each other, but more importantly, I became endlessly curious on how we interact with the universe, both in this physical plane and in the spiritual plane. It stirred in me many intriguing questions. How can we work in concert with the universe to attract and to experience what we desire? How do we play in it? And how come so few of us feel like we are winning in it? How come so many of us feel we are not living our destiny?

In the movies and the books I enjoy, a common theme is the hero's journey. It usually follows a path in which our hero seeks their destiny, as if it is some preordained life, they have no choice but to find and follow. As if there is no action they can do to change it. Chalking it up to the writer's own point of view, I thought this was a concept only for fictional stories.

To my increasing surprise, most of the people I spoke to shared that they actually felt like the heroes in these stories. Not only did they feel like they had no say in their destiny, they woefully felt they would never be able to live up to this destiny. It gave them an overwhelming sense of pain and loss, and ultimately failure.

If truth be told, I also shared this feeling of not living up to my destiny. So I turned my curiosity inward. What had happened and why was I feeling this sense. Was this just a childhood fantasy, was I delusional? Should I just let it go? And so, I did! For years I stopped listening to this feeling and went about life like so many others. Doing the things we seem to think are important: Getting the job, getting the money, getting the spouse, etc. But no matter how hard I tried to stop that feeling, it kept coming back. As a matter of fact, each time it seemed to come back harder, even to say, it was haunting me.

The irony was, it seemed to be my destiny to not let go of this "sense of destiny" and thank goodness I did not, or you would not be reading this book. So forgive me for saying so, but you choosing to have this book in your hand in this very moment and reading it has a "sense of destiny" to it. What will you do with it?

The first thing I let go of was the idea that either we had a pre-ordained destiny OR everything in life was only about our own free will. These conflicting concepts being an either/or proposition seemed out of line from what I experienced. Rather, I saw the world offering up the opportunity to combine the two concepts so we have free will AND destiny. The sitting around and awaiting our destiny was futile. Also, taking action without connecting to one's own sense of self and destiny was equally pointless.

This later point also brought about another discovery. The need for congruency. Have you ever spoken to someone who talks about how fit they want to be while munching on a jelly donut and drinking a large soda. Heck, I have been that person! Living a life that is disconnected with who we say we are results in a heightened and every increasing sense of loss and despair. In seeking out what destiny truly meant, I realized it is unique to every individual. That being the case, destiny is really a byproduct of the most important thing you hold about yourself, your identity.

Creating your destiny means living a life that is congruent to your own designed identity.

And that led to the biggest revelation from my experiences. Simply put, we are not here in this world to discover who we are, but rather to create who we are. Once we create that, the universe lines up to support who we say we are. After this "ah-ha" moment came the obvious question. "Great, but how?"

Through years of research, discovery and self-exploration, I pieced together concepts and teachings shared since ancient times and sequenced them into a methodology that I and others can use to take an active role in manifesting one's destiny.

Swords of Illumination is the culmination of my discoveries. It is about how you can create your experience of any event you will face this lifetime. It is a book about how to get that feeling back of a sense of destiny. It is a book about closing that gap between who you say you are and how you actually are in this world. It is a book about, having not lost that sense of destiny, how to take charge of it and begin living the life you were meant to live!

It is also an invitation to be reintroduced to the Master inside of you that has always been there and has never left your side. It will never leave your side for that is impossible! A Master so powerful that it literally has all the answers to the questions you could ask about finding your destiny and living it!

CHAPTER 1

Wrong Turn

"This is not what I wanted," he sighed. "Where'd it all go so wrong?" It was the 187th time he had repeated these lines since he began driving. The previous 186 times were met with the same response, silence. "This is not what I wanted. Where'd it all go so wrong?"

He had it all planned for as long as he could remember. He knew exactly where he wanted to be, specifically what he wanted to do, and precisely who he wanted to be. None of it happened. "Where'd it all go so wrong?" He lived a life of thunderous desperation. The desperation that arises from knowing your options are limited, your future is determined, and your life remains unfulfilled.

Eight hours ago, Tom Henderson set out in his car, made a left when he knew to go right, and just kept driving. He had no plan for where he was going. His only goal was to get as far away as possible from the point he started. The setting sun told him he was heading west, and the unlit road told him he was off the highway; that was the extent of the knowledge of his route. His path was quickly slipping in darkness speared by the headlights of his Audi—a car registered to him but still owned by the leasing company for the next two years, three months, and seventeen days.

Eight hours earlier, he told his wife he was going to the office. It had been some time since she protested his going in on a Saturday. It was a battle he always won with the refrain, *"You think I want to?"* She finally came to believe the answer was *yes* and let him be. It was the kids that had a harder time understanding. At six and eight, they were just young enough to want their daddy, but slowly creeping into the age of self-reliance that ushers a child's rapid ascent to adulthood.

"Daddy is very important," six-year-old Katie would say to no one in particular. "He has to go to work when no one else does." Tom liked the admiration, however misplaced. The truth was not so heroic. He went in on weekends because he was in constant fear of losing his job. Tom had steadily risen up the ranks at his financial services firm to a position that paid generously but was equally tenuous. His weekend trips to the office were to show the powers that be that he was, indeed, as his daughter said, "important." Important enough not to be cut when the inevitable mid-level management layoffs came.

He could not afford to lose his job and, more importantly, the salary it provided. He had a mortgage, college for the kids, and plans for a 65-year-old retirement. He also had fears. Fear of a market crash costing him his pension, fear about a volatile housing market, and fear about a serious illness of a family member wiping out his bank account. It wasn't like his life was rapidly spiraling out of control. His descent was slow, almost imperceptible. He could not recall a particular moment or event that initiated the plummet to his current state. It just gradually happened.

Tom got his MBA the same year he married Lynn. With a degree from one of the finest business schools in the country, Tom set out to stake his claim in the world. He had seen the toll *just getting by* had taken on his father. It sapped the light out of him and drove him to his grave a year before his only son's wedding. Tom grew up idolizing the man and sought to emulate him. But on the day of his funeral, he silently vowed never to be like him. He thought how the world had beaten his father down, but it would not serve the same fate to him. Tom looked at his life going forward with a tinge of revenge. He would beat the system to avenge what it did to his dad.

Lounging by the pool during their Jamaican honeymoon, he bragged that in fifteen years he'll own his own company, they'll have homes on both coasts, and their biggest problem will be where to go on vacation. Lynn smiled thinking about that future, and that smile motivated him.

He was fortunate enough to get a job right out of graduate school at a very reputable firm. He worked his way up to a valued associate. With each step along the way, he was rewarded with greater compensation. Paradoxically, each step was also met by equally greater financial obligations. The townhouse became a house. Annual trips to Europe became a child, then a second child. The sports car became a college tuition fund.

Slowly, each of the goals he had set out to achieve fell by the wayside. He was still working for someone else. Tom Henderson, Inc. was not even a blip on the horizon. Instead of staking his claim, he felt like a claim had been staked on him. The company owned him, his family owned him, and the bank owned him. There was little percentage left over for Tom to own of himself.

He stopped boasting to Lynn about his grandiose future plans. They both accepted that life was about getting through the next day, month, and year. Their life grew colorless, but they thought it could be worse. He could lose his job, and with it, the lifestyle they had not only grown accustomed to but that they also needed. Tom felt like he was digging a hole in a sandy beach. The larger the hole got, the more sand seeped in from the sides. He had reached a point where he was no longer making the hole any larger; he was just able to shovel enough to maintain its current size.

"I need a bigger shovel," Tom sighed at the breakfast nook.

"What?" Lynn asked as she fixed a button on Katie's coat.

"Never mind. I'll be home by five." Tom kneeled down to give his little Katie a kiss and pluck off her tiny nose. "Daddy has to go but I'll hold onto this to remind me of you."

Pinching her nose, Katie replied like she had before, "Hurry back Daddy. I might have to sneeze!" Then she said something that was never part of the usual repartee. Looking up with those big brown eyes, she said, "When I grow up, I want to be just like you."

It froze him. Staring back at her, he thought of how he thought the same thing about his own father. Tom recognized the same feelings his father must have had when his young son made the same vow. For the first time that day, he thought, *This is not what I wanted. Where'd it all go so wrong?*

Katie's eyes became brighter and brighter. He squinted to keep focus on the face behind it.

Seamlessly and suddenly Katie's eyes morphed into the headlights of a Mac truck, its horn screaming a warning at him. He slammed his brakes and skidded to a sudden stop.

The truck driver's reaction was to swerve into the opposite lane to avoid Tom. The semi roared past the immobile Tom, so close that he could make out the St. Louis Cardinals emblem on the hat that covered her long stringy hair.

Just as suddenly as the terrifying moment happened, it was quickly replaced by dead silence. He would think it was funny how much his hands were shaking if it weren't for the fact he couldn't make them stop. Putting the car into gear, he cautiously moved along—in the correct lane—and searched until he found a clearing.

His escape would have to stop for the night. Pulling off the road, he drove a little way into the wooded area and killed the ignition and lights. Tom remained sitting in catatonic silence; his hands strangling the steering wheel at ten and two.

He was tired, hungry, and scared. He came seconds away from certain death; however, that did not scare him. The questions racing through his mind were what frightened him. Why had he braked instead of swerved? Why didn't he just turn out of the way? Why didn't he see the truck earlier? Why can't he shake that icy feeling deep in the pit of his stomach? The feeling that he wished the truck had hit him.

He never fancied himself a quitter but in the last eight hours, he had essentially run away from home and attempted suicide by proxy. He was exhausted from all the noise inside his head. The incessant self-questioning of his life was deafening, and it had finally taken its toll. Catching a glimpse of himself in the rearview mirror, he stayed focused on the image reflecting back. In his amazement, the face that he saw before him was unrecognizable. Instead of seeing himself, Tom looked at a man miles away from where he wanted to be. He saw a man who was hungry, tired, and scared. He refused to believe that man was him.

"When I grow up, I want to be just like you."

Tom closed his eyes and trembled. The harder he told his body to stop, the more he shook. The trembling became fiercer. He closed his eyes tighter, his eyes stinging from the pressure of his lids. Despite his mental commands to his hands, the shaking continued. He could feel the entire car shaking from the force as the driver's side glass sounded as if it would explode at any second. The creaking of the car also became louder. Tom found the sounds morphing to have a human quality, almost as if the car was asking him if it could help.

"Excuse me, sir, can I help you?" It was the politeness of the sound from his car that startled him into opening his eyes. Tapping gently on the window next to him was a concerned-looking elderly Asian man. "Pardon me sir, but are you alright?"

Tom quickly rolled down the window. "Oh yeah, I'm fine. I was just, I was just catching some Zs. I, um, got tired and thought I'd pull over. You know, before I crash into something."

"A very wise move. It would be a shame if you hurt yourself." His salt-and-pepper hair indicated his old age, but Tom thought there was something in his eyes and reassuring smile that projected a youthful exuberance.

"Oh, I'd never do anything like that," Tom implored a little too loudly. "Well, thanks for your concern. Take care." He quickly closed the window.

"Would you care to join me?" Tom heard through the glass.

"Join you? Join you where?"

"Well, I'm a little tired too, and I thought I'd set up a little campsite just down the hill there."

Speaking louder so he could be heard through the closed window, Tom asked, "Where's your car?"

The man mumbled something Tom could not understand.

"It's where?" Tom asked.

The gentleman made a circular motion with his arm.

"It tumbled down the hill?!" Tom asked in response to the man's motion.

"This conversation might be easier on your vocal cords if you lowered your window," the old intruder yelled.

"Oh, yeah." Tom lowered the window again. "You lost your car?"

"No, I don't have one. Don't really need one."

"Yeah, okay. Well, I'd give you a ride, but I've got a thing about hitchhikers so..."

"Oh, I beg your pardon. I am not asking for anything, nor would I want you to do something you are not comfortable with. I thought you would like some company as you rested. You never know what or who you could run into out here in the middle of the night. Again, I am sorry."

"No problem. No offense taken, I'm just going to hang here for a little while, but thanks for the offer."

With a wave of his hand, the gentleman walked into the wooded area down the hill and out of sight.

Man. And I thought I had problems, Tom mused to himself.

You do have problems, the other side of his brain responded. *You've run away from home, you have no idea where you are, and now your car won't start.*

As Tom was thinking of his plight, he unconsciously began turning the ignition. He was no car expert, but he knew enough to know that the *click, click, click* meant his battery was dead. The reason he leased his Audi was to avoid maintenance, but now, at the worse possible moment, the thing he avoided reared its ugly head.

He removed his AAA card from his wallet and began dialing the number on his cell phone. As he fumbled with the numbers, it occurred to him that he didn't know where to tell them to come. He had long stopped paying attention to the road signs. Maybe the clerk can help him figure it out or trace his cell phone or something. *They can do that*, he tried to reassure himself.

Not if the cell battery is dead too. Among the many things that ran through his mind this day, recharging his cell phone did not make the list. Pulling the car charger out of his glove compartment, he plugged it into the phone and then into the car's USB port. Nothing lit up. He checked the connections. Still nothing. It took another five minutes of fiddling to figure out that it had nothing to do with the charger and everything to do with the fact he was plugged into a vehicle with no power.

Okay, now I'm in trouble, both sides of his brain concurred.

CHAPTER 2

Out of Tune

Tom cautiously eased down the tree-lined hill in the direction of the faint firelight below. He had no idea where he was or what he was doing but thought being lost with someone else was better than being lost alone. *I'll just wait for light and then go... somewhere*, he plotted to himself.

Also, there was something disarming and comforting about the old gentleman that made Tom feel secure in joining the stranger. "I'd hate for you to be out here all alone," Tom greeted the camper. "So, I thought I'd keep you company. You know, for your safety."

"Your kindness is much appreciated. Please come near to get warm. Can I get you something to eat?" The old man offered Tom some strands of thin brown links that he did not quite recognize in the dimly lit night.

"I'm not big on Asian cuisine, but thank you,"declined Tom.

"I get tired of it sometimes too, that's why I enjoy a good beef jerky." The old man took a healthy bite and savored his every chew.

"I'm sorry, I shouldn't have assumed. I'd love to try some," Tom replied sheepishly. The old man handed him the pack and Tom took a small bite followed by a larger and then a larger bite. In his desperate state, he had forgotten how hungry he was, and the artificially enhanced beef juices brought his hunger pangs to the fore.

The two sat together quietly, enjoying their meal, and

staring blankly into the small fire. While Tom's mind raced a thousand miles a minute, he noted that the old man's stare was one of complete calmness and contentment. To get out of the noise in his head, Tom broke the silence. "Nice fire you built. I was a lousy boy scout. Could never do the two sticks rubbing together thing."

"Oh, me neither," replied the old man and he showed him the lighter from his breast pocket.

Silence returned as Tom searched for another conversation topic. "So, do you just wander around the woods or are you heading somewhere particular?"

"I am heading somewhere," replied the old man as he stoked the fire with a long, broken tree branch.

After an unusually long pause, Tom finally asked the obligatory follow-up query. "And where is that?"

"I'll know when I get there."

"Oh boy, another one of those deep philosophical types, huh? All we are is dust in the wind, floating like that feather in *Forrest Gump*. I never did get that one. Come on, you've got to be heading somewhere, everyone is heading somewhere. Even homeless guys head for the shelter."

"Where are you heading?" the old man asked in a calming tone. He seemed to sense the blood pressure rising in Tom.

"Nowhere. I'm not heading anywhere, okay."

"Now, that's very philosophical and deep."

For an extended period, the two sat in silence with the only sounds coming from the crackling fire and rustling leaves. *What does he know about me?* Tom wondered to himself. *I don't need his sarcasm. I am on track to become vice president by forty, my house was just appraised at $850,000, and I drive an Audi A8. Son of a bitch doesn't* *even own a car and he is judging me?* Tom could feel his blood heat up but then immediately cool down by the cold night air blowing through his thin clothing.

Without saying a word, the old man handed Tom a blanket from his pack. Never taking his eyes off the fire, Tom took the blanket and wrapped it around himself.

Christ, I am pathetic. I am at the total mercy of this bum, he confessed to himself. The truth was he was angrier with himself than the old man. By now Tom's anger and despair had turned to embarrassment. As he sat staring at the fire, all he could think about was the depth of his fall and how he was going to explain it all to his wife, family, and friends. He was ashamed of the way he acted, running away from home like a petulant teenager. Here he was, miles from home, shivering in the cold night with a wandering hobo, wrapped in a blanket smelling of curry. He was hoping this was rock bottom because he could not endure anything more.

A shrieking, high-pitched sound broke the silence. Tom shot his head up to see the old man playing a flute-like instrument. He kept starting and stopping in a futile attempt to play a song that seemed self-composed. *Okay, this is the new rock bottom,* Tom sighed to himself.

"Would you mind?" Tom inquired in a surly tone.

"I am sorry, but I just started learning. Something I always wanted to pick up. Thought it'd get your mind off whatever you are thinking about."

"Oh, and you know what I'm thinking?"

"You are thinking about what has gone so wrong in your life that it brought you to this point. Why, despite doing your best and doing everything everyone told you to do, you are completely miserable. Why you feel like a failure to your friends and family and most of all to yourself. And what in the world did you do so terribly wrong that has you sitting in the middle of nowhere, alongside some crazy old man, listening to him play a terrible flute."

"Good guess," Tom responded in a hushed tone.

"If it is any consolation, you are not alone. Today, yesterday, tomorrow; there are, have been, and will always be plenty of people feeling the same despair as you are."

"My misery does not love the company," Tom moaned. He was not altogether surprised the old stranger had figured him out. He figured his despair covered his entire being. "Sometimes I feel like I literally can't walk straight. Like I'm walking a tightrope with howling winds pushing me in all directions and I frantically flail my arms to keep my balance. Finally, my arms got exhausted, and I couldn't keep upright, so I fell. I fell all the way here."

"It seems you need a different kind of life... or stronger arms." The old man's observation elicited a sad smile from Tom. "Your predicament is not unlike a great ancestor of mine. Tales of his life have inspired me since childhood, and like you, he once felt his life lacked purpose and spiraled out of his control. At his moment of deepest despair, he made a choice to travel on a fabulous journey, a journey that would culminate in his becoming a great samurai. Along the way, he discovered a different way to live that allowed him to walk life's proverbial tightrope with a confident gait."

"This is where you hand me a pamphlet about your temple and spend the next three hours convincing me that joining your cult and buying your tapes and books are going to fulfill my life. Thanks, but no thanks. Appreciate the help, but I'll figure it out on my own."

"That's exactly what he did," replied the old man. He picked up the flute and restarted his ear-splitting opus.

"Okay, okay. I'll listen to a little about this ancestor of yours if you promise to pull the plug on the concert."

The old man lowered his flute. "I understand I still need a few lessons. I shall cease and will refrain from boring you with my ancestor's tale. We can just sit quietly."

They returned to their silent conversation, but something in what the old man said kept gnawing at Tom. He knew his life was in shambles. It was fruitless to continue fighting the same old battles that resulted in the same losing end. He desperately needed answers. "What did you mean, 'That's exactly what he did?'"

"Excuse me?"

"I said, 'I'd figure it out on my own,' and you said, 'That's exactly what he did.' What does that mean?"

"No one can truly tell you how you should go about living your life or exactly what you should or shouldn't do. My ancestor became great not by following some prescript but by following certain principles and adapting them to fit his own way of life."

"Did he go to some school or get some training to become a samurai or was it all self-taught?"

"He went to a very famous school and learned from the greatest of masters. He acquired a wealth of knowledge and skill through his training there, but it was all useless until he figured out how to apply those skills and knowledge to his own way of life."

"So, his story really has no bearing on my life?"

"All our lives are unique, but the barriers and obstacles we face are shared and timeless. Whether it be ancient

Japan or modern-day America, men and women have always sought to answer the question, 'Where is my place in this world and how do I fit in it?' The startling thing about my ancestor's experiences is its similarities with today's world more than its differences."

"I can't imagine what a samurai warrior and an investment counselor have in common, but at least the samurai part sounds cool."

"There's your first thing in common with Yoshi-san. My ancestor thought being a samurai was 'cool' too. He was enthralled with becoming a great samurai warrior, for as long as he could remember…"

The old man smiled, his eyes brightening in the reflected firelight, as he began his tale about Yoshi Minamura. The old man sounded like he had told the story a thousand times, falling into a steady, yet mesmerizing cadence. Somehow Tom knew this story was a gift, a gift he desperately needed.

CHAPTER 3

Battle of Hamasuka

The smell in the air was the first clue that something was terribly wrong. The stiff summer breeze blew the scent of burning cedar before they even saw the smoke. Above the tree lines to the north, plumes of blackness began to merge into the low-lying clouds. Even the inexperienced in such matters could tell the source of this smoke was intentionally made and not the result of an accident.

Fifteen-year-old Yoshi Minamura gazed upon it with a combination of awe and exhilaration. He envisioned a glorious battle with warring samurai squared off in mortal, yet beautifully choreographed, combat. He envisioned himself riding into the scene, side-by-side with his hero, the legendary samurai Miyamoto Musashi. Together they would clash swords with each of the opposing samurai and deftly, cunningly, and swiftly vanquish them one by one.

After the victorious conquest, Yoshi and Musashi would earn respect and adoration throughout all of Japan. They would gain personal gratitude and reward from the shogun himself. Books, poems, and songs would be written about their exploits; and children long into the future will fall asleep to tales of the great Yoshi Minamura, just as he had fallen asleep hearing tales of Musashi.

Yoshi was awakened from this daydream by the clamoring of metal coming from behind him. He spun around to see before him a fully armored, battle-ready samurai. The red lacquered iron armor interlaced with golden silk cords sparkled in the mid-afternoon sun. The black coverings over his shins and forearms did nothing to inhibit the samurai's smooth gait and movement. The samurai's katana stuck out from under his gear like a menacing tail. His head was covered by an iron helmet with silver rivets, and his face was shielded with a mask protecting the brows, cheeks, and nose. Yoshi wondered if the power of his daydream had conjured up his boyhood hero.

Only the medallion hanging on the samurai's breastplate clued him in to who stood before him. He had seen that medallion a million times but always around the neck of the fair-skinned woman with the kind eyes, the woman who bore and raised him. The samurai stopped before Yoshi and took him in for a long moment. He then took off his helmet so he could speak to his only son face-to-face. "Son, whether I return or not, I will always be with you. Follow your path and I will be behind you."

With that, Kensi Minamura handed his son a key. Yoshi knew immediately it was to his father's trunk which contained Kensi's vast library of scrolls. These documents covered a wide scope of topics including historical tales, philosophy, and combat theory. Especially interesting to young Yoshi, they also contained the glorious tales of Musashi and other samurai and the lessons they had learned.

As a young child, his father first read the scrolls to him aloud, but after Yoshi learned to read, the two would sit reading them for hours and discussing the lessons they held. He lived for those conversations and learned more from them than anything taught at school. The passing of the key impacted upon him the seriousness of the situation. "I have told you many times that you have a destiny about you Yoshi, one far greater than mine. Remember, with knowledge lies destiny." The last line was a very familiar quote to Yoshi. His father often spoke it, but today it was presented with an unusual tone of finality.

"Father, let me come with you. You've shown me how to handle a sword and taught me many of the lessons of the great samurai. I am old enough to be of service. Please Father, I beg of you, let me share in your glory."

A wry smile slid across his father's mouth; a smile Yoshi had seen often just before one of his many lessons. "What I do now is not glorious. It is all I have done before this moment that has been great."

Kensi stood up straight and bowed deeply to his only son. In a dreamlike trance, Yoshi returned the bow and held the pose for an extended moment. Once he rose, his father had already put back on his headgear and taken his horse's reins from his wife. Kensi paused in a rigid stance for a moment before boarding the steed. His back was to her but in that silent exchange Yoshi could sense the dialogue between the two. He could hear his mother pleading with his father not to go, and his father professing his desire to stay. After that moment, Kensi Minamura—father, husband, farmer, samurai—mounted his horse and galloped north into the forest toward the growing cloud of black smoke.

"Why?" Yoshi asked his mother, searching for a myriad of answers with that one question.

"Hamasuka-san's farm is being overrun by a marauding band of rōnin," replied his mother as her gaze stayed fixed on the forest that had just enveloped her husband. It was a look of anticipation, as if she expected him and his horse to return at any moment.

"Let the daimyo fight them. He's our protector, isn't he?" The daimyo were powerful feudal leaders assigned to run a particular region of Japan. During the Edo period, the shogun was the supreme ruler of Japan. While an emperor still sat on Japan's throne, his status was an ineffective formality. Instituted by the great warlord Tokugawa Ieyasu, at the beginning of the seventeenth century, the Tokugawa Shogunate had absolute rule, led by a secession of sons from Ieyasu's lineage. The shogun parceled out areas of Japan to local daimyo whose loyalty was secure. Matters such as the one on Hamasuka's farm usually fell under the daimyo's responsibility, but his primary responsibility was to placate the ruling shogun and many other matters usually fell by the wayside.

"Our daimyo is either too fearful or too lazy to stop them, so your father has taken it upon himself to help make a stand. Several other neighboring farmers and merchants are joining the cause." Her gaze turned toward Yoshi and she gave him a reassuring smile, whether it was for him or her, Yoshi did not know. "Your father is a great and noble warrior. I have every confidence in his victorious return." With that, she returned to the main house.

Yoshi had heard the terrible tales of this particular group of rōnin. Samurai without masters, rōnin were generally held in low regard in Japanese society. They were considered dishonorable men for losing their masters, and often the shame of this failure led to ritual suicide or hara-kiri. Those who chose to live spent their lives constantly searching for a new master or daimyo to serve, or they spent their time cultivating pursuits in arts, literature, martial arts, and area other personal growth. His hero Musashi, perhaps the greatest rōnin of all, chose the path of personal growth.

The group attacking the neighboring farm chose another path. These disenfranchised rōnin had banded together under the leadership of a mysterious rōnin known only as Jaiko. The group began pillaging and raiding outlying villages and farms during the past two years. The tales of death and destruction were the talk of the schoolyard but never spoken about at home. When he would bring the subject up with his father, he would always change the conversation toward chores and lessons Yoshi had yet to complete. Yoshi thought his father was so afraid of these rōnin that he feared even thinking about them. Until today. He witnessed the awe-inspiring transformation of a simple farmer into a fearless warrior, from a humble father to a glorious samurai.

"Mom, I am going to Gensi-kun's to help him with some chores," he shouted to his mother. Gensi was a good friend and would cover for him if he were forced to give an alibi. Yoshi saddled up the horse his father bought him last summer and galloped away from the home, then circled back around toward the Hamasuka homestead.

He had no idea what he was hoping to accomplish by going to the battle scene, but he knew he had to witness it. There was a newfound pride he felt for his father, and he knew he had to bear witness to his father's glorious victory in battle. As the sun began to slip under the western mountains, Yoshi broke through the forest and into the clearing that marked the beginning of the Hamasuka family property.

Immediately upon entering the glen, Yoshi met the plaintive wail of a charging warrior. It was all a blur as the warrior grabbed hold of Yoshi's right leg and dragged him off his steed. This was the first moment it occurred to Yoshi that he should have come armed. *Some samurai you will be*, he berated himself.

Once he hit the ground, Yoshi quickly broke from the warrior's grip and stood up into a fighting defense position, prepared to use the little self-defense his father had taught him. His attacker's appearance startled him more than the takedown.

The warrior's armor was torn asunder, and the left side of his face was crimson red. His right arm below the elbow was bent outward from his body in a gruesome and wholly unnatural angle. "There are too many, too many to stop. I have wife, children, crops. Must get back. You understand right. You understand I was a warrior. I was a warrior."

The part of the injured man's face that was visible turned ashen as he turned back toward the forest. After a few labored steps, he collapsed face-first onto the ground. Yoshi ran to him and rolled him over to see the last breath of life escape him. With eyes wide, the dead warrior looked up at Yoshi with a quizzical look, as if he was asking, *Why me?*

This was Yoshi's first face-to-face encounter with death. Although he read and heard about it countless times in colorfully grand accounts, it was always described in more heroic terms than the reality facing him now. His moment of reflection was soon broken by the thought that his beloved father was in the midst of this battle. Determined to help his father, Yoshi searched around the fallen warrior and found his wakizashi. It was the shorter sword of a samurai, but at least it would give him something to use in the fight. He leapt back on his horse and raced headlong toward the smoke and commotion just over the hill.

Reaching the top of the hill, Yoshi dismounted and laid in the tall grass to get a sense of the scene. He was amazed to witness the macabre dance of battling warriors. There was a peculiar arrangement and rhythm to the pairs of samurai pitched in mortal combat. A quick survey of the field told Yoshi that the rōnin clearly held the edge and were driving the few remnants of the farmer's defenders toward the riverbank to the east.

There was a lone Hamasuka defender who was faring much better than the others in the face of the challenge posed by the advancing rōnin. While the others retreated in panic, he had an air of calm and control about him, even as he fell back. As he faced off with an opponent, this samurai waited for his adversary to make the first move, but then, from that point on, the advantage was his. With liquidity to his movements and strikes, he overwhelmed and vanquished his foe in just a few strokes, then immediately set himself to face yet another warrior. The problem was that there were too many rōnin and not enough Hamasuka warriors to fend them off.

It did not take long after Yoshi reached his hilltop observation spot for the last of Hamasuka's defenders to be killed or to escape across the river, save the fierce lone warrior. From his vantage point, Yoshi could not tell if his father was among the ones slain or if he was able to retreat. To his embarrassment, he silently prayed that his father turned coward and fled away back to their home. As he crept closer in the grass, the sunlight's reflection caught something on the lone samurai's chest. The shape and symbol were unmistakable even at this distance. It was his mother's medallion.

His father was surrounded by a ring of rōnin pointing their blades at him. His situation looked absolutely hopeless, but none of the warriors would attack. They held firm as if waiting for something. That something soon arrived in the form of a regally tall rōnin warrior. It was clear from the respect the others showed that he was their leader. "That must be Jaiko," Yoshi whispered to himself.

He was covered from head to toe in black lacquer armament that was polished to a shine bright enough to give off a reflection. His headdress was adorned with red silks that gave the appearance of fire coming out of his helmet. At Jaiko's side was another samurai in similar dress, but Yoshi could tell from the way he walked he was much younger, perhaps closer to his own age.

The rōnin opened up the circle to allow their leader to enter with his young apprentice. Yoshi's father stayed in his defensive pose as he studied the duo. Jaiko gently pushed aside his apprentice and unsheathed his katana. He took up an eerily similar posture to that of his father and remained still. The two stayed locked in the same position staring at each other as if waiting for someone or something to initiate the action but nothing came. This rōnin leader seemed to be taking the same tact as his father, wanting his opponent to strike first.

Yoshi's head was spinning. Cold sweat was pouring from his brow, and he felt all the contents of his stomach were about to escape out of his mouth. *What can I do against so many? How can I help? Why can't I move?* All these questions bombarded Yoshi as he remained motionless in the grass watching the two samurai facing each other.

Finally, before his mind could tell his body what to do, Yoshi stood up out of the tall grass. Unfortunately, that was the only action his jumbled mind would allow his body to do. The rōnin surrounding his father took no notice of the short, stocky kid standing up nearly a stone's throw away. The first person to notice Yoshi was his father. With the quickest of glances, they made eye contact. For the first time in his life, Yoshi gazed at those eyes and saw complete fear. His gaze quickly disengaged from his son's face and returned to his opponent, and with an ear-piercing wail, he rushed to attack the rōnin leader.

The rōnin quickly parried Kensi's initial attack and the two subsequent ones. On Kensi's third attack, the rōnin quickly dropped to his knees avoiding Kensi's blade and responded with a vicious slash at his charging opponent's left leg. Yoshi's father immediately fell, his leg slowly turning a bright shade of red as it barely hung on above the knee. Kensi quickly got back up and stood ready to engage his opponent, standing on his one good leg. Jaiko seemed to be taken aback by the rapid recovery and willingness to fight off his formidable foe.

With tears welling up in his eyes, Yoshi realized it was now or never. He raised his sword and took two steps toward the fight, but suddenly froze in his tracks. His father extended out his armed telling Yoshi to stop. This movement startled the group and the surrounding rōnin looked up to see Yoshi standing still in the tall grass. Commotion ensued as several warriors raced to engage young Yoshi. But they too froze in their tracks by Jaiko's barking command to halt.

Never taking his eyes off Kensi, Jaiko could tell exactly what was happening. He knew the boy in the tall grass was his adversary's son and Kensi would do anything to avoid harm to him. Jaiko also knew he wanted this victory in front of his men to assure his standing as their superior. He signaled with his hand for Kensi to come at him. Yoshi sensed his father understood this was a suicidal invitation. Yoshi also read in Jaiko's offer a de facto agreement that if they fought, Kensi's son would be spared.

With all the might left in his body, Kensi Minamura made his last attack. From the depth of his soul, he yelled "May the gods keep my family whole and safe!" He lunged forward toward Jaiko. On only one good leg and severely weakened by the extreme blood loss, he was no match against the rōnin leader. With a blow that was imperceptible to Yoshi, Jaiko quickly sidestepped Kensi's advance and sliced him halfway through his abdomen. Yoshi's father fell to his knees, his head bowed, and his lifeless hand still clinging to the sword by his side. Jaiko never looked back at Kensi or his son. He simply walked to his horse, mounted it, and ordered his troops to follow.

Yoshi's legs could not move, just tremble. He shook as the pain and anger and sorrow all screamed to detonate out of him. But his terror was so great he could not muster a single sound.

As the rōnin slowly followed behind Jaiko, a lone figure remained behind, staring at the fallen Kensi. The figure then turned to the son of the vanquished. From his attire, Yoshi recognized him as Jaiko's young apprentice. Although most of his head was covered by his helmet, Yoshi could make out his eyes clearly. They were young eyes yet lacked a youth's vitality. In fact, they lacked any discernible activity.

They were devoid of any emotion or expression. These eyes had witnessed death firsthand but lacked any recognition of it. A chill of fear pulsed throughout Yoshi's body. The eyes would eventually turn from Yoshi and follow the band of murderers into the forest, but the sight of them would stay with Yoshi for the remainder of his days.

Early on, those eyes would wake Yoshi in a cold sweat of fear. Eventually, he would use it as a source of inspiration to follow the lessons of his father and adopt the way of the samurai to become a warrior worthy of his father's name. Not for glory, nor fame, nor fortune. But for vengeance.

"Okay, so this is a story about a kick-ass samurai," interrupted Tom. "I thought this was going to be a tale of self-discovery, but I see it's more like a Tarantino film."

The old man shook his head and laughed. "I made the same assumption when I first heard this tale. But as you will hear, it is about so much more than that. Yoshi had set out to become a warrior and held a preconceived belief of what that would entail. But just like a young man ready to take on the world upon graduation from the university, the expectations and the actual journey often take you in two different directions."

"I can relate to that. So, he doesn't become a samurai and avenge his father? No offense, but I'm not in the mood to hear a real downer story."

"Oh, this an 'upper' story I assure you. Yoshi will become a samurai. He will achieve all that he desires, just not in the way he expected. You see, it is not just about becoming something, it is about being something."

"You lost me with the Eastern philosophy mumbo jumbo," Tom confessed.

"Your current occupation? It is what you wanted to do when you graduated college?" the old man asked.

"As a matter of fact, it is. I guess I'm lucky in that respect."

"So, you are what you set out to become."

"Yet I'm still not happy." A flash of recognition came to Tom. "That's what you mean by being."

"As Yoshi would find out, life is not just about the destination. Once you get there, one does not just stop living." The old man settled in as he prepared to continue the story. "But before one realizes this, life's path can be a very bumpy road." Tom was still a bit confused but eager for the old man to continue with his story about the young Yoshi Minamura.

CHAPTER 4

Where Wisdom Lies

oshi Minamura was glad it was raining. The misty sprinkle blended with the tears running down his cheek and masked his heartbreak from the gathered crowd. Even at a memorial for one's own father, public displays of emotion by men were looked on as weak in feudal Japan, and on top of the ache of his loss, Yoshi did not want to endure the sting of embarrassment. The rain provided a perfect cover; a gift from the heavens that he believed was ordered down by his father.

It had been three years since his father's death on the Hamasuka farm, and his family had gathered for the annual Obon festival to commemorate the passing of loved ones. The Obon was an occasion to celebrate the spirits of the departed while also serving as an opportunity for family members to visit and reconnect with one another. There had been several memorials since the passing of his father and Yoshi dreaded each of them. They forced him to reflect on his life and whether he was living up to the standards set by his father—topics he desperately wanted to avoid. As the Buddhist priest prayed aloud, Yoshi's mind was jarred open and demanded he take stock of the last three years of his life.

"You have a destiny about you Yoshi." His father's slogan echoed in his mind every day since his passing. It rang in his mind when he woke up. It spoke to him as he tended to his family's farm. It screamed at him as he trudged through his monotonous daily chores. Since the

day Yoshi returned his father's body to his wailing mother, he committed all his energies to helping his mother by taking up the role left vacant by his father. His efforts were rewarded with the farm enjoying tremendous prosperity and steadily increasing harvests and profits.

At his school, he was recognized as one of the most accomplished students in both academics and physical skills. His mastery of the sword garnered both high regard and a bit of jealousy from many of his peers. To his neighbors and friends, it looked as if the young boy was growing into a respectable member of society and a credit to his slain father. More times than he cared to recall, a family member or neighbor predicted that he would grow to be one of the finest farmers in the region. Each time he heard the compliment, it stung him like a slap across the face.

Spying his reflection in a still pond, Yoshi saw someone he was far from admiring. Over time, his resentment steadily grew to anger. His ire stemmed from a sense of being let down. Let down by fate, who took his father from him and put him in charge of the family. Let down by himself, who could not find a way to live a fulfilling life. Eventually, his anger turned to his father.

The secret he was ashamed to share was that he hated who his father was. Not as the man, but as the meager farmer. Ever since he learned of the tales of the great Musashi and other great warriors, he envisioned himself growing to be one. But every boy's model of manhood ends up being his own father, and that example was a man toiling behind oxen twelve hours a day.

"You have a destiny about you Yoshi."

Was it just words? Yoshi wondered. Maybe his father

was just teasing him with his vision. Maybe this is all he was supposed to be. Just another version of his father. At the age of eighteen, Yoshi felt like a man at the end of his journey. He felt old.

"You are looking more and more like your father every time I see you." The comment from Koji, his mother's oldest brother, awoke Yoshi out of his trance. Another affirmation of his plight. "I am sure he would be proud of you."

Proud of me?! Why?! Proud that I have taken up his cursed life? Proud I am nothing but a farmer. I live my life in a hopeless state, the flame of optimism and desire slowly extinguishing inside me. If that is his idea of pride, I would gladly take his scorn!

Yoshi ran this diatribe in his mind before quietly acknowledging the compliment with a polite bow.

The oshō concluded his prayer service and the group of family and friends moved to the south bank of the stream on the family lands. Each family member placed a floating lantern with a candle lit center into the stream. Silently, all watched as the glowing vessels slipped down the waterway, taking Kensi's spirit back to the world of the afterlife.

The congregation meandered back to the Minamura family home to continue the observance. Yoshi played the role of host as best he could as he made idle conversation with relatives and neighbors.

"Yoshi-san, come here," beckoned his uncle Koji. "Do you remember your cousin, Makato? You were just a little boy when you last met." It had been a long time since Yoshi had seen his cousin. The man no longer resembled the scrawny boy of his youth. Although Makato was three years older, Yoshi recalled being bigger than his Uncle Koji's only son.

When they played together, they would often have simulated fights. Although physically smaller, Makato would always play aggressively. This inevitably led their fights to escalate past the level of simulation and into actual blows. Though he never started the fight, Yoshi ended up finishing it with his superior strength and skill. The end of their playtime left the older cousin in tears and Yoshi the recipient of a stern punishment from his parents. *"You should know better,"* was the response his father gave to Yoshi's plea for understanding.

The Makato that stood before Yoshi today was a physically filled-out man, who was much taller than Yoshi. But it was not his stature that impressed Yoshi. Catching the light of the midday sun was a sword secured in his waistband, the sword of a samurai.

While Makato listened quietly, Koji bragged about how his son had just graduated from a fine samurai academy in Edo. Makato's accomplishments at the school had caught the attention of the local daimyo and led him to hire Makato to serve him. "Our family has been blessed from on high to have a true warrior in our lineage. Perhaps, if my son were already a samurai during the battle at Hamasuka's farm..." Koji's thought was extinguished by the icy glare shot at him by his sister's son. Yoshi had to endure many slights, real and perceived, but it was evident this one was not to be tolerated.

Makato quickly moved to ease the obvious tension. "Yoshi-kun, it is so good to see you again. I am glad we survived our childhood without killing each other, or rather you killing me." They laughed and it served Makato's purpose. "Please show me around your farm."

Yoshi was grateful for the opportunity to leave the family reunion. He feared he could not accept one more comparison to his father. As the duo strolled along with no particular agenda, Yoshi switched the conversation from a tour of his homestead to an inquisition of Makato's rise to a samurai. His cousin eagerly relayed the story of how his father was able to get him admittance to a very popular school. He figured it cost his father a fair sum in gifts and bribery. Once at the academy, Makato was able to make his father's investment pay off. "I felt it my duty to not just succeed for myself, but for my father too. It made for a lot of pressure, but I am glad I did it."

Yoshi was glad he was not alone in feeling paternal pressure. "What do you do now?"

"I live the life of a samurai. I serve my masters to their satisfaction and pray I always live up to their expectations or else..."

"You come back here to be a farmer like me," Yoshi completed the sentiment.

"It's not so bad you know," was Makato's half-hearted response. Yoshi could tell he shared the dread of living out his days as a farmer. The difference was Makato's father gave him a chance at a different life.

The two walked back to the family gathering in silence until Yoshi finished their conversation with an unsolicited confession. "I will become a samurai someday and avenge my father's death."

Makato was taken aback by the matter-of-fact way Yoshi made the statement. Thinking it was a request for help, he offered some. "I can see what I can do about getting you into the academy in Edo. I am confident a good word from me could help."

Yoshi respectfully declined. "Makato, I appreciate the offer, but I know this is something I have to seek on my own."

"Still stubborn like when you were young, Yoshi-kun." Makato smiled as he accepted Yoshi's explanation. "You should have let me win one of our fights, but even then, your pride wouldn't have it."

While taking up his cousin's offer was alluring, Yoshi knew that to become the samurai he craved to be, he needed to go to a great school and learn from true masters. He did not tell Makato, or anyone else, but his heart was set on one place and one place only, the School of Aspen.

His father often spoke of the legendary school hidden amongst the aspens. A shroud of secrecy covered the tales about the school and the training methods it employed, but no one disputed its results. The School of Aspen was renowned throughout the entire country for training the finest samurai in the land. It was rumored that the Shogun Tokugawa Ieyasu studied there and had sent his sons to the school to be trained.

At the core of the school's mystique was the belief that within the walls of its main temple was the sanctuary housing the fabled Swords of Illumination. The swords were believed to have been forged by the hands of the greatest samurai of Japanese history. Yoshi's father would tell him a samurai must possess these weapons to obtain true greatness. Kensi shared little else about the swords or the powers they held. *"If you prove yourself able, you may someday wield these swords,"* Kensi would respond to his son's pestering.

Despite his inquiries, no one he had ever encountered could tell him any more about the swords or the School of Aspen. The common refrain Yoshi received was, *"Only an elite few have gazed upon these masterful weapons and even fewer have held them."*

Yoshi did learn from his father that entry into the academy was by invitation only. When young Yoshi pressed his father on how to get such an invitation, the elder always responded, *"When you are old enough to know where your destiny lies, you will gain what you seek."*

"With knowledge lies destiny, right? That is what you always tell me."

"That's right. Now, how about we read some tales of the great Musashi?"

Yoshi's inquiries about the School of Aspen always steered the father and son to the old trunk in the attic. Passed on to Kensi from his father as it was from his father before him, the trunk held a collection of writings from the great philosophers, priests, and samurai of Japanese history. The thirst for knowledge was an inherited trait of the Minamuras, and Yoshi was the latest in the lineage to carry the gene. Yoshi loved the moments he and his father would sit and read the scrolls. To the young Yoshi, they held fanciful tales and the opportunity to spend time with his father. As he grew older, he came to see the critical lessons and knowledge imparted by these testaments. None enthralled him more than those of the great samurai Miyamoto Musashi.

Musashi was the rarest of samurai, one whose exploits on the field of battle were exceeded only by tales of his eccentric lifestyle. Unlike most samurai, he refused to stay in the employ of a single master. He spent his life traveling from one manor or school to another, always seeking to test his skills as a fighter, acquire more skills, and hone the ones he already possessed. Late in life, he would slip away to write his great manifesto, *The Book of Five Rings*, a tome on battle and life philosophies that a samurai should live by. Kensi's chest contained a rare copy of Musashi's book along with other descriptions of his life.

Since his father's death, he spent nearly every evening reading from the scrolls, immersing himself in each word, each story, and each lesson they had to offer. He became so well-versed in the scrolls that he could recite them from memory. He filled his mind with every bit of knowledge in the hopes that wisdom would come to him, and with it an invitation into the School of Aspen. After three years, Yoshi was still waiting.

A week after the Obon festival, Yoshi was going through the paces of his daily assignments at the farm, but his mind was far from the land he was working. Instead, he was wielding his sword side-by-side with Musashi as they fought off hundreds of faceless warriors. He was studying with the great philosophers of Japan. He was being lauded in songs and poems for his exploits. He was also digging up dirt that had already been seeded.

Awaking to his *real* world, Yoshi looked down to see his absent-mindedness had just undone several days of recently completed seeding. With a frustration that extended far beyond his current error, he let out a howl that shook the nearby birds from their perches.

Walking back to the house, he encountered his mother. *"I have to get out of my mind,"* he told her. She knew exactly what he meant. It was a term the family used when they needed to let go of a problem and let a solution find them instead of chasing one. This was Yoshi's way to tell her he was taking a long walk. Ever since his clandestine departure on the day of his father's death, he checked with her before leaving the house. Although he was old enough and his role as head of the household did not require such permission, he still felt it necessary as penance for his past deception.

"Your father is proud of you Yoshi," his mother responded. "He tells me every night in my dreams that he is." She put down the tea kettle and rose to face him. "He also tells me you are destined for a great journey and the time is near for it to commence. Solve the puzzle and it will begin." He returned her bow and departed.

"Solve the puzzle and it will begin?" he asked himself over and over as he walked the hillside to the west of his family farm. The ground below him was worn as he had taken this same path many times when he needed to clear his head. But today, he could not shake clear the commotion raging inside him. His questions soon turned to accusations. *Why all these riddles and puzzles and clues? If he loved me so, why not just give me the answers? Why not hand me the sword and send me off to the school?* He found his frustration grow with each step. No longer able to keep his thoughts in his head, he screamed them aloud.

He stopped and spun around, engaging the imaginary ghost of his father. "You told me you will always be behind me! Well, where are you? If you really were a great teacher, you would have led me, not have me endure this floundering." Yoshi stood waiting for a response. None came.

"Lead me!" he cried out once more. No response.

"Fine, then I don't need you following me!" Yoshi suddenly sprinted off, not along the well-worn path, but off into the brush. He was running from his father, cutting to the left and right, feigning one way then another, making every effort possible to elude the formless figure chasing behind him. His pumping heart became audible as his pace quickened. The brush was high here and his raised forearm was the only thing he could see before him.

Suddenly one of his galloping steps did not meet the earth. The momentum of his step plummeted his foot down, pulling the rest of his body with it. It did not occur to him that he had fallen down a hidden sinkhole until the second after his shoulder exploded in pain as it absorbed the force of his weight crashing down. Luck and a soft, soggy ground conspired to prevent any serious injury. Stunned and confused, Yoshi moaned for a bit as he rolled on his back. Opening his eyes, he stared at the cloud-pocked sky above, the winds slowly morphing the white pillows into a distorted smile. "Very funny, Father." Yoshi cursed. *That'll teach me, he thought. No matter how far I run, I'll always end up lying on my backside, right beside my destiny.* He laughed aloud at his humorous thought. He couldn't stop laughing like a little boy being tickled.

His explosion of laughter was an erupting valve, releasing the pent-up steam of emotion from his day, his year, his lifetime. *Oh, here I lie with plenty of knowledge, so I guess this is my destiny?* he chuckled. *Reading all those scrolls with their wealth of knowledge and insights... and it all just led me here, lying on my back in a muddy pit. All those scrolls...* Suddenly, he froze. His face lost its supply of blood as it pumped to his brain. A realization slowly crept into his consciousness.

"With knowledge lies destiny," is what his father told him. *Where else could this knowledge be he was talking about but within the scrolls in the old creaky chest... what lies beneath that knowledge is my... destiny!*

Covered in mud and drenched in sweat, Yoshi ascended from the hole and ran to his family home. "Forgive me for my appearance," he bowed to his startled mother greeting him at the door. Yoshi climbed up to the attic and stood before the chest containing the scrolls. Of the hundreds of times he had gazed upon it, this was the first time he could remember studying it. Generations of wear had scarred it with scratches and dents all across its wooden frame. If he had stumbled upon it for the first time, he would have thought it was something that had been discarded, awaiting its fate in a pit of fire. The observation allowed him time to calm down. Removing the key he always kept around his neck, Yoshi slowly kneeled beside the chest and methodically slipped the key into its lock. He turned it slowly, half expecting an explosion. Instead, he was greeted by the dozens of bound scrolls resting exactly as he had last left them.

"When you are old enough to know where your destiny lies, you will gain what you seek," his father told him when pressed on his invitation to the School of Aspen. "With knowledge lies destiny, right? That is what you always tell me," he whispered in response to this memory. "It has to be here."

Slowly, he removed each scroll one at a time, and once the chest was empty, he scanned the bare bottom with his eyes opened as wide as physically possible. As if reaching into a substance he didn't know was hot or cold, Yoshi gently ran his fingers along the bottom and corners of the chest. He fiddled all around the edges, tugging at each corner. Nothing gave way.

"It has to be here," he mumbled again. "With knowledge lies destiny." He quickly turned the chest upside down and began the same examination of the underside. This time, in an even more meticulous manner, he spent time investigating the edges. He pulled on each corner. Nothing on the top right. Nothing on the top left. Nothing on the bottom right. Nothing on the bottom... wait. *There was something not right*, he thought. *What was different about the last corner I pulled at?* He re-examined the bottom right corner and this time he recognized what his eyes had already seen. There was a speck of white on an otherwise black bottom. He tugged again on the corner. With a slightly stronger pull, the panel gave way slightly. Following it up with a few more progressively harder tugs, the entire bottom panel eventually came off.

Yoshi fell back and looked upon the object stuck on the bottom of the case. It was covered in a white cloth and tied with a red silk band. Gently, he removed it from the chest and laid it before him. Slipped between the ties and the cloth was a folded parchment. The paper looked weathered and was sealed with a blackened wax stamp. He removed the document and examined the seal. Embedded in the wax was the outline of a tree.

Yoshi took a deep breath before cracking open the seal and unfolding the document. His mind immediately embedded the image of the document so that it would stay in his memory for all his days. It took only a few seconds for him to read the entire text.

To the bearer is offered an invitation, an invitation to embark on a grand journey. This journey will illuminate a world far different than the one most experience. It will provide you with knowledge, skills, and confidence. Tools necessary to live a life of fulfillment and balance. To live a life of service. To live the life of samurai.

To this end, you have been given a great gift, the Sword of Illumination. It is a true samurai's greatness weapon and will serve you as you battle a variety of foes. To wield it, you must master it. To master it, you must live it. To be samurai, you must adopt it.

Use this sword and you will gain entry to the place you seek. The School of Aspen.

He untied the band and unwrapped the cloth from its contents. The dim light of the attic could not hinder its brilliance. Yoshi saw his own amazed eyes looking back at him in its reflection. It was the most splendid sword he had ever seen. Removing it from the cloth and moving it to the light for a more careful examination, he discovered an engraving along one side of the sword. It read:

Sword of Identity
Who am I in this moment?
Have my actions reflected who I am?
Hold who you are in your mind at all times and your actions will manifest accordingly!

He was feverish with excitement. For the entirety of his young life, Yoshi yearned for this moment. He held in his hands the invitation to the School of Aspen and a life as a samurai.

"Every ending is a beginning. Every beginning is an end." The ancient quote he recalled from one of the scrolls summed up his current feelings. Obtaining this invitation was his overriding goal for all the days he could remember; but now that he possessed it, he felt he was standing at the beginning of a very long trail. He could not see where the trail ended but prayed it would lead him to greatness.

An overwhelming need to share the moment came over him. Yoshi believed the reality of the moment needed verification and no person would be better to share in this momentous occasion than his mother. Flying down the stairs, he burst into the living area only to find a note from his mother which read:

I've gone to the market. Will be back soon.

Not soon enough for Yoshi. He had to share this moment right away lest it dissolve into a dream. He rummaged through the attic and found one of his father's old belts. He sheathed the sword in the case it came with and slipped it into his father's belt around his waist. With steps that barely touched the ground, Yoshi flew down the road toward the village market.

The village was bustling with people finishing their late afternoon chores and shopping. Popping his head up and down and side to side, Yoshi frantically searched for his mother. Being careful not to bump others, he slipped between the teeming crowds. Racing around a corner, he barely averted crashing into an old farmer, brushing gently the man's loose-fitting clothing. The old farmer had a weathered face that looked older than his years. His clothes were also marred with stains and holes. In his right hand, he held a set of oxen reigns, sans the oxen. In his left, he carried a pitchfork which he used more as a walking aid than for its intended purpose. "A thousand pardons, sir. Please will you accept my apology?" Yoshi asked of the stranger as he bowed to him.

The farmer's reply came abruptly in the form of a hard smack upside Yoshi's bowed head. Yoshi's face shot up to see the disheveled form before him. "Who do you think you are messing with? You think I am just some low-life farmer, huh? I don't have to take your abuse; I can fight back you know. I will not be insulted by some little boy." The old man took two steps back and raised his pitchfork. Yoshi spied that the tips of the fork were dull and rusty as was the wavering man who held it. He had never met the irate form before him and was taken aback by the extraordinary venom cast upon him. A crowd began to encircle the two as the old man continued to vociferously challenge Yoshi.

"Come, boy. Take your lesson like a man, for it will be the last lesson you learn." The old man spun his words into action as he took a meaningful, yet feeble, stab at Yoshi. It was clumsy and clearly telegraphed, allowing Yoshi to easily dodge it.

Yoshi now realized this man meant him serious harm. He grabbed the handle of his new weapon and began to draw it out. *This man has no idea who he is facing*, the irate young man spoke to himself. *He will now see.* Before the slightest portion of the blade was exposed, Yoshi suddenly paused. He ceased his internal conversation, stepped back, and surveyed the surrealism of the scene. On the most exciting day of his life when all he wanted was to share in his great joy, a man he had no quarrel with was pointing a pitchfork at him. As the chants of "coward" rang out from his adversary, Yoshi knew the obvious response was to engage this man and easily dispel him. To protect his honor in front of the growing crowd of villagers around him, it was clear he must fight. *Besides, does not the invitation say I must use this sword to gain entry?* Yoshi thought. *This is the perfect opportunity.*

As he tightened his grip on his new *gift*, his mind transported him back to a sunny afternoon of his youth as he played with his cousin. Pretending to be great samurai warlords, they held broken tree branches as swords, smacking them against each other in faux combat. For reasons inexplicable to Yoshi, Makato grew more agitated and started clubbing at Yoshi with greater authority. Yoshi knew he was quicker than his older cousin and could easily avoid his blows. But he also knew he had the strength and skills to defeat his cousin, and he felt compelled to show off his power. Beating down Makato would prove Yoshi's superiority.

Striking down this old farmer would also prove Yoshi's superiority. Yet, he could not unsheathe his sword.

The sword. What was written on the sword? Yoshi attempted to recall.

Who am I in this moment?
Have my actions reflected who I am?
Hold who you are in your mind at all times and your actions will manifest accordingly!

The sword was more than just a weapon to be used in combat. It was a guide, a principle, to be employed. *Who am I in this moment?* Yoshi fashioned himself to be a great samurai. *Would a great samurai engage in battle without a just cause? Would he fight and slay a lesser foe just to show these witnesses his prowess with the sword? Was his self-confidence so fragile that it could be shaken by the rantings of a madman?* Yoshi's response to all these questions was an emphatic *No.*

He gently released the handle of his sword. *My actions will reflect who I am,* he thought to himself while bowing to the man. "You are obviously a great and skillful warrior and I have no wish to engage you. I beg you grant me leave and I wish you a good day." With that said, Yoshi walked into the crowd and away from the scene. The old man was left dumbstruck. Yoshi could hear him yell out something about Yoshi making a good decision to run away, but Yoshi blocked it from his mind as he heard another voice.

"You knew better," was his father's response.

Finally, he found his mother at the spice stand. When she turned to him, she let out a small gasp and her face turned ashen. "Mother, what's wrong?" Yoshi quickly grabbed her arms to steady her before she fell.

"Yoshi. Oh, Yoshi, it's just you. For a moment I thought you were your father." She caressed his face. "Today, right now, you look so much like him. You look so much... older."

"I found where my destiny lies," Yoshi responded tapping his new sword.

"Then it is time. Your father told me this day would come when you would have to leave us. Knowing it will happen and being prepared for it does not make it any easier for me. I just pray I have prepared you well enough."

"Mother, please know, everything I accomplish and achieve I will owe to you and Father."

As they strolled home together in the dimming twilight, Yoshi took the time to embrace and enjoy this moment with his mother. He listened intently to each word of advice she shared. He memorized the shape of her face and the shine of her hair. He did not want any aspect of this time to slip from his consciousness. He knew his journey would take him far from here and far from her. Memories like this would comfort him as he began his great journey.

"Why didn't Yoshi's father just tell him where the sword was? Seemed like a lot of jumping through hoops for nothing," Tom said with a tinge of frustration. "I mean, if my father held some sort of key for my success and didn't tell me I'd be pretty pissed."

"What was your first car?" the old man asked.

"Oh, it was an '81 black Camaro. Really sweet ride. What does that have to do with anything?"

"How did you get it?

"I worked my butt off at the local grocery store as a stock clerk and bagging groceries. Worst job of my life."

"But it was worth it, right?"

"It got me that car, and that car got me... well... I had a good time with that car."

"Your father, he could have bought it for you though?" the old man asked.

"Yeah, he could have. Sure, would have saved me a lot of time and kept my back from killing me."

"But it wouldn't really have been your car. Although he gave it to you, there would always be that sense that it was his car, and it was on loan to you. By buying that car yourself, you owned it outright, and you got to pick exactly what you wanted."

"I see your point." Tom laid back and looked up at the stars in the clear night sky and pondered the thought. "He had to find the sword in his own time and in his own way. It's just hard to figure out your own way."

The old man smiled. "That's what Yoshi was about to find out."

CHAPTER 5

School of Aspen

Dear Yoshi,

I write this note to you as I prepare for a great battle, unsure of my return. I go into this fight with no desire for death, but rather a passion for life. The fight I wage today is in preservation of others' lives as well as my own, for if I refuse to act when I know I can make a difference, a part of me would die. In time, you will understand this

I asked your mother to hand you this note on the day you found where your destiny lies. It had been a hope of mine to be with you upon this discovery. But an even greater hope, and my greatest dream, was that your calling led you to a life in pursuit of knowledge and excellence.

A father's goal is to provide his son a path to a prosperous life. All my words and deeds were to set an example for you, but your life will be determined by your own decisions and actions. Your journey will be unique and determined by who you are. No one can set your destiny without your permission.

You alone have set into motion the wheels of fate that send you to the School of Aspen. This great academy will offer you the knowledge, skills, and training necessary to make you samurai. The proper use of that knowledge, skills, and training will make you a great samurai. I have every confidence that will be your ultimate outcome.

My final advice to you is to always seek. Seek knowledge. Seek guidance. Seek friendships. Seek love. Never stop the search.

In you, I live.
Your father

Yoshi had read the note a hundred times since his mother handed it to him. He sighed deeply and fought back tears as he carefully folded the paper and slid it next to his breast.

From the pack slung over his shoulder, he removed another parchment, studied it and then considered the overgrown path ahead of him. The paper was a map to the School of Aspen that Yoshi had found tucked in the shroud that contained the Sword of Identity. He could not believe he failed to notice the map when he first found the sword and thought he was lucky to have not accidentally discarded it. But as Yoshi stood on the side of the Tokaido Road, he questioned his luck and the wisdom of the map. The map called for him to depart the well-travelled thoroughfare and trek on no discernible path.

Yoshi had traveled the Tokaido Road on several occasions. It linked the cities of Edo and Kyoto. The road had been established and maintained by the Tokugawa Shogunate as a way to promote travel and commerce between the traditional capital city of Kyoto and the growing home of the shogunate, Edo. More than just a road, the Tokaido Road had grown in lore through its epic description in popular art and literature. Men felt a sense of adventure and inspiration from traveling on the road, and Yoshi was no exception. His previous journeys on the Tokaido Road filled his mind with the imagery of being a great warrior on a treacherous mission or of a learned philosopher musing about the meaning of nature. When Yoshi stepped foot on the road two days earlier, he realized that on this journey he did not need to conjure up his imagination. The Tokaido Road was truly leading him on his greatest adventure.

When the map told him to turn off the road, he expected to be on to another paved and clear path, but the paper in his hand was directing him onto a route that could barely be called a path.

The ground ahead appeared never to have been traveled. He sighed, shrugged his shoulders, and concluded he was in no position to question, and there was no way he was going to turn around now.

For the next two days and two nights, Yoshi carefully followed the directions on the map. The paths took a winding route through forests, along riverbanks, and eventually, steeply up the mountainside just to the west of Mount Fuji. Eventually, he found himself surrounded in a forest of aspens, which according to the map meant he was close.

The aspen is an unusual tree in that a single tree sprouts roots that form genetically identical trees. From that one tree, a grove of Aspens can spread for more than 100 acres. While the trees themselves live up to 150 years, the root systems can last for centuries. His father often spoke of aspens as an example of how all living things are interconnected to each other. *"Do not be fooled by their quaking leaves, Yoshi. The aspen is a powerfully strong tree. From the roots created from just one seedling, centuries of trees are formed. Let that be a lesson. One thing can affect many."*

Sitting under one of the aspens, Yoshi relived that lesson as he ate a rice ball wrapped in seaweed, the last meal prepared for him by his mother. Looking at his map, he was at the location the school should be, but the path had ended long ago, and he saw no evidence of any structures or man-made tracks. As he continued his examination of the map, he heard a faint sound in the distance. He immediately shot up since unlike all the sounds he had heard for the past two days, this one did not resemble anything derived from nature. Silence, then he heard it again, this time slightly louder.

He was confident it was man-made since nothing he knew in nature made a metallic creaking sound. He thought for an instant it might be a wagon heading for the school. With the sound bouncing off the tight group of surrounding trees, Yoshi found it difficult for him to pinpoint its origin.

Suddenly from the corner of his eye, he caught a flash of red in an otherwise brown and green forest. It reappeared quickly and then as quickly disappeared behind another row of trees. Grabbing his pack, he sprinted in its direction. The flash of red was moving at a rapid pace just within Yoshi's eyesight. He picked up his pace to catch up, maintaining his sights on the flashes of red while also weaving between the trees. Ahead there was a small clearing of trees and the red image appeared unfiltered for a brief moment. The sight stopped Yoshi in his tracks. The source of the creaking appeared to be a man, dressed in a red robe, running through the woods. What stunned Yoshi frozen was that it looked as if he was running in midair. In the brief time Yoshi witnessed the man, his legs were pumping furiously but were almost two feet above the ground.

"What sort of mystical place have I come upon," he whispered to himself. Curiosity taking control of his legs, Yoshi resumed his pursuit of the floating man in red.

He raced through the trees, moving in any direction that would make the creaking sound louder. Running at full speed into an area of denser forest, he feared he was getting more lost than found. The tall trunks of aspens littered his route as Yoshi weaved in between them. Holding an arm in front of his face to block the lower-lying branches, he dropped his outstretched limb just in time to see the wall of stone immediately in front of him. Straightening his legs with all his might, he skidded to a stop just before slamming into the barrier.

He stood before it in awe. Made of huge stones stacked in a perfectly fitted puzzle, the wall stood several feet higher than Yoshi. It ran as far as the eye could see in both directions.

The creaking sound ceased and there was no sight of the red figure. Deciding that the last of the sounds came from his left, Yoshi followed along the edge of the wall in that direction.

He jogged for nearly twenty minutes until the stone barrier abruptly ended and was joined by an equally massive iron gate. Covered with a pagoda roof, Yoshi took several steps back from the gate to read the inscription on the top. It simply read, *Knowledge*. He smiled realizing this was the place he had sought for so long.

Putting aside any thoughts of the strange red figure, Yoshi took a deep breath and walked up to the large gate. Before he could pull on the thick rope leading to the large metal bell at the top of the entrance, the large iron doors slowly opened, its hinges echoing across the forest behind him. The iron gate revealed a long row of stone steps that gradually rose up into the distance. Descending from those steps was a solitary figure draped in a red robe. For a moment, he thought this could have been the figure he had pursued in the forest, but that idea vanished when he got a closer look at the man.

About seventy years of age with a clean-shaven head, the man Yoshi immediately assumed to be a monk bowed deeply to him. Yoshi returned the gesture and removed the invitation from his breast. Bowing again, he offered it up as a sign of his right to be admitted.

"There is no need to show your invite. Your appearance at our gates is evidence enough of your worth to enter the School of Aspen. Welcome, Yoshi-san."

"How did you—"

The monk abruptly cut him off with his own introduction. "My name is Daichi, and it will be my honor to introduce you to your new home." The monk turned and walked back up the stone stairs, taking each step gingerly and with care.

Yoshi's first impressions led him to find the monk to be peculiar in form and behavior. His robes were dirty and ill-fitting, hanging on him rather than worn. His gait and slightly hunched back showed he was not in the best of health. As he turned to return up the stone steps, he started whistling an odd and out-of-tune melody. Yoshi instantly created a story in his mind that his guide was an old monk—perhaps even an old samurai—who had fallen on hard times. With no family to care for him, the School of Aspen, in an act of charity, had provided him a home.

Yoshi hesitated in following Daichi, lost in his thoughts. Sensing the new pupil was not coming along, the monk stopped and turned back around. "It may seem difficult at first, but everything is difficult at first," the monk said with a smile.

Slightly embarrassed, Yoshi smiled and nodded. He

recognized the old monk's comment as a quote made famous by Musashi. With that, he started his ascent, realizing these were his first steps toward becoming a samurai. As they continued up the tree-lined stone walkway, Yoshi spotted a second gate at the end of the steps. This gate was made of wood and adorned with images of the great samurai of Japanese history. Right above the gate and painted with crimson red characters were the words, *The School of Aspen.*

The wooden gates opened to reveal a magnificent courtyard humming to life with the sights and sounds of students buzzing across it. As the two entered the school, Yoshi marveled at the enormous temple on the opposite end of the courtyard. A procession of a dozen monks solemnly crossed the courtyard and entered the shrine while others knelt before the statues it housed, deep in prayer. "This is the great temple of the School of Aspen. It is in the very heart of the campus as a reminder of the place spirituality must play in a samurai's life."

At the west end of the courtyard stood another shrine. Less ornate than the temple, Yoshi could immediately tell it was dedicated to all the great samurai throughout Japanese history. His guide confirmed his assumption. "The shrine honors all those who have come before us and have departed into the heavens." Yoshi's heart skipped a beat when he saw intermingled with all the other dedications a shrine to his childhood hero, Miyamoto Musashi. The reality began to filter throughout him that he was embarking on the same journey as his idol once had. It took all his might to keep his legs from giving way.

Yoshi followed the old monk as they ventured to the

east side of the courtyard and through a sliding wooden door. The duo was met by the deafening sounds of bamboo and wooden swords cracking against each other. The thunderous sounds of swordplay were only outdone by the barking commands of the instructor's criticism and encouragement. Yoshi marveled at their speed and skills as he and the guide traipsed along the edge of the dojo courtyard. Watching these students spar, a sudden fear of inadequacy overcame Yoshi. He did not see a single student in the bunch that he felt confident enough to battle against. The breadth of the task he was about to undertake was becoming apparent.

Leaving behind the sparring students, Daichi and Yoshi traveled down a gravel pathway carved in the grassy field. The guide pointed out a meditation area replete with fine white, perfectly raked sand and a flourishing koi pond. As they left behind the area, Yoshi spied the first really shocking sight of his brief stay at the school. Trotting and chanting in a tightly aligned formation was a group of nearly thirty women.

"Close your jaw, Yoshi-san lest one of our female samurai shuts it with the butt end of a wooden sword. The lessons taught at the School of Aspen are for all samurai... of both genders." While not found on the front line of the battlefield, Japan had plenty of female samurai. They were expected to fight every bit as hard as any of their male counterparts. Usually, they would be called on to fight at the most desperate of times, as the final line between the enemy and the rest of the household. Yoshi was slightly embarrassed by his unsophisticated views. He simply never thought of women as fit or able to be a samurai. It was his first lesson at the School of Aspen.

Crossing a bridge over a large stream that was almost a river, the two came upon the living quarters for the male students. The monk showed Yoshi to his designated mat among a long row of others. "This is where you can stow your belongings and where you can sleep, in whatever little time you will have for that."

The duo quickly left behind the barracks and returned to the center of campus. Instead of entering the dojo center, the guide led him through a gate within a low-lying wooden fence. The buildings in this courtyard were open-air shelters packed with students. They were either writing or attentively listening to an instructor. Walking in between the structure, Yoshi could listen in on some of the seminars. He was captivated by the variety of topics covered, from philosophy to war theory to history. Lagging behind his guide, Yoshi wished the tour would discontinue and he could take a seat with his fellow students. He was so eager to absorb the knowledge being offered. "Keep up Yoshi-san, you will spend plenty of time here and we still have much to cover."

The monk led Yoshi out of the learning center and across the rest of the campus. He showed the new student all the other buildings at the school including the lodging of the senior senpai and elders along with the other shrines, memorials, and meeting areas. Daichi informed him of the daily schedule for each student. Beginning with the ringing of the campus' main bell right before dawn. The day is full of classroom study, physical exercises, combat training, and other school-assigned duties. In the evening, he will have some personal time for self-reflection prior to getting precious few hours of sleep. Yoshi could sense the tour was nearing its conclusion as they ended up back near the center of campus.

"And that temple to the north, what is that?" Yoshi asked.

The entrance door to this temple was far less ornate than any other entrance in the compound. There was absolutely nothing remarkable about it, which made it grab Yoshi's attention.

"It is odd you should inquire about that temple. It is not part of the usual tour, but since you asked, I will go off script. That is the Ishuiado Temple, the sacred resting place of the Swords of Illumination. We do not usually do this, but I will show you."

As Daichi led the way past the white rock garden to the steps of the temple, Yoshi noticed an older gentleman speaking to a pair of monks. All three turned their attention to Yoshi and bowed to him. Yoshi paused and returned the bow. When he looked back up, he recognized something familiar about the older gentleman. He initially brushed off his first impression of where he knew the man but then took a second look. The smiling face that returned his gaze confirmed his initial thought; it was the old farmer from the marketplace! A sudden breeze literally knocked the dumbfounded Yoshi back a step.

The farmer along with the two elder monks walked over to Yoshi. Falling to his knees, the farmer cried, "Thank you. Thank you." The other words he uttered came out too fast to be coherent. The monks helped the old farmer up off his knees. "May the gods grant a thousand blessings to you and your heirs, Yoshi-san." A still silent Yoshi stood, mouth agape, as the trio walked off.

"He has suffered greatly in recent years. His land was raided by rōnin. His wife and two daughters were lost to illness. His attack in the marketplace had nothing to do with any anger toward you but toward his life. After your encounter, he sought out one of our monks and regaled him with the tale of your restraint."

"I could have killed him," Yoshi softly replied.

"But you didn't. Why?"

"I thought about the engraving on the sword. Killing him wasn't who I was."

The old monk smiled. While he had been friendly and congenial the whole day, this was the first time Yoshi saw real affection from the old monk. "And that is why you are here," he explained. "Obtaining the sword did not grant you access to our school. It was your application of that sword that earned you an invitation."

"But I didn't use the sword."

"Oh, you did. The Swords of Illumination are forged of iron and steel, but their true strength does not come from their ability to cut and slice. Their usefulness comes from applying the lessons etched upon them. Once you have demonstrated the knowledge of the sword and, more importantly, the application of that knowledge, the sword will be taken from you, and you will be invited to accept the next Sword of Illumination."

"The next sword? There are more?" Yoshi asked.

Without a response, Daichi pushed open the Ishuiado Temple's doors. Both paused in silent meditation before the altar at its entrance before proceeding further. Through a stone corridor lined with lit firesticks, the two traveled until reaching a wooden door. With a hefty push, the monk opened the door to the chambers. Yoshi adjusted his eyes to the sudden brilliance that was upon him. From a dingy hallway, he entered a round chamber room laden with radiant golden panels and adorned with wall ornaments honoring the various Shinto gods. Hung across the walls were dozens of swords, sheathed into golden pockets within the walls.

"The Swords of Illumination," gasped Yoshi.

"Actually, these are merely replicas of the first Sword of Illumination, the Sword of Identity. Just like the one you carry at your side. When a samurai in training has shown mastery of the Sword of Identity, the sword is taken from him and returned here where it will be held until another person is deemed worthy to receive it."

"This sword is not mine to keep?"

"The sword will always be with you in that you will be able to use the knowledge you take from it. But we believe knowledge is strengthened when it can be shared."

"The roots from a single seedling, just like an aspen tree," Yoshi mused.

"I am amazed by your insight. Your father must have been a great teacher. That is why the elders gave him the Sword of Identity. They were confident he would prepare its eventual recipient well."

"I wish he were here to share this moment with me," Yoshi sighed as he remained staring in amazement at the swords surrounding him.

"Are you ready to begin your lessons Yoshi-san?" the monk asked.

"Yes," a confident Yoshi replied. He unsheathed his sword, bowed, and offered it to the monk. Simultaneously, the monk took out a rag, bowed, and offered it to Yoshi. Embarrassed, Yoshi looked up.

"I assumed you were ready to take the sword from me and pass it on to the next one," a reddened Yoshi responded.

"One, you humble me to think that I am the one who decides if and when you move on to the next sword. There are higher authorities than me who make that decision. And two, here is a bit of advice not given on the typical orientation tour. Never assume anything."

Yoshi sheathed his sword and took the rag from the monk. "Your first task, young student, is to polish each sword in the chamber. Make sure each is clean enough to blind you with its reflection. When your task is complete, return to the dining area and your dinner will be ready." The monk walked toward the door and without turning said, "...or your breakfast."

Daichi departed, humming that same odd, out-of-tune melody. Yoshi counted the seventy-six swords in the surrounding walls. He picked up the polishing agent off a table in the center and removed the first sword.

The sword's engraving read the same as the one he discovered in his father's chest:

Sword of Identity
Who am I in this moment?
Have my actions reflected who I am?
Hold who you are in your mind at all times and your actions will manifest accordingly!

He would read and re-read this quote hundreds of times. By sword number forty, he was saying it out loud just to give his ears something to do in the silence of the chamber.

By the sixty-second sword, he was almost singing it. As he completed the last polishing wipes on sword seventy-six, Yoshi could think of nothing else but those words.

CHAPTER 6

Sword of Identity

Yoshi stumbled out of the temple into the night air. He had no idea what part of the night he was entering. All he knew was that his fingers were aching, his eyelids were heavy, and his belly was barren. After several wrong turns, he found his way to the dining area. Placed out in the middle of one of the benches were two rice balls illuminated by a single candle. He rushed over to the table and inhaled his late dinner/early breakfast. He was so focused on satisfying his hunger, several minutes went by before he noticed the note that lay beside the candle.

Thank you for your help today in maintaining our swords. Please enjoy your meal and get some rest. Morning exercise begins promptly when the sun breaks the horizon.

That could be in five hours or twenty minutes for all Yoshi knew. Whatever the case, he needed some sleep. He finished the last bit of his meal and returned the dish to the kitchen area. Using the candle as his guide, he found his way to the barracks. Spying the only empty mat in the group, he tiptoed to it, navigating the space between slumbering students. As soon as his head hit the ground, sleep overtook him.

It felt like it was closer to the twenty minutes rather than the five hours as the hustle and bustle of awaking students aroused him from his sleep. The student to his right quickly bowed to him and signaled for him to join him. Yoshi, still bleary-eyed, got up and raced out with the rest of his new mates.

This is how each day would begin for the next thirty in a row. The mornings were filled with exercise that included calisthenics and running. This was followed by classroom lessons in philosophy and war theory. The afternoons were for combat and sword training. The day concluded with the designation of chores, such as cleaning and general maintenance of the school. The evenings were set for reflective time, reading, and conversation.

Yoshi committed himself with great zeal to each task. He immersed himself in every exercise and heeded every lesson. He thought himself a sponge soaking up every bit of knowledge he could absorb. The one thing lacking from this incredible experience was communication, particularly his communication with others. Since his first interaction with the monk that greeted him, Yoshi barely spoke to another person since he arrived. It was not from a lack of effort or because others were especially rude. Yoshi just never felt comfortable engaging any of his fellow students or the senpai, the senior-level students, who also served as instructors. He constantly awaited someone else to make the first initiation of conversation. He was still waiting one month into his studies. Initially, he chalked up his lack of engagement with others as being the new guy in school; however, two weeks after his entry into the gates of the School of Aspen, a new student arrived and was received with much greater fanfare.

The entry-level trainees were divided into two groups. The new student was placed in the other group from Yoshi so what he knew of him was only from word of mouth. That word told of a brash, confident young man who had rapidly set himself apart from the rest. His ability with the sword was astonishing, as he bested every one of his classmates and even several senpai. Rumor had it that he would be promoted to the next sword within days, an astonishing feat since it took most students several months to achieve that goal.

This recent rumor sent Yoshi into a funk. For several days, he mulled over his failure to connect with anyone and the reason everyone viewed the new student as such a success. It was not being boastful to say he had ascended to become one of the finest students in his groups. On several occasions, instructors singled him out for his grasp of the lessons taught in class. His excellence in combat training had made his fellow students wary of facing him. When the senpai sought volunteers to face off against Yoshi, no hands rose, forcing the senpai to select the unfortunate opponent who would soon provide an example of a vanquished foe.

One evening during the self-reflection period, Yoshi wandered off by himself to the meditation garden. He needed to *get out of his mind*, and he wanted solitude. He found a spot to lie down beside the koi pond. Staring up at the cloudless night sky, Yoshi began another round of mental shadow boxing.

Why have I not been promoted to the next sword when I have utilized its lesson in the face-off with the farmer? he asked himself. *The monk had clearly stated moving on meant showing mastery of the lesson of the sword. Had I not shown that? How was this new student so readily showing his mastery of the sword?*

During times like this back home, when questions ravaged his brain, he would visit his father's old chest of scrolls. Even though the scrolls were still in his family's attic, the stories they told remained in his memory, as clear as if he was reading them from the paper. He laid back and closed his eyes. In the library of his mind, Yoshi chose a scroll about his hero Musashi. He recounted the tales it told about the great samurai and his many legendary battles and victories. He smiled thinking of how Musashi used a combination of guile and skill to defeat his foes in glorious fashion. *Oh, it would be great to live the life of a samurai,* he thought to himself. A strange voice suddenly shot him up onto his feet.

"Are they saying anything interesting tonight?" It was the odd old monk, Daichi, who had guided him through his orientation. The last time Yoshi had seen him was right before his all-night polishing session with the Swords of Identity. The scent of oil and grease immediately flooded his memory.

"Who?" A confused Yoshi looked around seeking others.

"The koi. What kernels of wisdom are they speaking of this evening?" asked Daichi.

"Honestly, it had not occurred to me to ask them for help."

"Then who are you asking?" The old monk sat cross-legged by the side of the pond, a good thirty meters from Yoshi. Yoshi could not tell if the monk was respecting Yoshi's space or laying out his own.

"What makes you think I need help?" Yoshi's feeble attempt at pride was deflected right back at him by Daichi's arched eyebrows. "Okay, perhaps I do have some questions. But as a samurai, I will be faced with many puzzles, and I will have to solve them on my own." He wanted to impress upon the monk his fortitude and strength. He failed.

"The only samurai that have no need for guidance are the ones etched on the walls of the great shrine," the monk coolly replied. "Should I have the carpenter begin to add your likeness to the wall?"

"Those are only for dead samurai." Yoshi got the point as soon as the last syllable escaped his lips. To avoid his lingering embarrassment, Yoshi quickly changed the conversation. "So, Daichi-san, besides orientation tours, is there anything else you do here at the school?" Yoshi was making idle chatter with the idea of changing the subject away from him. He still held the belief that Daichi was a ward of the School of Aspen who was given menial jobs to keep him busy in his old age.

"I do a great many things. I enjoy each day. I explore, study, laugh, and sing. And on occasion, I help people who seek help."

"What sort of help?" Yoshi could not stop himself from asking although he was not sure he wanted to go down this road.

"Each person has their unique needs so the help I provide can vary. I offer guidance and advice on how to remedy their problems."

"So, you provide answers to life's mysteries?" he asked somewhat derisively.

"I don't provide answers. I just ask the right questions," he responded ignoring the mocking of the young student. "My aid enables people to seek out their own solutions."

Yoshi contemplated the monk's response. "To seek," he repeated under his breath. A chill coursed through his body and the image of his father invaded his vision.

"My final advice to you is to always seek."

Yoshi looked upon the old monk in a new light, thinking that he might have judged him incorrectly. "That can be quite valuable I think," Yoshi finally acknowledged.

Yoshi caught his reflection in the koi pond. He looked at the rippled image of himself and wondered how others saw him. He thought whether they made the same misjudgments about him as he made about the old monk.

"What do you see?" the old man quietly asked.

"Oh, nothing," Yoshi replied, brushing off the question.

"What do you want to see?" the old monk persisted.

Yoshi paused. If he saw nothing, then would others see the same? He knew beneath that reflection was a man of great talent, confident in his ability, and with a distinguished air that commanded respect. "I want to see... me."

He drew out his Sword of Identity and re-read the engraved words.

Who am I in this moment? He had always been secure in his belief that he was a great samurai in waiting.

Have my actions reflected who I am? Since he entered the School of Aspen, what had he done to reflect his belief in who he is? The answer that came back was a resounding, *Nothing.* He has carried himself as only a student in the shadows, meekly waiting for the light to be turned on him. He had taken no steps to manifest the image of what he wanted to be. If he did not behave like a samurai or show the confidence that he deserves to be at the school, why would anyone treat him as such?

Hold who you are in your mind at all times and your actions will manifest accordingly! If he believed in himself, truly and wholeheartedly, his behavior would stem from that confidence. And even if others judged him incorrectly or with disdain, he would be true to himself.

He was thunderstruck at the realization. He turned to Daichi who was now standing and smiling at him. "I just ask the right questions," the old monk repeated.

"Do you offer this help to anybody, even lowly students?" Yoshi imagined that a man of Daichi's age and experience probably does not waste his time with mere students. He was happily surprised at the response.

"If it is your choice, I will be happy to offer you some time in which we can converse about whatever subjects you choose." The old monk spoke bluntly and firmly. "I have only two conditions. First, you come to me with an open mind and, second, you keep a true commitment to our work. Not because you have to, but because you want to."

Yoshi bowed in agreement and offered many thanks. As he jogged back to his barracks, he felt a burst of energy. He had someone to seek advice from and he felt confident it would be an invaluable aid in his quest to become a samurai. He did not realize it would mean so much more.

The next morning Yoshi could barely contain the excitement of his self-discovery and the opportunity to put it into action. He decided that he would put into practice his new identity during the morning breakfast at the conclusion of exercises. *In reality, I am putting on my old identity*, Yoshi thought to himself.

During dining time, the senpai sat in a separate dining hall from the other students. This morning, they would get a new dining mate. He could feel the questioning eyes upon him as he carried his meal into the hall. He scanned the area for an open seat and spied one among the most senior-level samurai of the School of Aspen. *Well, if I'm going to join this crowd, might as well start at the top,* Yoshi thought and moved with confidence to the table.

"May I join you on this glorious morning?" Yoshi inquired. One of the eight samurai seated at the bench gave him silent approval and Yoshi joined them. At first, he sat quietly, engaging in their conversation without saying anything. He wanted to speak but not just for the sake of hearing his own voice. Then the conversation turned to something Yoshi knew about, farming.

One of the senior senpai was complaining about the poor harvest of apples he experienced while working on a farm. He could not understand why every year the crop had steadily diminished in size and quality.

Yoshi could not stop the chuckle that escaped before it became audible. For as long as he could remember, he did all he could to leave his life as a farmer to become a great warrior. Now, here he was sitting at the finest samurai academy in the land with a group of future great leaders, and the very past he was running from returned to his present. The surrealism was almost too much to handle.

"What is so funny?" asked the senpai with a bit of irritation.

"Pardon me, but I am not laughing at you, but with you," Yoshi quickly covered. "You see, I grew up on a farm and have experienced the disappointment of poor harvests." He proceeded to hold court for the next several minutes explaining that most of the time, the issue lies with the soil quality. He regaled them with methods and techniques taught by his father on how to detect deficiencies in the soil quality and remedy them. "The manner in which life grows is based directly on its foundation, its soil. Start with a secure foundation that is properly cultivated and nourished, and your bounty will be great. In farming as well as in life."

The last comment was a direct line from something his father told him once. He thought it amazing that it would jog loose from his stored memory at this given moment. The senpai quietly stared at Yoshi, but the one seeking advice broke the silence. "That makes sense... on many levels."

The conversation turned into a lively discussion of the point Yoshi had introduced. Yoshi felt emboldened to share more of his father's philosophies, on both farming and life. He remained amused throughout the meal at how the two subjects interchanged, begrudgingly thankful for all those hours of drudgery in the field.

The morning was a greater success than he ever dreamed it could be. The senior samurai seemed to genuinely appreciate Yoshi's insight and company. As his day went along, other students and senpai greeted him in a friendly and respectful manner. *Words travel with the mountain wind*, Yoshi thought, remembering a line from one of his scrolls. He could feel the energy of everyone's attitude toward him lifting him up, giving a spring to his step and strength to his posture.

During the evening's reflection time, Yoshi could not wait to share with his fellow classmates his revelation. He believed they were struggling with the same identity questions, and Yoshi was eager to see that spark of awareness in their eyes when he told them what he learned.

With an almost sing-song quality to his voice, Yoshi told a circle of his mates about his journey to the School of Aspen, the scrolls of Musashi, and the encounter with the irate farmer. Most importantly, he related his conclusion that one needs to believe in who they want to be and must follow that vision with actions. At the conclusion of his rousing tale, he was met with silence. He expected to be showered with gratitude from his comrades for showing them the way. Instead, he was met with muted comments such as "That was a great story," and "Thank you for sharing it with us." While their appreciation was genuine, Yoshi could tell from the blank looks in their eyes that they did not understand what he was telling them.

The jubilation of the day was diminished a bit by the failure to get his point across to them. He pounded himself with questions. *Why didn't they understand? Was it the way I told the story? Was I wrong in my beliefs?* The old insecurities began to creep back in, but his confidence bluntly blocked them from taking hold. *No, I know what I did was right. I showed myself to be who I am. My actions reflected who I am.*

"Yoshi Minamura," barked the senior senpai who entered the barracks. "Grab your sword and follow me!" He had just been called out and he had no idea of the reason. His mates looked at him with concern, and he shared their anxiety. He grabbed his sword, steadied himself the best he could, and walked out of the room. *Well, if I am going to fail, at least I failed on my terms*, he thought to himself in an attempt to bolster his confidence.

The senpai did not speak as he led. To Yoshi's surprise, they veered away from the main campus and up the steps to the Ishuiado Temple. He had not entered the temple since his first day at the school and his marathon polishing session. After the duo paid respect to the shrine at the entrance, they walked to the other side of the shrine. The senpai then pushed a false wall and directed Yoshi to enter. Upon passing through the wall, it was closed shut and Yoshi was left alone in pitch black.

After what felt to be an excruciatingly long time that was probably only a few seconds, a single flame brought light to the room. Several other flames came to life until the room was completely illuminated. The room before him was not as decorated as the chamber with the Swords of Identity. There were no golden panels and while it had tapestries adorning the walls, they were not of gods but of samurai warriors. In his quick glance around the chamber, he recognized one of the renderings as Mushashi.

In his peripheral sight to his left, he could see another young man standing alongside him. He could not get a good look at him to recognize his face, but Yoshi was impressed by his rigid, unwavering stance.

Yoshi's eyes turned to the door before them as it opened. In a solemn processional, twelve elders in hooded robes entered the room and lined up. In unison, the twelve bowed, and Yoshi and his partner returned the respect. One from the group stepped forward and gestured for Yoshi and the other to kneel down. "Present your swords," the elder commanded.

Both unsheathed their sword and with bowed heads presented them to the group. The swords were quickly taken from them. The thought crossed Yoshi's mind that this was his dismissal. Perhaps the story he told to the senpai was somehow offensive, or he should not have shared his experience with the other students. *No, everything you did was in keeping with the lesson of the sword. You were true to yourself. Do not begin doubting yourself now, Yoshi,* he castigated himself. Yoshi looked up to see the elder who had been speaking was now right in front of him and the other young man.

"You two have been called here tonight to take one more step on the path of enlightenment and balance. By being here, you have shown to yourselves that you understand the great gift of the Sword of Identity. In time, you will learn its true power. It is now time to receive the next level of enlightenment."

Two others in robes stepped forward, kneeled before the young students, and, with bowed heads, presented a new sword still encased in its sheath.

"Before you accept the next Sword of Illumination, you are both permitted to ask one question of this council in order to gain additional knowledge. Togo-san, you may go first."

The young man, Togo, replied without a moment's hesitation. It was as if he had scripted his response. "What can I do to accelerate my learning process in order to become a samurai as quickly as possible?"

The leader of the council responded just as quickly in a monotone, almost detached voice, "The answer you seek is in the experience itself."

"Thank you," Togo replied without a hint of confusion.

Yoshi, on the other hand, was confused. Of all the questions to ask this great council, why choose that one? Was that what the council wanted to hear? Did they want questions that exhibit the student's eagerness?

"Yoshi-san, what is your question?"

Yoshi pondered it for a moment. He decided he might

never get this chance again, so he decided to ask the question that was most pressing on his mind. "When I came to understand the life lesson of the Sword of Identity, when I realized that I could create who I am and I could live the life I chose through my actions, I was overjoyed. In my exuberance, I wanted desperately to share this insight and knowledge with my fellow students. However, upon telling them what I learned, they failed to grasp its meaning and ignored what I had to say. Can you help me understand this?"

Yoshi thought he detected a glimmer of a smile slip on the leader's face. "Oftentimes, others cannot learn from your experience processed through your words. They must seek their own words through a personal verified experience." The leader began to turn away but paused for one more comment. "Yoshi-san, you are already further down the path of the next sword than you know." With that, the leader led the group of twelve elders out of the room.

Yoshi immediately unsheathed the sword and read its engraving:

Sword of Mission and Purpose

"So Yoshi became what he thought he was," Tom said, feigning his understanding.

"He chose to see himself as a samurai and because he accepted it and embraced it, he was in turn accepted by others," clarified the old storyteller. "When creating an identity, there are three things to remember. First, you have free choice in everything. Yoshi was free to choose to be a samurai. Second, who you say you are is who you'll be.

Yoshi acted and spoke like an equal to the other senpai and, therefore, became one. Third, and most importantly, until you accept it, no one else will. Once he saw a samurai in his reflection, everyone else did too."

"I think therefore I am," Tom replied.

"I think and do, therefore I am," corrected the old man.

"One thing I don't get though," Tom said. "If he proved he understood the lesson during his encounter at the marketplace, why did he have to do it again?"

"That Camaro you owned... just because you drove it once did not make you a good driver, did it?"

"I drove it a million times and my mother would still question if I was a good driver. But I think I see your point. I work as a financial advisor. I assist our firm's clients with creating a portfolio to meet their needs. When I select investments, I don't look for one-year successes, but those that have a proven track record over a long period of time."

The old man smiled. "I am woefully uninformed about the world of finance and money, but that is the idea. Success is not achieved by doing something only once, it is in the ability to duplicate those actions where true mastery is achieved."

"It's the difference between being Bruce Springsteen and being Billy Ray Cyrus," Tom mused.

"Are they stockbrokers?"

The sound of his own laughter startled Tom. It had been a while since he truly laughed at something, but something about this old stranger was putting him at ease. And something about this tale was starting to make sense.

CHAPTER 7

Sword of Mission & Purpose: Part I

U pon graduation to the second Sword of Illumination, students at the School of Aspen moved from the shared barracks and were provided their own private room. Small in size and without any amenities, it served as a place for the warrior in training to enjoy some degree of privacy. Walled off by thin rice paper panels, the room had just enough space for a mat and some personal effects.

The first thing Yoshi did upon entering his new quarters was to put up his new sword on the wall. Standing before it, he quietly reflected on its inscription.

Sword of Mission and Purpose
Why am I here and what is my path?

While escorting him back to the barracks, the senpai informed Yoshi that his first order of business should be to answer the sword's query. The answer would serve as his mission statement and guide him through his studies at the school as well as in his life beyond. A litany of possible answers had been buzzing in his head ever since he first read the inscription, but now was the time to concentrate and settle on an appropriate response. As he knelt before the sword, he felt the weight posed by the significance of this decision. This identity statement must be something he truly believed.

Why am I here and what is my path? Since the day he saw his father slain, Yoshi had dreamed his path would lead him into the armament of a great samurai, allowing him to exact his revenge. But since he had begun his training at the School of Aspen, his mind and soul had been exposed to numerous other pursuits, pursuits that seemingly ran counter to his vengeful endeavors. He thought about the genuine feeling of excitement he had in wanting to share his insight about the Sword of Identity with his fellow students. He reflected on the joy of reading from the scrolls in his father's chest and engaging in the discussion of its lessons. Finally, Yoshi recalled the warmth he had felt from the old farmer's gratitude for his display of understanding and patience. He felt uneasy and confused that the embers of revenge may be cooling and feared this was an act of treason against his father's memory.

The next afternoon he shared his concerns with his new mentor. "I will still have the murderer answer for his crime," he argued, more to himself than his audience. "But there has to be more to my life than just seeking revenge. I do not want my father's murderer and my existence to end at the same moment."

"That is a wise observation, Yoshi-san," the old monk replied. "One that many make too late in life." The two sat on a hilltop, basking in the early afternoon sun. Below a group of recently arrived students were going through rudimentary combat skill lessons. Their yells sounded muffled to the ears of Yoshi and Daichi, caused as much by the students' exhaustion as by their distance. Daichi's eyes never left the group, but Yoshi sensed he was looking through rather than at them.

"So?" Yoshi finally asked after an extended pause. "What should I do?" Yoshi came to the monk to hear his advice but found the conversation decidedly one-sided.

"*What should you do* is the question, isn't it?" the monk asked his young questioner.

"Oh, is this an example of you asking the right questions?"

"No. This is an example of you answering the right questions." The monk smiled to ease the bluntness of his assessment.

Yoshi bowed his head in frustration. He thought about the times his own father never gave him a straight answer to a question. It infuriated him then as it did now. *Why can't he just tell me what to do!* he shouted in his mind.

On cue, as if he heard Yoshi's cry, the monk spoke. "Every time I escort a new student through the grounds of the school, I feel I witness the beginning of life. Each student enters here with the same goal in life, to be samurai. Yet it is the life led once they have achieved this goal that is true living. This school. These swords. It is about creating a perpetual, worthy life, not one that ends at just being samurai. So the question again is... *what should you do?*"

The old monk sprung up and brushed the grass from his robe. Yoshi continued staring into the distance, perplexed by the monk's comments. "What else is there beyond being a samurai?" he whispered.

"I can give you an answer to your question. You would accept it and do all you could to adopt it into your life. But eventually, it would corrode you. Your true sense of self would rebel against this foreign body inside of you. This mission statement must derive from you alone. No one, not even the sagest man in the world, can answer it for you. Your statement of purpose defines who and what you are. It will be the seed that germinates your sense of self, and every action you take will stem from that core." The monk departed leaving the young student alone with his meandering thoughts.

A breeze kicked up a leaf from one of the aspens and blew it onto Yoshi's leg. He picked it up and twirled it in his hand. He reflected how from a single seedling, millions of these leaves were born. He mused about how powerful that single seed was to affect so much of the environment and life around it. *"The vastness of one's accomplishments is measured by the vastness of its influence."* It was a quote he recalled from an old scroll and was about to dismiss it as another obscure proverb when it suddenly hit him. *"That's it!"*

Yoshi rushed back to his quarters. Once there, he settled down and closed his eyes to lower his racing heart. He realized the importance of this moment of self-discovery. He calmly and deliberately took out a sheet of paper, some ink, and a brush. He thought it would be best to literally write down his identity statement. The written form had the permanence and heft that Yoshi sought from his statement. It made it more of a pronouncement as if he was declaring this statement to the world. As if the words were being dictated to him from another source, he wrote it out without a second of pause.

Upon completion, he held it up for inspection, evaluating the language and penmanship. Satisfied it met the standards of such an important document, Yoshi pinned the statement just below the hanging sword. He set it up to serve as a reminder every morning when he rose and every evening when he lay to sleep. His declaration read:

I am Yoshi Minamura. I seek to enrich my soul through the obtaining of knowledge and wisdom. In turn, I shall share this enlightenment through my actions and words in order to serve the world around me.

The old monk was right. This statement was the seed inside him that would spring all his actions. In turn, he sought to be like the aspen seed, to influence his environment in a positive and nurturing manner. This would serve him beyond being a samurai.

Filled with a new sense of confidence that only the direction of purpose can give, Yoshi left his new room and trotted to his afternoon lessons. His thoughts were interrupted by a deep voice. *"Because people don't listen."* Yoshi was startled not so much by the comments but by the voice, since he did not detect anyone approaching him. He stopped to take in his fellow student.

"It is because people don't listen. The answer to your question at the sword ceremony about the students failing to grasp your meaning and ignoring what you said. It is because people don't listen."

After a few moments of study, Yoshi realized the intruder was Togo, the student who joined him at the graduation ceremony. Yoshi had learned that he was also the much-heralded student admired by all his classmates. Togo walked with an exaggeratedly straight posture that accentuated the height advantage he had over Yoshi. His frame was lean and covered with wiry muscles. Togo stared at him with eyes of pure focus and commitment. Yoshi thought them familiar but could not place in who else's face he had seen them.

"Oh, they'll hear you, and they will follow your commands if you lead them," continued Togo. "But no one ever really listens except to the fist and sword."

Togo continued walking to the class and Yoshi followed. "I beg to differ. I think if done properly and articulately, one can pass on these lessons to people. Are you not listening to the advice given to you?"

"I am not people," he answered as they both entered the class and occupied seating areas for the next round of lessons, thus concluding the debate.

For the next couple of weeks, Yoshi focused on putting into practice his mission statement, both because he wanted to live by it and also to prove Togo wrong. Since he was now a second-level student, he was expected to help the newer students and provide assistance when requested. He made a point of introducing himself to every one of the new students and extend an offer of assistance. Every time he did this, the student responded with great gratitude and a genuine interest in taking Yoshi up on his offer. But so far, none had come to him for help.

He did get a request for help but from an unexpected source. The senpai, who Yoshi engaged in the lively conversation about farming several weeks earlier, approached him at the conclusion of his philosophy class. "I've given our little conversation much thought, Yoshi-san," the senpai said as an introduction.

The senpai asked Yoshi to follow him as the two ventured outside the main compound and across a wide plain. On the other side, Yoshi spotted another set of wooden gates. Although large, they were not as grand as the main entrance to the academy. As the senpai pushed open the doors, Yoshi was startled as a wave of nostalgia and dejection swept over him. Before him was a moderate-sized apple orchid, not dissimilar to the one located on his family farm.

"The School of Aspen does more than produce great warriors," explained the senpai. "We also conduct commerce with the neighboring villages by providing an assortment of products, both agricultural and manufactured. More than a money-making enterprise, we find that having our students hold employment outside of their studies helps build character, knowledge, and understanding of how society functions."

"And so, you want me to work the fields of the orchard? I have plenty of experience in this and don't see how this will help me grow," Yoshi said.

"We are hoping your experience will help the apples grow. Our harvest has not been up to previous years, and we need you to run the operations to ensure a bountiful crop."

"Won't this affect my studies to become a samurai?" Yoshi asked searching for any excuse not to follow this order.

"Consider it part of your studies as a samurai. I know the elders take success at your job into consideration when promoting to the next level."

Initially, Yoshi thought his past had come back to curse him, but now he saw the blessing of having this experience. If running a farm would get him to the next level, then he would operate the most efficient and productive farm this school had ever seen. He immediately met with the farm's staff, whose ages ranged from pre-teen to over sixty. With an exuberance his new staff might see as madness, he let them know that his goal was to double the production of sellable apples for the upcoming harvest.

After introductions were completed, Yoshi made a brief announcement. "This is a goal that is completely achievable if you heed what I say and give maximum effort," Yoshi explained. The glossy-eyed response he received from his audience did not boost Yoshi's confidence, yet he was committed. Being a farmer was the last thing he ever expected to do again, but he was willing to undertake any task to achieve his ultimate goal.

As the senpai bid his farewell to Yoshi, he offered one last bit of advice. "I noticed you have not signed up for the Tournament of Tests. You should, Yoshi-san. It's another way into the hearts of the elders."

Every two weeks, the school pitted students against each other in various tests of physical and mental ability, called the Tournament of Tests. Attended by the entire student body, these events had a festive air about them and were looked upon as entertaining distractions from all the hard work. The school's elders also attended and watched the proceedings from a designated box above the field. Their presence was a reminder that while entertaining, the participants were under constant evaluation.

Yoshi had shied away from entering in order to spend time on his studies. He also wanted to allot his time and energy to helping the younger students, but he had not received an outpouring of requests. Realizing that his performance in these contests could enhance and accelerate his chance of promotion, Yoshi signed up the next day for his first set of contests.

With a new focus, Yoshi spent the next three months consumed with studies, work, and competitions. In classroom lessons, he was often the first to offer a response to the question and provided answers even his instructors found compelling. After class, he was approached by some of his fellow students seeking his insight about the day's lessons. While he was happy to help and provide answers, Yoshi's responses lacked the depth and understanding he knew he could offer because he felt a crunch of time pressing on top of him. There was always another chore to accomplish or another place he needed to be. He did the best he could to live by the principle of his mission statement, but there were just so few hours in his packed day.

After his afternoon lessons, Yoshi often raced off to the farm to monitor and supervise its progress. He had restructured the farm's operations, changed the time and manner of pruning, and restructured the harvest methods. He added a new type of fertilizer to the soil. Instead of treating it weekly, he had the staff do it every two days. He was not one to just delegate these duties. He worked elbow to elbow with his staff, helping them with the assignments. No longer did he spend time during the evening's reflection period thinking and discussing issues and lessons with other students as was suggested by the senpai. His work on the farm kept him busy right through the evening, providing only enough time to catch a few hours of sleep before rising for his morning exercises and training.

To add to his already hectic schedule, Yoshi enthusiastically entered as many competitions in the Tournament of Tests as he could. Initially, he faired modestly but each defeat made him work harder in his training for the following test. Upon entering his fourth Tournament of Tests, he won his first victory in the riddle-solving test. It was especially satisfying since solving a riddle found him his original invitation to the School of Aspen.

Two weeks later, Yoshi scored his first victory in

Kenjutsu, the martial art of fencing. These competitions were not for the faint of heart or body. Students engaged in combat with either a shinai—a bamboo sword tethered together in segmented portions by rope or string—or the bokken—a solid wooden stick shaped into the style of a katana sword. The selection of these practice weapons was determined by the student's ability and the discretion of the ranking senpai at the practice or tournament. The students squared off with the victor of each match determined when a student yielded or was judged unable to continue by the presiding senpai. It was not uncommon for students to spend a day or two in the infirmary after these competitions.

His first triumph gained him notoriety throughout the school and filled him with self-confidence. The self-confidence fed upon itself. For four consecutive tournaments, Yoshi bested his competition by utilizing a blend of the arts taught at the school, the lessons his father taught him, and the techniques he read from Musashi. After first using this tact, he feared he'd be scolded by his instructors for deviating from the way they were instructing. He was surprised that, to the contrary, they encouraged his adaptation of new styles and applauded his ingenuity. Applause also came from an unlikely source.

"I am impressed," Togo told him after his fourth victory in a row. "And I am not often impressed. I look forward to the time when I can test my ability against you on the field of battle."

Their interactions had been few but always polite, although Yoshi felt he was being judged when in Togo's presence. This was probably due in large measure because he was judging Togo at their every encounter. Togo had been impressive at the tournament's challenges right from the start. He had yet to be defeated in any test of combat, defeating his opponents in increasingly easier fashion.

"The tournament is not really a battle," retorted Yoshi. "I have witnessed battle firsthand and, I assure you, it resembles nothing to sport."

The young man bowed in respect. "Forgive me for any offense. I look forward to... playing with you someday."

Someday arrived the day of the ensuing tournament. A palpable energy encompassed the student body when the matchups were posted in the morning. The undefeated Togo would face the up-and-coming Yoshi in a battle using shinai. In these engagements, the objective is to knock your opponent off his feet or to get him to yield. While designed to simulate a real sword battle, the bamboo shinai are used so as not to cause severe bodily harm. Despite the precautions, the hollow swords are wielded with such speed and strength, especially by warriors as adept as Togo, that many a warrior-in-training left the practice ring battered, bruised, and dazed.

As soon as he saw he would be matched up with Togo, Yoshi began to physically and mentally prepare for the fight. Feeling this was something he needed to do on his own, Yoshi refrained from seeking out Daichi for advice. Instead, he spent the mornings practicing his stances, parries, and thrusts. He visualized how the encounter would go, anticipating Togo's moves and his own counterattacks. When the time came to meet Togo face-to-face at the center of the tournament, Yoshi felt they had fought a thousand times.

Although days after the showdown, several senpai told Yoshi the crowd was the loudest they had ever heard. Yoshi heard nothing the moment he entered the ring. The two bowed to the senior senpai officiating the match and then to each other. Togo's eyes had that same look of pure focus and commitment that Yoshi recognized earlier but still could not place. When the senpai ordered them to engage, Yoshi expected a whirlwind coming from Togo, just as he had done to all his previous opponents. Instead, Togo remained in his stance without moving a muscle. Yoshi thought this to be a sign of hesitation, perhaps even fear, by Togo. He took the initiative and launched into a series of attacks. Slicing and spinning with a speed and agility he had never before achieved, Yoshi pressed the action against Togo, who was able to match Yoshi's every strike with a defensive parry of his shinai.

When Togo launched his counterattack, Yoshi was able to land his first serious blows, first knocking him solidly in the right shoulder and then with a swooping swipe while he knelt that caught Togo flush on the left kneecap. He buckled for a moment but quickly steadied himself and prepared for Yoshi's advance. Sensing he was moments from victory, Yoshi stormed toward Togo, but this time Togo raced to meet him. He came at Yoshi with such speed that they ended up with their faces just inches apart. The mutual exertion on their met shinai was the only thing keeping them from colliding. Yoshi focused on the eyes of his opponent to sense his next move. His assessment proved wrong.

Yoshi did not recall what he felt first, the lightning bolt of pain to his right brow or the crippling blow to his left ankle. He was not sure what had happened until it was retold to him after the fight. Togo, in one simultaneous motion, struck with his head and with his right leg: the former connecting just above Yoshi's right eye, the latter stomping on Yoshi's left foot and holding it in place for a second before releasing it. The combined effect of both blows sent Yoshi staggering backward, his sight temporarily blinded. He never saw the final blow but felt the explosion on the right side of his head. His body hit the ground a half second later, and for the first time that afternoon, he heard the roar of the crowd.

The victor bent down and helped up the fallen Yoshi. As he did so, Togo whispered words into his foe's ear. While the audience interpreted those words as encouragement, Yoshi never shared with anyone the actual quote.

"This isn't playtime. This isn't a game," Togo whispered. "It is always war."

Three nights later, as Yoshi walked back to his room after another long night at the farm, he spied the same senpai who escorted him to his sword ceremony. Joining the senpai was Togo, the Sword of Mission and Purpose firmly in his hand. Yoshi felt the excitement bubbling in his stomach. "This must be the night we get promoted," he exclaimed to himself as he raced back to his room and awaited the senpai escort. Despite his one defeat to Togo, he had accomplished so much. The farm was rapidly improving its operations, surpassing even his lofty goals. He was clearly the most prepared and learned student in his class. His achievements at the tournaments were superior to the vast majority. Some of the students he defeated had gone on to the next level. Yoshi thought surely, he will be promoted tonight.

Sword in hand, Yoshi sat and waited. Minutes became hours and still no escort. He read again the engraving on the sword.

Sword of Mission and Purpose
Why am I here and what is my path?

In his haste, it had been weeks since he read the engraving, or the mission statement posted on his wall. In fact, as he sat waiting for someone who never came, Yoshi could not recall the last time he read either one of them. But tonight, all he could do was read his statement. As he began to succumb to his exhaustion, he heard the words he read all night echoing in his head.

I am Yoshi Minamura. I seek to enrich my soul through the obtaining of knowledge and wisdom. In turn, I shall share this enlightenment through my actions and words in order to serve the world around me.

"What have I done to live up to this?" he asked as he fell asleep.

"That's what I'm talking about," yelled Tom, not as much to the old man but to the world. "He did everything asked of him. He busted his hump and achieved everything he wanted. He didn't succeed by tripping someone up. No, he went about it all the right way, with hard work and dedication. And what does he get in return? Nothing."

The old man sat quietly listening to Tom, not daring to interrupt his explosion.

"I give my best at everything I do. I work hard and no one in that office knows more than me or has a better record of accomplishment. I give my family everything they could want, everything I didn't have growing up. I follow the law and I pay my taxes. And you know what, it's never enough."

Tom's voice was rising with each sentence. "I'll never get ahead in life. I'm stuck here; no promotion, no company, no payoff. And to make matters worse, I'm one pink slip away from losing it all. But the jerks in the world, they win. The guys who go about it the wrong way, the ones who cheat, scheme, lie; they all get what they want. You tell me, with all your wisdom, how is that fair? Why do nice guys finish last?"

The old man did not respond to Tom's questions. They sat there for a while just staring at the fire. The old man was calm, silent. Tom thought he might have something to say, especially in light of some of the points Tom just threw at him. But the old man offered no words. No words save for the next part of Yoshi's story.

CHAPTER 8

Sword of Mission & Purpose: Part II

With sunlight baking his back and the breeze blowing his straight black hair, Yoshi was in utter bliss as he rode atop his new prized pony. Galloping over the hills near his family homestead, he held not a care in the world and the world had no cares for him. It was the nirvana only a youth could enjoy but lacked the age to appreciate.

Returning to the present, an older Yoshi opened his eyes as he lay in a grassy patch. His gaze turned to the band of students playing flutes in melodic unison. The serene tunes emanating from their instruments ushered him back to that blissful moment in his memory. Lately, Yoshi found himself stealing away a few minutes almost every mid-afternoon to hear the group play. It grew to serve as a pleasant, and much-needed respite from his grueling day.

The group was led by one of the female samurai in training, Kira. Yoshi had learned from others that the school had never had a musical group, but that Kira had taken it upon herself to start one. Her mother was an accomplished musician renowned across the northern area of Japan, and it was apparent she passed on those skills to her only daughter. Kira was a second-level student just like Yoshi and was also an exceptional student in the philosophy courses they shared. Their interactions were limited to post-class small talk about the day's lessons.

When Yoshi first began to enjoy their music, the group numbered two to three but had now grown to an even dozen. Their playing had steadily improved, and Yoshi found the performances to be a highlight of his day. While he was never much into music, Yoshi discovered he enjoyed its magical ability to transport him to places he'd rather be.

The sun's position in the sky reminded Yoshi it was time to leave for his job at the farm. Walking at a brisk pace to the compound's south gate, he passed another student-led group, but one he wanted no part of hearing much less joining.

Togo, his recently promoted rival, was demonstrating some of his hand-to-hand combat techniques to some new arrivals to the school. It was not so much a lesson as an opportunity for Togo to boast of his rapid ascension at the school. It also served as a chance for the new students to curry favor through their adulation.

Yoshi had no time or patience to listen to their fawning. He had even less stomach to hear any advice from the acclaimed student or, even worse, any false compliments directed his way. He would not escape without hearing both.

"I am just surprised that Yoshi has not ascended with me to this level," Togo shouted loud enough that he knew Yoshi could not avoid hearing. "Yoshi, please join us and I can offer some tips for your next engagement."

Since Togo was at the higher level, he was technically Yoshi's senpai and he had to follow his instruction. For three weeks now, Yoshi politely joined whenever Togo called on him and he feigned an earnest interest in the advice and lessons Togo gave. Yoshi saw these educational encounters as another intentional head-butt from Togo, but this time meant to bruise the ego rather than the forehead.

Yoshi could not muster the will to partake in the charade. "Togo-san, I ask permission to respectfully decline your generous invitation. My duties at the farm require my immediate attention. While I know there is much I could learn from you today, I regret I cannot join you. May I take your leave?"

Togo studied him for a moment. "Your commitment to the apple orchid is impressive. I believe after your time here at the School of Aspen, you will become the greatest apple warrior of all time. Picture your opponent as red, round, and juicy, and you will never lose a battle again." The group laughed at Togo's wit. Yoshi did not. "Of course, you have my permission to slay that ripened fruit. Be careful none squirt you in the eye."

"Thank you, Togo-san," Yoshi replied and departed. He could still hear the group's laughter echoing in his head as he reached the gates of the farm.

His face reddened by both anger and embarrassment, Yoshi stomped up to the fire to warm himself up and cool himself down. He did not have time to accomplish either when he was interrupted. "I wonder if you could use an extra farmhand," the quivering old voice asked. Yoshi turned to see the old farmer from the marketplace, sans pitchfork, bowing to him. He was overjoyed to see the man, not just for the company but since it recalled one of his prouder moments. His bruised ego needed it, and the greeting pushed his recent troubles to the background.

"Of course, it would be an honor to have you work here," Yoshi replied. "However, I have only one condition."

"Whatever it is, I will do my best to fulfill it."

"This should be very simple for you," smiled Yoshi. "Just tell me your name."

The old man laughed. "We have been through much that I assumed you knew all about me, including my name. It is Hideki and I am at your service."

He was happy to have the old farmer and his wealth of knowledge and experience on his team. *He will be a valuable comrade in our wars with the apples*, he thought to himself.

Yoshi introduced Hideki to the other staff and proceeded to integrate him into the operations as quickly as possible. With each introduction, Yoshi asked the farm hands to get Hideki up to date on how they run things. After the third time he mentioned this, one of the staff, Shingo, interrupted. "With all due respect, Yoshi-san, we really don't know how everything operates."

"What do you mean?" a stunned Yoshi replied. "We seem to be working quite smoothly and effectively. Our harvest will exceed expectations, and you tell me you don't know what you are doing?"

Another staff member interjected. "We know what you tell us to do. Our achievement is due to your great knowledge and direction. But if we are to be honest, we could not do any of this without you."

"You have told us what to do, but never have told us why we do it," added Shingo, the original interrupter.

Throughout the rest of the day, Yoshi replayed this conversation over and over in his head. He responded to his staff that he would take the time to provide explanations in the future. They explained that they were not angry or upset over his methods, but welcomed the understanding he could provide. The staff might not have been angry or upset, but Yoshi was... at himself.

"They will follow your commands if you lead them," Yoshi remembered Togo telling him in their first conversation. He soured on realizing that he had become what he professed he would not be. Instead of living up to his mission statement of improving the world around him by sharing knowledge and enlightenment, he had been imposing his will on the world around him to get what he needed done.

His last obligation for the day was to meet with Daichi at the mediation garden for their regular chat. Lately, he found these sessions served as a pressure release for all his pent-up frustrations. The old monk was providing a patient and non-critical ear to receive Yoshi's laments and complaints. Yoshi greatly appreciated the monk's service. This evening he looked forward to unleashing another round of his frustrations.

As he waited for the old monk, Yoshi stared at his reflection in the koi pond. The last time he gazed into the pond, he saw a samurai warrior. Tonight, that vision seemed like a distant memory and now, he found he looked upon the haggard visage of an apple farmer. Yoshi tossed a pebble to scatter the unseemly image. As the waves surrounding the point of entry subsided, an unexpected object floated over and into Yoshi's line of sight.

Floating by was a small paper boat. It was made with surprising detail. Yoshi's eyes tracked the line it came from and settled on the image of the old monk crouched at the other end of the pond. Focused on the object in his hands, Daichi worked with great earnest on another one of his vessels.

"You enjoy boats, Daichi-san?" Yoshi greeted the old monk.

"Not just boats, but all forms of man-made transportation," he replied without looking up from the task at hand. "I am infinitely fascinated with the devices and machines we use to propel ourselves forward. We want to design machines that will take us over long distances with ease and speed. It's part of man's quest to never stay in the same place."

"I can attest to that," Yoshi sighed. The continuing source of his ill mood was the fact he felt his progress and the school had become stagnant. He had no vessel to move him forward. "I seem to be going around in circles," he lamented to the old monk.

Daichi finished his project and held up his work to admire it. It was even fancier than the last one with a high center mast and an elongated tail extending from its stern. He gently laid it on the smooth pond surface and, with the slightest whiff of his breath; he sent the ship on its one-way journey.

The young pupil silently kept watch on the departing boat. It started straight but soon its voyage was directed by the whim of the environment. A slight gust pushed it in one direction. The wake of a koi swimming past pushed it in another direction. Ultimately, it just meandered around the pond in a general loop, always getting near the other end of the pond, but never reaching it.

"With no rudder, it will never get to the other side." The old man sensed the question in Yoshi's mind and answered it without his asking. Yoshi's question, though, had nothing to do with the boat.

"How do I get a rudder?" he blurted out. Yoshi felt just like Daichi's boat, driven by external forces. Work. School. The opinions of others. Here he was at the School of Aspen just floundering about in no discernible direction.

The old monk stood up and walked up to Yoshi, getting so close Yoshi could see the crevices of his wrinkles and smell the fish from his dinner. The old man grabbed hold of the sword at Yoshi's side as the young student stood frozen, at a complete loss for the intentions of the old monk. Was he going to strike him? Was he going to confiscate the sword? Before he could ask, Yoshi felt the sword move but not out of its sheath. Instead, he looked down to see the monk moving it from side to side... like a rudder on a boat. The old monk let go of the sword and left Yoshi behind. As he walked away, he whistled a tune that sounded strangely familiar to Yoshi. It was only after the old monk disappeared into the evening that Yoshi recalled where he had heard it before. It was the tune played by Kira's musical group that afternoon.

Yoshi reached down and drew out his sword and read it again.

Sword of Mission and Purpose
Why am I here and what is my path?

He had the rudder all along, but he was just not using it. He had spent considerable time and thought developing his stated mission and purpose. He was confident it represented who he truly was and aspired to be through his life. "But there is a difference between believing in it and acting on it," he said aloud to the koi swimming below him. He realized he had fallen far off the path he had set out for himself with his mission statement. It was time to grab hold of the rudder. But before he started steering, he wanted to talk to someone who seemed to be headed in the right direction.

The next day, Yoshi summoned up the courage to speak to Kira about her motivations.

"I never really thought about why exactly," Kira said. "I guess it's just something I love to do and if I can share that with others, all the better."

"So you are not doing this because the senpai asked you or because it was part of any assignment?" Yoshi continued as he walked her to her mid-afternoon music group.

"Oh no. In fact, I wonder if the senpai think it is taking time away from my other duties. It really isn't and I don't believe there's been a drop in my performance. Sometimes I get the impression if people see you do something different, it must mean you are doing something wrong." Kira giggled. "Forgive me. I'm beginning to sound like a philosophy instructor."

"You are forgiven," Yoshi laughed back. He found her remarkably easy to speak with and very wise. Her wisdom did not surprise him; the way he felt in her presence did. Her voice had a soothing, melodic tone to it, much like her music, and when she smiled her eyes lit up in a way that made his heart beat a second faster. "I will let you get on with *doing something wrong.*"

"You should come by to hear us play sometime," she invited.

"I'll seek to squeeze in the time," he called off as they departed.

Time was a critical issue for Yoshi. He wanted to

structure it so he would have enough of it to do the things he was passionate about without neglecting his other responsibilities. In his zeal to be everything to everyone— good student, good warrior, and good farmer—Yoshi concluded he was failing at being good to himself. Not in some selfish manner, but rather failing himself in that he was not being true to his identity and who he wanted to be.

During the next couple of weeks, Yoshi took great effort and time to educate the farm staff on how and, most importantly, why he ordered the things he did. As he provided the new information, he gave them additional responsibilities. He no longer felt like he had to do everything which then freed him up to become a supervisor, counselor, and leader.

His efforts were validated on the day an infestation of harmful beetles began to attack the orchard. The staff promptly addressed the issue and contained it even before Yoshi was informed. "We showed those bugs not to mess with the Apple Warriors," Hideki said as he relayed the story to Yoshi. Yoshi laughed. He had taken the moniker Togo derisively gave him and he turned into a team name for his farm hands. It helped give them a sense of unity and purpose. Now that the Apple Warriors had their sense of purpose, it was time for Yoshi to regain his.

It all happened quite unexpectedly. He knew he had a passion to share his knowledge and help others, but he was not sure how he could go about it. Walking across the compound one afternoon, he saw Daichi awkwardly carrying a large box. He looked like he was struggling, so Yoshi approached to offer assistance. When he got a clearer image of the box the monk was hauling, Yoshi's face turned pale.

"Ah, Yoshi-san. How fortunate. You are just the person I was going to see," the cheery monk greeted him. "We received this package today addressed to you."

Yoshi casually took the crate from Daichi and opened the top plank. The contents inside brought a burst of joy from Yoshi. Easing out of the box, Yoshi held his most prized possession—his father's chest of scrolls. Setting down the trunk, Yoshi grabbed the note affixed on its top.

My dear son,
Your father's chest looked terribly lonely without you. I assumed you might be lonely without it too. I hope it brings you some companionship.
Your dedicated mother

Tears welled up in Yoshi's eyes as he folded the note.

"Is everything all right?" Daichi asked.

"Better than you can imagine." Yoshi took the chest and raced back to his room, clutching it as if it was going to be taken away from him. Like catching up with an old friend, he spent the entire evening reading the scrolls he knew so well. He whispered thanks to his mother a thousand times for sending them. In all his previous correspondences home, he never made mention of any despair or confusion on his part. He always painted the rosiest of pictures. *I guess mothers know*, he thought.

But more than just comfort, the arrival of the scrolls gave Yoshi an idea on how to start living up to his mission statement. If these tales and lessons had been such a valuable influence on his life, wouldn't it also help others to read and discuss them? He wanted to avoid the mistake he made the last time he shared insights with his fellow students. When they failed to accept his advice, he was crushed with disappointment. He thought back to what the elder monk said to him at the last sword ceremony. *"Oftentimes, others cannot learn from your experience processed through your words. They must seek their own words through a personal verified experience."* Yoshi knew he could not unwrap these scrolls for others; they had to want to do it themselves. He would not force feed it as before but provide it to those who were interested. Yoshi thought finding interested students would be the hard part. The next day would prove him wrong.

Kenjutsu combat lessons were being supervised by Togo, as the usual instructor was called away for a special assignment. His educational style was one based on pointing out the mistakes students made rather than offering solutions. In these settings, Togo tended to shy away from interacting with Yoshi. He didn't know the reason why, but Yoshi was happy to avoid him. On this particular day, Togo made a point to belittle the performance of a student who was struggling mightily with his opponent. The student, Haru, had constantly been one of the poorer performers in combat class and Togo's berating only seemed to exacerbate Haru's failures. Through it all, Haru never showed any signs of despair as he kept getting up off the ground and giving it his best effort. His fortitude earned him no ease from Togo's insults, but it did earn him respect in the eyes of Yoshi.

"Yoshi-san, I have a question for you." The limping Haru caught up with his comrade after the class. "I have noticed in your sparring some techniques that the instructors do not teach, yet they seem quite effective. Where did you learn them?"

Yoshi proceeded to tell Haru about how he adapted his style from lessons he learned from Musashi's style and other tips he took in from his father and others. "How about if you meet me this evening and I can show you these moves in greater detail," Yoshi offered.

Haru gladly accepted and the pair met in a clearing just past the koi pond. Yoshi explained his style and he found Haru to be a studious listener and quick learner. With the time being both enjoyable and helpful, the two agreed to meet again the following evening and again the night after. Soon, their one-time meeting grew into a daily occurrence. The meetings evolved from mere lessons on swordplay to discussions of all aspects of a samurai's life. For one meeting, Yoshi decided to share with Haru some of the scrolls from his father's chest. Haru took to them immediately, getting much pleasure and knowledge from reading them. Yoshi, in turn, enjoyed the response and added insight Haru provided with his interpretation of the scrolls.

After a couple of weeks of these meetings, Haru exhibited a marked improvement in Kenjutsu class. Togo kept eagerly waiting for moments to offer his un-constructive criticism, but those opportunities became fewer and fewer. His improvement did not go unnoticed by his classmates. When they asked him about it, he suggested they talk to Yoshi. Gradually, others who thought they needed extra advice—along with those who just wanted to find out how someone could improve so rapidly—asked Yoshi if they could join in the evening meetings. Yoshi was more than happy to accommodate, as each new person that joined the group seemed to bring additional energy to the proceedings. As opposed to classes or work settings where the attendees had to be there, everyone that gathered at Yoshi meetings wanted to be there.

During the next several weeks, Yoshi's evening meetings grew from only Haru to nearly three dozen students. The scrolls were loaned out and lessons lively discussed. Combat techniques were tested out in an environment where students could bring their own ideas and styles to the forum. Yoshi told his mates that his style was right for him but encouraged them to make changes to fit what best suited their unique way.

Prior to these meetings, Yoshi felt his days dragged as he went about his various assignments, but since the first meeting with Haru, the excitement of doing something he loved to do brought vitality and energy to everything else in his life. His conversations with Daichi morphed from complaint-filled to real give-and-take conversations about the lessons of a samurai. "It is apparent that by teaching others, you are learning more," Daichi observed during one of their talks. "Your purpose suits you well." Even Togo, by his almost complete avoidance of Yoshi, was acknowledging the change.

Despite his busy schedule, he did make time to listen in on Kira's music class. It was a soothing respite in the middle of the day, and he secretly enjoyed being in Kira's company, albeit at a distance. The distance closed when one evening, she became the newest member of his gathering. "I figured if you can take the time to come to my classes, the least I could do is return the favor," she said to a bewildered and embarrassed Yoshi.

"I didn't think you noticed I was there."

"I knew you were there from the first day you came." Kira smiled and selected a scroll from the chest. "I look forward to sharing what I think about this."

In all the excitement that his new sense of purpose had given him, he no longer fretted if and when he would be granted the next Sword of Illumination. So, it came as a genuine surprise when the senior senpai knocked on his door and requested that he follow him and bring his Sword of Mission and Identity.

Just as before, he was led into the pitch-black chamber that was illuminated by a gradual lighting of flames. With him this time were, as best as he could tell, three other students. The twelve robed elders entered the room as before and one stepped forward to command all to kneel and present their swords. The swords were quickly and deftly removed from the students' hands. Yoshi could tell from the voice it was a different elder than the one who spoke at the previous ceremony.

"You four have been called here tonight to take one more step on the path of enlightenment and balance. By being here you have shown to yourselves that you understand the great gift of the Sword of Mission and Purpose. In time, you will learn its true power. It is now time to receive the next level of enlightenment."

Others in robes stepped forward, kneeled before the students, and presented the new sword still encased in its sheath.

"Before you accept the next Sword of Illumination, you are permitted to ask one question of this council in order to gain additional knowledge. Yoshi-san, you may go first."

Yoshi took a deep breath and thought about all he experienced these last several months and the subjects that they presented. He thought of his lowest moment during this period and then spoke. "How come doing everything the right way doesn't ensure success?"

"The right way for you or the right way for others," the elder responded in more of a statement than a question. "People fail to succeed when they are incongruent with who they are. If your stated purpose is to do and be one thing, and yet you act, however well-intentioned, in ways that do not support this, you will be out of sync with who you are. If you say you are this, then be this. The perceived failure stems from the neglect of *your* way. Stay congruent with who you say you are, and your mission and path will be illuminated for you."

After all the others had asked their questions, the swords were placed into the hands of the kneeling students. Yoshi anxiously withdrew the sword and read its inscription.

Sword of Roles
Who am I in the specific moment of now?

"So, it's as simple as do what you want to do?" Tom asked with an incredulous look on his face. "That might be feasible in the make-believe world of fairy tales and Asian proverbs, but it doesn't cut it in the real world."

"And why not?" responded the old man.

"It just doesn't, that's why. I don't know anybody except maybe the super-rich that can get away with doing whatever they want. The world won't let you."

"That is a very sad point of view to have."

"It's a very real point of view to have," Tom sharply quipped.

"I believe the concept Yoshi learned is that being true to who you are is key to unlocking endless opportunities. Yoshi did not stop going to school, tending to his job, or any of his other responsibilities. Instead, he incorporated his personal purpose and mission into each of those. When he did that and embraced how he wanted to live his life, opportunities came to him. His life found fulfillment through sharing his knowledge and helping others."

"But that other guy was a jerk and still got promoted."

"The Swords of Illumination are not about judging someone on whether they are good or bad. Togo had dedicated his life to success at all costs. He focused his energies to accomplish that goal and incorporated it into every aspect of his life. He lived his mission statement. Because he stayed true to what he said he was, he exhibited his mastery of the Sword of Mission and Purpose. Once Yoshi showed that same commitment to his own purpose, he was invited to the next level."

Tom settled down and soaked in what the old man just said. "It is a matter of staying on point, so to speak, to keep with the game plan through everything you do?"

"Great way to put it."

"But I'm so many things. I'm a father, a husband, an employee. All those things require me to be different."

"You are getting ahead of the story," the old man laughed. "Who you are doesn't change, but the roles you play do. This is precisely the lesson Yoshi is about to learn."

"Which explains his receiving the Sword of Roles. Maybe I should just settle down and listen a little more."

They both shared a laughed and settled in as the old man continued his tale.

CHAPTER 9

Sword of Roles: Part 1

Sword of Roles
Who am I in the specific moment of now?"

He repeated the engraving on his sword over and over again as he trekked to the farm. The air had a slight briskness to it, harkening the advent of autumn. It also reminded him that it had been two months since he received the sword, and he still felt no closer to understanding its message.

I am a samurai, was the only answer he could come up with, yet he felt far from being one.

Since he received the Sword of Roles, nothing had progressed as he had hoped. The excitement brought on by refocusing his schedule and initiating the evening workshops had dissipated. Just like an arrow shot from a bow, he had started with great momentum but over time and distance, he crashed to earth. As the weeks went on, he was finding it harder and harder to manage all his responsibilities.

Harvest time was drawing near for the apple farm and while he had given the staff a greater amount of autonomy, he was still looked upon to make the bulk of the decisions. He had not yet fully overcome his anxiety about being a leader. These workers looked to him for direction on what to do and how to do it, but Yoshi felt he was the one in need of direction. *Did I come to this school to be a student or a teacher?* Yoshi bemoaned in the privacy of his mind. He also felt that tending to the farm took valuable energy and time away from his training to be a samurai. No matter how hard he sought to push it away, Togo's teasingly dubbing him the apple warrior still stung Yoshi. It stung because he started believing it.

Yoshi also found his greatest accomplishment slowly turning into his greatest burden. The evening gatherings had grown into an enormous success. It was not uncommon to have more than 50 attendees. Senior senpai joined with lower-level students to review the school's lessons, share battle tips, and discuss philosophies. But all these participants expected Yoshi to have more answers than he possessed. During moments when he was bombarded with questions, he yearned to scream out, *How should I know? I am a student too!* The same issues of status that plagued him at the farm were bothering him with the study group. Yoshi felt pressured to have all the answers. Students expressed shock when Yoshi asked a question during class. To avoid such embarrassment, he refrained from asking any questions lest he appear 'not to know everything.'

Of all his relationships with his fellow students, one grew to be the most important one. Kira, the musically skillful student, had become a regular attendee to his study group and her input was insightful and invaluable. She brought a different approach to the proceedings, from her unique perspective on the lessons to her cagey style in combat. After the group would break up for the evening, Yoshi and Kira would often take the long way back to their respective rooms, spending the extra time discussing, and often debating, various topics. She was the only one who didn't think or expect him to know it all. He found that equally challenging and refreshing. He also could not deny that his feelings for her were growing stronger by the day.

But whenever Yoshi felt inclined to display his affection for Kira, he hesitated. He reminded himself that he was a samurai in training. His mission statement called for the acquisition of knowledge and wisdom, and for him to share it with the world. It left little time for affairs of the heart. There was no doubt Kira held all the qualities he desired in a woman, the most attractive being her intellect and wit. Despite feelings to the contrary, Yoshi vowed to remain steadfast in keeping the relationship appropriately distant. He just did not see himself ready for anything more.

Burdens of work, school, and relationships had taken their toll and he felt a bit of his spirit fading. During times of self-reflection, Yoshi looked on the positive side of things. He did not think his life was terrible. He felt he was exactly where he wanted to be, just not *how* he wanted to be.

He read the sword once more before sliding it back into its sheath.

Who am I in the specific moment of now?

He offered a litany of answers.

I am a student.
I am a tutor.
I am a friend.

Finally, a clear answer came to him. *No, I am a farmer.* As he entered the gates of the farm, he sighed in resignation. The thought barely exited his mind before he was bombarded with inquiries by the staff about what they should do. The apples that should have been plucked today were not as ripe as they should have been. They were already three days behind and the crop needed to be sent to market by the end of the week. The question was whether to keep them on the trees for a day or two longer and risk not having them harvested in time for market, or pluck them now with the chance that the quality will suffer and harm the farm's reputation with its customers.

Yoshi did not have the answers, so he requested, "Give me some time to think," as he wandered away from them and out of the farm area. He walked in no particular direction, just as long as it was away from the problem at hand. Getting away from the problem took him south of the farm to an area with high, overgrown brush. Lost in his thoughts, he suddenly caught sight of a startling vision.

Gliding just above the tall grass was the seemingly bodiless head of the old monk. When he first glimpsed Daichi, Yoshi thought the old monk was merely walking along a path behind the tall grass. After taking a few more steps, Yoshi stopped suddenly. Something about what he just saw struck him as completely odd and yet familiar.

He returned his gaze toward the old monk and tracked his head floating above the grass. Floating was the only term he could apply to it since Daichi's head did not move in the typical fashion of a man who was walking. As Yoshi sought to make sense of what he saw, he remembered why it seemed familiar. It looked the same as the mysterious floating man he encountered in the forest that led him to the gates of the School of Aspen. His astonishment would be compounded a second later when Daichi emerged from the grass and into the clearing.

Yoshi stared as the old monk rode a mode of transportation unlike any he had ever seen. Forged completely of metal, it had two wheels, but rather than side to side; they were arranged one in the front and one in the back. Metal poles linked the two wheels to an elevated seat in the middle. In the front were two poles in a shape of a "T" and when the rider swiveled them, the front wheel moved accordingly. Below the seat were two pedals not unlike those found on a spindle for weaving. These pedals were joined together with one higher than the other and in turn, the melded pedals were joined by a taut chain to the back wheel. Sitting high on top of the seat and pushing his legs up and down in a marching motion, the old monk propelled this device. It moved him forward without a horse in sight.

Daichi rode along in a wide circle all around the clearing, moving his legs up and down in a fluid manner and maintaining a remarkably controlled and straight direction. It was remarkable because the wheels on this device were not particularly smooth. While evidently designed to be round, the wheels were bent and dented and should not have produced the smooth ride they were giving the old monk. Despite the apparent hindrance, the old monk rode straight with his head facing skyward and singing aloud a strange, probably self-composed, melody. Yoshi was mesmerized by this completely foreign display. Although fascinated by the strange device, he was apprehensive to ask about it. He feared the old monk would encourage him to ride it; he feared it because he already felt overwhelmed by everything else in his life.

Yoshi's silent observation of the monk was abruptly shattered. "You want to ride it? It's easy once you know what you are doing," said the monk.

"Are you talking to me," Yoshi blurted out.

"I see no one else I should be talking to," chuckled the old monk.

"Please forgive me, I am not sure where my head is today," an embarrassed Yoshi replied. Daichi drove right up to Yoshi, stopping a few steps before him.

"I see it! It is right above your shoulders," the monk replied with sincerity. "Does it move from there often?"

Yoshi paused at the unexpected response. Recognizing the joke, he laughed. "Lately it has been all over the place."

"Life can be dangerous if you don't bring your head along." The old monk dismounted his device and inspected it.

"Seems life can be dangerous riding that thing," Yoshi retorted as he joined in the inspection. "I have never seen anything like this. Did your fascination with transportation make you create it?"

"I put it together, but I am no creator. That distinction is beyond any mortal man. Although, the universe did give me some inspiration as I watched a watermill."

"A watermill?"

"The water propels the wheel in the mill to spin and thus generate power for grounding grain or pounding metal. I watched the gears spin and thought, 'What if energy was placed in the opposite direction?' Giving power to the gears to turn the watermill."

"I would have never thought of it like that," Yoshi observed, impressed with the old monk's insight. "How did you come up with that?"

"Can I tell you a little secret? It's not that amazing. It's just a matter of looking at things from a different perspective."

Yoshi chuckled slightly to himself. "That's great advice." Yoshi was not thinking about it in the context of mechanical engineering. He was thinking about how he might use it in his own day-to-day life.

"It's only great if you use it. Let me know if you do." With that, the old monk mounted his watermill and rode off to a tune Yoshi had never heard. Yoshi wanted to continue the conversation but remembered that people were waiting for him back at the farm, or specifically, waiting for answers from him.

Shaking his head as if the physical action would somehow clear his thoughts, one thought remained in his mind, *A different perspective.* Daichi's inspiration caught Yoshi's imagination. *That's a fascinating way to look at a situation,* he spoke in his mind's voice. *If only I could...* It hit him. He could do that. He could do that for this very issue. "Look at it from the market's perspective," he said aloud as he raced back to the farm.

Yoshi thought as if he was the seller of his product. If sellers get the apples a day or two late, they might lose a day or two worth of customers; but if they sell poor quality apples, they'll lose those customers forever. When he arrived back at the grove, he instructed his team to wait until he thought the apples were appropriately ripened before harvesting, no matter how long the delay.

Satisfied with a concrete answer from their superior, the workers went about their duties. Yoshi felt a sense of confidence overcome him. While he was not one hundred percent sure he was making the right decision, he acted as a leader. His actions felt right and not in conflict with who he was and wanted to be. He shrugged at his realization. "I am a farmer," he laughed as he answered again the question he posed in the morning.

Three more days would pass before Yoshi was satisfied that the apples were ready for harvest. Working all night and day, they gathered the crop and prepared it for market. As he watched the last of the horse-drawn carts ride away in the mid-afternoon sun, he stared at the turning wheels and thought of watermills. His laughter brought odd stares from his staff.

His little victory at the farm was a huge boost to Yoshi's self-esteem and carried over to his workshop that evening. He felt strong. He felt confident. He felt like a samurai. He thought nothing could ebb his exuberance. He was wrong.

"Quite the little following you have here Yoshi-san," the new visitor commented as he surveyed the gathering. Yoshi immediately recognized the voice of Togo before he spun to greet him. "I was waiting for my invitation, but it must have gotten lost by the messenger."

"Our group is open to anyone at the school. Forgive my negligence in not giving you a personal invitation, but I was not aware you were interested in getting extra work with our group," Yoshi replied with deadpan sarcasm. He felt the blood inside him slowly simmer. Togo's mere presence summoned the ugly head of Yoshi's insecurities.

"You are right, I don't need the extra work," he replied tapping his sword. Yoshi now noticed it was a new sword; Togo had graduated past the Sword of Roles already. Yoshi's mind was spinning with questions about how Togo could advance so easily. "But I am sure that the help you are offering here will make a little difference with some of these students. All samurai need teachers."

Togo punched the word *teachers* and it stung Yoshi. It was clearly another dig at Yoshi and Togo's perception of his role. First it was apple warrior, now teacher, but never samurai. The insult injured Yoshi more than he expected and now his blood really began to boil. Unconsciously, his hand slid to the handle of his katana.

Togo noted the movement and acted on it with words. "Perhaps, the great teacher Yoshi would like to demonstrate some of the techniques he teaches in his classroom."

"I would enjoy the opportunity to impress you with my curriculum," Yoshi replied as his pulse pounded in preparation for a rematch with Togo.

"Great. I would love to see it. The best vantage point for me to enjoy the demonstration of your skill is as an observer. Let's pick a sparring partner from your merry band." Scanning the crowd that had quietly gathered around them, Togo eyed the match-up he wanted. "Haru-san, please come here."

The original member of Yoshi's study group rushed forward and bowed to his senior senpai. "I have been thoroughly impressed with your performance in Kenjutsu class in the recent months. Your progress from ineffective punching bag to adequate warrior has been nothing short of a miracle from the gods."

"Thank you, Togo-san," Haru smiled in response.

"Your tutor, Yoshi-san, has offered to demonstrate to me some of his skills and I can think of no better person for him to showcase his ability than with his most prized pupil."

Togo signaled for two bokken, the hard wooden sticks carved into the shape of a katana sword, to be brought to the pair. As the wooden weapons were handed out, Yoshi wanted to decline to spar against his friend; however, his aversion to engaging Haru was overridden by the rage burning inside him to show Togo that he was indeed a warrior. "Are you sure about this?" another student asked as he handed the bokken to Yoshi. Yoshi did not respond as his eyes stayed on Togo.

Yoshi gradually turned his focus to Haru. As he gripped the bokken, he felt the substantial weight difference between it and the bamboo shinai. He could sense his opponent's discomfort underneath his apparent brave face. He felt Haru's apprehension was a mixture of facing a friend and mentor, coupled with the elevated seriousness brought by the introduction of the wooden swords. He also knew Haru wanted desperately to impress Togo, a senior senpai, but for a reason less selfish than Yoshi's. The two bowed in silence to each other, then turned to Togo and bowed. When he turned to face Haru again, it was still Togo's smirk that blazed in Yoshi's eyes.

Haru was indeed much more skilled since they began working together. Yoshi quickly initiated the attack and Haru defended Yoshi's initial onslaught. It was when Haru attempted an offense of his own that the tide turned irreversibly in Yoshi's favor.

Fueled by an explosion of the rage he had felt over the past months, Yoshi parried away Haru's clumsy assault and unleashed a torrent of blows against his overmatched opponent. Behind every one of Yoshi's blows was a flash of one of Togo's slights or a recollection of one of Yoshi's moments of self-doubt. Yoshi's momentum drove Haru back and through the circle of students surrounding the pair.

Yoshi sensed Haru's nervousness at failing before the judging eyes of Togo and his peers. Barely able to keep the mighty blows of the bokken from hitting him, Haru attempted to turn the tide with one last attempt at offense. Haru raised his bokken for a blow but before he could strike, Yoshi spun and struck a blow to the right side of Haru's body. Haru immediately dropped the bokken and crumbled to his knees in anguish. Heaving heavily, Yoshi stood over his foe, his grip still tight on the faux sword preparing for another blow. He withheld his attack as a group of students rushed to Haru's aid. Yoshi calmed down enough to look at the splintered half of the bokken that remained in his hand. The force of his blow had torn the bokken in half. Yoshi would later learn it also broke three of Haru's ribs.

The sound of a single person clapping broke Yoshi's trance. "Well played teacher-san," a smiling Togo cried out. "I guess Haru-san needs some additional homework. Keep up the good work. You may yet become a samurai." Togo departed in one direction while the students guided a wobbly Haru toward the barracks.

Standing alone in the spot he delivered the crushing blow, Yoshi felt sick to his stomach. He allowed his personal issues to cloud his actions and now someone was hurt because of it. The adulation from Togo notwithstanding, he felt farther from being the samurai he wanted to be than at any moment since his arrival at the School of Aspen.

"It's not your fault."

Yoshi turned to meet Kira's gaze. In the glow of the setting auburn sun, she looked as beautiful as he had ever seen her. "Injuries can happen when you spar. Better here for Haru than on the field of battle." Her words were comforting but they rang hollow. Yoshi knew she secretly agreed that he went too far.

"A samurai controls his emotions. He learns not to feel but to act. I allowed my feelings to dictate my actions. These students look up to me and I have failed them with my demonstration."

"Aren't you being a little too hard on yourself Yoshi-san?" Kira said with a light smile. She stepped closer to him. "You have not failed all your students." Kira's soft brown eyes locked onto his and for the first time, Yoshi saw a reflection of the same passion he felt for her. He desperately wanted to reach out and hold her; shut everything and everybody out. His heartbeat was so loud he feared she could hear it.

"Kira-san," he whispered.

"Yes," she replied breathlessly.

The moment was there to profess his feelings, but the embarrassment of his most recent display of emotion was just too fresh. "Thank you for your kind words and support. Forgive me, but I must go now." Although he didn't see it or feel it, he sensed Kira reach for his hand as he turned away. He did not dare look back as he briskly walked away.

Yoshi tossed and turned all that night. A kaleidoscope of imagery invaded his dreams. He dreamt of Musashi's battles, his father's lessons, Haru's crumpled body, apple trees, Kira's smile, and Togo's new sword. The scenes all mixed and blended in no discernible pattern. In all of them, he sought to be the same person—Yoshi, the samurai in training. He fought alongside his heroes, he battled Togo, he triumphed over giant apples, and he politely evaded the amorous advances of Kira.

But even in the fantasy of his slumber's story, Yoshi could not succeed. The more he sought to be the samurai he thought he should be, the more his dream world pulled him in other directions. His mother would beckon him from battle. The apples cried to be harvested. The allure of Kira's music compelled him to watch her.

The chiming of the morning bells startled Yoshi awake. He knew his dreams were just a precursor to the issues he now faced in the light of reality. "How can I be the same in every situation?" he asked himself as he dressed for the day. He re-read his mission statement and placed it in his breast pocket. He stared at the engraving of his sword.

The Sword of Roles
Who am I in the specific moment of now?

He answered as honestly as he could. "I am... confused."

"It's a bicycle," Tom blurted out after a momentary pause in the old man's story.

"Excuse me?"

"The old monk. He was riding a bicycle. Why didn't you just say it was a bicycle?"

"This tale takes place nearly two hundred years before the popular introduction of bicycles in the world. No one had ever seen it, so they didn't know what to call it."

"Are you telling me this old monk invented the bicycle?" Tom asked.

"I am just re-telling the story of what happened. I am not saying he built the very first one, but who am I to say he did not?"

Tom silently agreed with the point. It's a big world and just because some European was credited with the invention of the bicycle did not mean they were actually the first. But there was something else about this part of the tale that rattled in Tom's mind.

"I think this Yoshi and I have more in common than just an aversion to riding bikes," he uttered as the old man offered his canteen of water. After taking a drink, Tom continued. "I know what it's like to struggle to be everything to everyone. I try to be consistent with everything I do and everyone I meet, but the demands can be so different. They really tear at you."

"Then don't do it," the old man nonchalantly replied.

"Don't do what?"

"Don't be consistent. You can't act the same in every relationship you have. As a father you act one way to your children, but you would never act that way at work."

"Obviously, I change who I am depending on where I am. It's just I have a hard time juggling who I am at a given moment. It's constantly changing, sometimes from minute to minute. It gets so I have difficulty knowing exactly who I am. Then my head explodes, and I end up freezing my butt off on the side of some road in the middle of nowhere."

The old man silently got up and disappeared into the woods. Tom called after him to come back. He offered his apologies if he said anything offensive. He pleaded for several minutes but to no avail. Just when Tom had given up on talking the old man back, he suddenly reemerged from the woods. In his arms were several tree branches. He laid them neatly on the fire, building up its flames.

"This will help with the freezing your butt off. Perhaps more of Yoshi's tale will help with the head explosion."

CHAPTER 10

Sword of Roles: Part II

After hearing his presence acknowledged, Yoshi slid open the rice paper door, slipped out of his shoes, and entered Haru's room. It was the first time he had seen his friend since the sparring match that left Haru injured and confined to bed rest. Yoshi had delayed this visit for more than a week. His shame for his actions kept him away, but now it was his shame for neglecting a friend that brought him to Haru's side.

"I brought you some of my father's scrolls," Yoshi offered as he knelt beside Haru. "I thought these tales might keep you company during your recovery."

"Thank you, Yoshi-san. I look forward to reading them and to rejoining my classmates as soon as possible."

The two sat in silence for several moments. Neither one knew what to say. An uncomfortable tension existed that both of them wanted to extinguish but neither knew how. Yoshi took a stab at dousing the embers. "Haru-san, I apologize for my actions. It was never my desire or intention to injure you. My zeal was misplaced and excessive. I've come here to ask for your forgiveness and to pray for your full and speedy recovery."

Haru stared silently yet intently at the ceiling above him, not making any eye contact with Yoshi. Yoshi thought he detected a tear forming in Haru's eye as he finally spoke. "I shall not accept any such apology from you Yoshi-san. For to do so would accept that I am not the warrior that you are." Haru turned to face Yoshi. "You had no unfair advantage over me. We fought on equal footing and with the same weaponry. You bested me in battle, this time. Fortunately, with more effort, I shall improve. More than anyone else here, you have taught me that. But while the wounds you inflicted on the field were painful, the wounds you inflict today with your words are even harsher."

"I never meant to..." Yoshi went to finish the apology but was abruptly cut off.

"Meaning or not, you speak to me as someone of a lesser station than yourself. If you have not noticed, I too am training to be samurai. I have been accepted to this same great academy just as you have. I have always admired you for your skill and knowledge; but more importantly, I have respected you for treating me as an equal comrade, unlike other senior senpai. Your apology today, however well-meaning, suggests you think of me as something less than that." Haru's voice began to rise, and his face grew flush. "Why should you not have engaged me with your full fury? Did you think I would not be able to handle it? Do you think of me as a child? I assure you my enemies on the real field of battle will take no such position. I can accept you defeating me in battle; I cannot accept you treating me with diminished respect."

Yoshi was stunned by Haru's reaction. He had come here to apologize to a friend and had now unwittingly made matters worse. He mumbled a few more apologetic words and took his leave from Haru, stumbling out into the cloudy mid-afternoon air.

Later that day, Yoshi sat with Daichi by the koi pond. He started their conversation by explaining how he used the *different perspective* approach at the farm to great success. Still smarting from Haru's wounding words, Yoshi had no desire to share this latest embarrassment. He spoke with an exaggerated joy, attempting to put on a false front that everything was going well. Yoshi glanced over at the silent monk beside him, expecting him to question his exuberance. Instead, he found him smiling as he gazed upon the koi in the pond. He seemed totally entertained with the fish as if it was a grand theatrical performance.

Daichi picked up a pebble and tossed it into the pond. The rock broke the plane of the water's surface, sending the koi scattering away. Within a few moments, the koi returned to the spot of the disturbance as if investigating a scene of a crime.

"Cats are not the only ones so curious," Daichi observed as he broke the silence. "The fish, they flee the commotion to their environment, but soon they are compelled to return to see what happened."

"Are they not just acting on instinct?" Yoshi asked. "It is not as if they want to know what happened."

"Perhaps they don't, but you do." The old monk turned to Yoshi. "Like the fish, we first run from the rocky seas but something inside us demands an investigation of the cause."

"But it will not stop more pebbles from disturbing the peace," countered the student.

"At least we will know it is just pebbles," Daichi said, and Yoshi knew the monk sensed that his pond had been disturbed.

"I sought the forgiveness of a friend today and instead received his scorn," Yoshi finally confided. "It was a large stone thrown in my pond." Yoshi related to Daichi the story of his predicament with Haru and how it all developed, from the taunting of Togo to the cracking of the bokken on Haru's ribs.

"Who is Haru to you?" the monk inquired of Yoshi.

"A fellow student... and I thought a friend."

"And when you faced him in that sparring session, who was he to you then?"

"Still my friend, which is why I was so sorry to hurt him."

"Why would you attack a friend with a bokken? With friends like you, who needs enemies?"

"Well, I didn't attack a friend," Yoshi protested.

"So at that moment, you did not treat him as a friend?"

"Right."

"Then why feel sorry for hurting a friend?" Daichi asked.

"We were sparring as part of an exercise." Yoshi hated the fact his confidant was taking the side of Haru. Times like these made Yoshi reconsider meeting with this crazy old man. "When I faced Haru, I was not fighting him as a friend, but as a combatant. Can't you see that?"

"Yes, I can. Can you?"

Angered by the incessant nature of this conversation, Yoshi stood up and stormed off. After a few paces, he regained his composure and turned back to the monk. Standing up also, the monk smiled and dropped a pebble into the pond.

Just like the koi, Yoshi meandered back to investigate. "I apologize for the outburst."

"I think you have apologized enough for one day, Yoshi-san."

Putting his arm on Yoshi's shoulder, Daichi guided

him around the pond. "At the moment you bowed to Haru and lifted up your bokken, you ceased being his friend and classmate. You became his opponent and acted accordingly. Do you think you should have laid your bokken down and let him strike you?"

Yoshi shook his head.

"You acted like the warrior you are training to be, and so did Haru. When you apologized to him, you inadvertently suggested that there was only one person acting as a warrior."

Yoshi reflected on it for the moment. Just like he did with the apple sellers, he looked at it from Haru's point of view. He surmised he would feel slighted if Haru apologized for beating him and understood how it could be seen as condescending.

"You have had enough reflection for one day my friend. Know this. The answers you seek are to the questions most present to you."

Yoshi's mind and body were too worn down to contemplate any more of the old monk's vague advice. He proceeded to deal with the rest of the day's duties by focusing on each task immediately before him, pushing out all thoughts of Daichi and Haru and everything else. As he retired to his room for the evening, he found it surprising how quickly and efficiently he worked when he just focused on the moment at hand. He chalked it up to the ramblings of a tired mind.

As he removed his sword from his waist, he unsheathed it and read the words on it again.

The Sword of Roles
Who am I in the specific moment of now?

He then heard Daichi's strange advice about the question being most present to him.

Some advice. I've been seeking to answer this question for months now, Yoshi thought to himself. He thought about how the answer to the sword's query was constantly changing. "How do I know who I am?" he asked in a voice louder than he expected. At that moment he took his mission statement from his breast. It clearly spelled out exactly who he was, or at least wanted to be. He wondered how he could live up to this ideal while also being a samurai and a farmer and everything else he was expected to be. Exhausted by all his confusion, Yoshi laid his head down and fell into a troubled slumber.

Yoshi's lack of sound sleep was catching up to him. Exhausted after another tough day of lessons and work, he seriously contemplated skipping the scheduled meeting with his old advisor in favor of a mid-afternoon nap. Before he could take any action on this hesitation, he heard the monk's voice say, "Follow me." At first, he thought the voice came from his head and was startled to see that it really came from the monk standing behind him.

Without a word, Yoshi followed Daichi out of the gates of the School of Aspen, through a path in the woods, and eventually ended up by a stream flowing down from the large mountain to the north. Upon reaching the stream, Daichi bent down and with cupped hands scooped some water and drank it. Staying crouched down, the monk left his hand in the stream, allowing the cool water to rush past it.

"Water is water," the monk finally said after not speaking for their entire journey. "It can fall from the sky, rush down a stream, or freeze into ice. It can move around rocks or carry tree branches. Water can replenish my thirst or kill me by drowning. It can do all these things and so much more, yet it is always water."

"It can also help inspire a mode of transportation," Yoshi added.

"Precisely." The old monk smiled. "It can be anything, but it is only one thing."

"I suppose this is allegorical to something that I should know," Yoshi asked more than stated. "If I may be blunt, how does this help me understand the lesson of roles? The sword asks who I am in the moment of now. But I am constantly changing."

"Are you really?" the monk replied. He stood and walked past Yoshi, tapping him on his chest. The monk kept walking back toward the school leaving Yoshi alone by the stream. Yoshi felt where the monk tapped him. It was right over where he kept his personal mission statement. He took it out and read it again. This time he didn't need to go further than the first sentence to get the point.

I am Yoshi Minamura.

Slowly at first, then in a rapid secession of thoughts and ideas, Yoshi began to finally understand what the old monk meant. Just like the water, Yoshi's identity remains constant. The statement he held in his hand clearly states the person Yoshi believed he was. What changes is his behavior according to the environment he is in or the situation he is facing. As a student he must behave a certain way that is different from when he is running the farm, and that way differs from when he is conversing with friends. He realized he had been focusing so hard to be the same person in all the areas of his life when in fact he was the same person. It was his behaviors that had to change.

Yoshi took out his sword again and re-read it with a new understanding.

Who am I in the specific moment of now?

He shook his head in embarrassment. The answer was with him the whole time just like the monk had said. The roles he plays are dictated by the moment, but they do not define who he is.

Seeking validation on his self-discovery, he chased after Daichi. He ran in the direction the old monk departed and kept in that direction for several minutes. Scanning through the trees and shouting his name, Yoshi looked feverishly for the monk. He finally understood, or thought he understood, a key lesson and wanted the satisfaction of showing his comprehension to his master. Reaching the gates of the School of Aspen, he re-entered the compound looking for the old monk.

His search for Daichi stopped abruptly when he came across Haru. With the aid of a monk, he was gingerly taking a walk through the school's courtyard. The two caught each other's eyes and Haru gave an acknowledging bow of his head toward Yoshi. Recalling their uncomfortable encounter, Yoshi wanted to turn and continue on his way. His heart overrode that instinct and directed him to engage Haru.

"I am glad to see your recovery is progressing Haru-san," Yoshi greeted him. "I deeply admire your determination to heal. I believe it will be in no time that we can return to our lessons, conversations, and sparring."

Haru gave a smile that erased away any bitter tension

between the two. "Just make sure you have a sturdier bokken. The one you had last time was too flimsy that it should break from one soft blow."

Yoshi grinned and bowed to Haru and the monk assisting him. By treating Haru as an equal rather than an inferior, Yoshi realized that he was showing him the respect he deserved. He also felt the power of behavior and how changing it can change how he is perceived at any given moment. Leaving his encounter with Haru, Yoshi thought about how understanding this simple fact can help in so many areas of his life. He felt exhilarated by this awareness as it would serve him well. It turned out it would serve him sooner than he could imagine.

He heard the loud bickering even before he reached the wooden gates of the apple grove. Yoshi recognized the voice of old Hideki, but he did not know the owner of the other and louder voice in the argument. As he was about to intercede between the debating duo, Yoshi was intercepted by a young female farm hand, Mitsuki, who gave him a brief overview of the situation.

The man arguing with Hideki was named Jungo and was a frequent customer of the farm. He was also an equally frequent complainer. Every year when he picked up his crop of apples for market, he would find some fault in his purchase. He typically berated the staff long and hard enough that they always conceded and gave him whatever discount he demanded. Mitsuki explained just like the blooming of the cherry blossoms, Jungo's tirade was an annual rite of passage.

"Unfortunately for poor Hideki-san, he thinks he can

talk Jungo-san out of his complaint," Mitsuki explained to Yoshi. "He will give in as the rest of us have."

Yesterday, Yoshi would have either slyly avoided the confrontation or acquiesced to the irate seller's demands. Yoshi was a samurai in training and had no desire to deal with such a matter. That was yesterday. Today, this moment, was different.

"Jungo-san," Yoshi greeted the two in a loud and booming voice. "What a great pleasure for us that you have come to our humble farm for another year of crops. We are honored by your patronage." Jungo was momentarily stunned silent by both the loud voice and the unfamiliar face.

"Oh, forgive my manners," Yoshi continued. "My name is Yoshi, and I am the new manager of this farm. I'd be happy to help you with any concerns you might have."

Regaining his irate position, Jungo prepared his attack on his young and inexperienced foe. "I have been a loyal and constant customer of this farm for many, many years and I have never been treated in such a horrific manner. Quite honestly, I will have to discontinue this relationship unless I am satisfied."

"No problem can be so terrible that we should lose such a valued customer as yourself," Yoshi responded still in a booming voice. He put his arm on Jungo's shoulder. "How can we please you?"

Jungo took a breath and unleashed his tirade once more. "I can easily tell that the crop of apples you have provided me has been harvested at least a week too early. They have not been allowed to grow to the proper maturity and clearly, their quality and taste will suffer. I will be lucky to sell half of these apples and will likely lose the customers I do sell them to."

Yoshi knew that Jungo's complaint was completely baseless. He had purposely delayed the harvesting to ensure that the crop ripened sufficiently. Just as he must have done in the past, Jungo was fabricating an excuse in order to increase his profits. Yoshi had never dealt with such a blatant attempt at deception. While he did not want to lose a customer, he also sensed that Jungo could not afford to lose the farm as a supplier.

He led the disgruntled customer off to the side, out of earshot from anyone else. Standing before him with eyes locked into his, he spoke. "As you have said, you have years of experience, far more than I have. However, we both know that there is absolutely nothing wrong with these apples."

Jungo let out a breath as he prepared his counter, but Yoshi quickly and boldly cut him off.

"No, Jungo-san, I will have no more of it. I would not expect you to permit me to come to your stand at the market and berate your selling techniques. I should think you would not expect me to allow you to do the same. My offer is this. You accept these delicious and ripened apples. You can purchase them for the already agreed-upon price. You will make a healthy profit and have happy customers. In acknowledgment of your loyal patronage, I will allow you to visit our farm next year at the time of harvesting and to offer your advice on what you consider the best time to pluck the crop." Yoshi looked firmly and resolutely into his customer's eyes. "The alternative is to leave here with an empty wagon. As always, the choice is with you."

Yoshi's heart was beating out of his chest, but he stayed

steadfast and showed no display of the nervousness he was feeling. He had never played the heavy prior to this moment. While he was not sure of its outcome, he found it both exhilarating and terrifying.

Jungo wrinkled his brow and stroked his chin as if he was in deep reflection. They both knew he could not afford to leave empty-handed, but Yoshi offered him a way out while saving face and the apple seller took it. In a voice loud enough for the others to hear, Jungo responded. "I would be happy to advise you next year on your harvest. I appreciate your realization that you can use my expertise and advice. In turn, I will do you the favor of purchasing your apples at the price you asked."

Yoshi thanked him once again for his wisdom, counsel, and patronage. The farm staff quickly loaded up Jungo's wagon. They did this not because of their zeal to be of assistance to him, but due to their overwhelming desire to see him go. As the staff watched their problem disappear down the road, Hideki asked Yoshi, "Do you really want him to help with the harvest next year?"

"Do not worry. He will come to purchase our apples, but he will not come to harvest. He will be conveniently busy at that time."

"You really shook him up," Hideki observed as Yoshi retired from the farm.

I really shook myself up, he thought to himself. Reflecting upon it later that evening, Yoshi realized he did not particularly enjoy playing the heavy, but knew it was the right thing to do in that given moment. While he understood behaving differently did not change who he really was, he fretted about whether that excused any behavior he displayed. Could he basically do anything he wanted and justify it by saying, *That's not who I really am.*

In his dreams that night, he found himself playing all types of characters. Some were good and kind while others were evil and harsh. He did heroic deeds and terrible acts during his slumbering hallucinations. When he awoke, he marveled at the excitement he felt in wearing all those hats. Unfortunately, he was still unsure of what it all meant.

Yoshi was forced to mull these ideas alone for several days as he had not seen Daichi since their meeting by the stream. Each of the next several evenings, he had the same dream experiences and awoke with the same questions. He thought he would burst if he did not share it with the old monk soon.

"Miss me?" Daichi suddenly appeared beside Yoshi as he walked from his lessons at the dojo center to the farm.

"As a matter of fact," a surprised Yoshi responded. But before he could get the rest of his sentence out, the old monk handed him a bow and arrow.

"Follow me," the monk commanded. The two left the walls of the School of Aspen and headed into the southern forest. Yoshi had not walked through this area since he first arrived at the school.

"I have so much to share with you. I finally realized the lesson you taught me by the stream and I..."

"Quiet," Daichi yelled in a whispered tone. "You'll scare them away."

For several minutes, Yoshi followed the monk as the two crept in silence between the trees. He had no idea what the monk was looking for and wondered if his guide knew what he was seeking. Suddenly, the monk froze and crouched down. He beckoned with a waving arm for Yoshi to join him by his side. As he approached, Daichi pointed out what he had been seeking. In the small clearing ahead was a baby deer, not much more than six months old. She stood in the sunlight breaking through the treetops. But she was clearly lost, calling out for her mother to no avail.

"Shoot it." The monk's request hit Yoshi like a punch in the stomach. "Use the bow and arrow and shoot it."

"What? What for?" Yoshi stammered. "We have plenty of meat at the school."

"Because I said so. Did you not agree to listen with an open mind?" The monk was stern as his eyes never left Yoshi.

He recalled the vow he made but this request made him painfully uncomfortable. Yoshi thought that the monk had been right about so much thus far, so he hesitantly raised the bow and arrow and aimed at the shaking fawn. His eyes began to cloud and lose focus, his hands trembling. An impassioned argument broke out in his head.

There is no need to kill this fawn. It is not sport or food. There is no glory or need in doing this!

The other side responded, *The monk told you to do it then do it. Besides, do you not realize you can do anything, be anything, and it does not change who you are? You are not your behavior. You are just playing another role, another character. Play your part. Kill the deer!*

Cocking the string tight, Yoshi steadied his aim. His eyes cleared and the deer was right in his sights. His two fingers on the bow's string slowly eased their grip. One more command to his fingers and the arrow would be released on its deadly path to the fawn's heart.

This isn't me, Yoshi's mind shouted.

Everything is me, he retorted back to himself.

"Not this," Yoshi said aloud for the monk to hear. He lowered the bow and arrow and sat in silence staring at the doe.

"I am sorry I failed you, Daichi-san," Yoshi said, breaking the silence.

"Enough with apologies." The old monk sat and spoke in whispered tones so as not to disturb the fawn. "You are not sorry, or you would have shot the arrow. It just wasn't who you are."

"But I thought that was the lesson of the water and of the Sword of Roles. That no matter what I do, I am still Yoshi, the same person I vow to be. I should be able to kill that deer and it does not change who I inherently am."

"And yet, here you are with the arrow by your side. So, why did you not do it?" The monk asked the question not in an accusing manner but in a matter-of-fact way, like there was a simple answer.

Yoshi blurted out the only answer he had. "Because it did not feel right." After reflecting on his response for a moment, Yoshi continued. "That doesn't sound like a very good excuse, does it?"

"But it is the right one because it is true to you," the monk explained. "Do not ignore your feelings, Yoshi. They let you know when your actions are incongruent with who you are. You are right when you say you can do anything, be anything. But when those actions run counter to your identity, then your feelings serve as an alert system. The pain you feel in your heart lets you know that this particular action does not correspond to your identity."

"So, I can't be everything," Yoshi surmised from the old monk's explanation.

"That is not true. Just now, your aim was straight, your form solid. If you released the string, you surely would have killed the deer. You can do it. You chose not to." The old monk inched closer to Yoshi to make clear his point. "The gift is the ability. The skill is the awareness of the gift. Wisdom is to know when to use the gift, and when not to." Daichi deftly rose without disturbing a twig and turned to depart. After a moment's reflection, Yoshi followed him.

After taking a few steps from the clearing, Yoshi froze at the sound of the air splitting. He spun around in time to see the arrow lodge deep into the side of the fawn, making a sickening thud. The stunned deer staggered a few steps, eyes wide in fear, and finally slammed hard to the ground. Out of the opposite side of the clearing, Yoshi spied a rustling of branches. Lunging toward the culprits, Yoshi's arm was grabbed by the old monk. "That is who he is," Daichi whispered into Yoshi's ear.

Out of the clearing came an all too familiar face. Togo.

"I always believed you are what you do," Tom mused. "I mean, the first thing anyone ever asks when you first meet is, 'What do you do for a living?'"

"It seems quite shallow, does it not?" replied the old man. "I should hope we are much more than what we do for a living."

"But that's not how people see you."

"Our behaviors are how we are perceived by others; however, our behaviors are not who we are. You are Tom and are always Tom. Depending on where you are and who you are with, you might act differently, but you are still Tom."

"It's a matter of the roles I play, right?"

"Yes, but it is more than that. Just like Yoshi, you can do anything, act in any manner. In any given role you play, you have the power to change how you behave in that role. And just like Yoshi's moment with the deer, if you do not feel right about your behavior, if it runs counter to who you are, you can change it. Just stay true to yourself."

"I see," Tom responded without really seeing.

"Do you cheat on your wife?" the old man blurted out.

"What? No! What kind of question is that?" asked a stunned Tom.

"Why not?"

"Why not? Because I love her and we've made a vow to each other, and I wouldn't want to hurt her, and what the hell are you asking?"

"But you could cheat on her if you wanted, right?" the old man persisted.

For a split second, he thought of Heather, the redheaded receptionist at his office. She had been overtly friendly to Tom since she joined the company six months ago. She made a point of delivering his messages in person and always stopped by his office to ask if he wanted anything when she went to lunch. He often heard the other guys at work comment on her looks and sexiness, and he concurred wholeheartedly with the assessment. If he were honest with himself, he'd admit that the thought had crossed his mind about pursuing her. He was confident that she was attracted to him and would be willing to have an affair. But it never went further than a passing thought.

"Whether I could or not is irrelevant. I don't." Tom replied.

"It's not irrelevant. It is something you can do and choose not to. For the right reasons, I might add. The lesson Yoshi is learning is that he has the power to change his actions and behaviors. He also has to behave and act according to who he is."

Tom abruptly excused himself and headed into the woods to relieve his bladder. After taking care of what he needed, he took out his wallet and removed a picture from it. In the moonlight, he could make out his wife's face. The old man was right. He could, but he won't. Because he loved her. Because it was not true to Tom.

CHAPTER 11

Sword of Roles: Part III

I t took several days for Yoshi's anger over the deer hunting episode to subside. Once he let go of the rage, he focused on the wisdom behind the experience. He realized there were benefits to be gained in exploring the different types of behavior he was capable of.

For several weeks, he experimented with changing his behaviors according to the various situations he faced. He stretched himself by behaving in ways he had never considered just to see if they suited who he really was. On one particular day, Yoshi decided he would boast about all his accomplishments to whomever he met. To classmates, senpai, and even Daichi, Yoshi regaled them with tales of the grand successes he achieved. He bragged about the farm's profit margin under his direction, the compliments he received in class, and the speed he dispatched a recent sparring partner. He found it remarkable that during these bragging sessions, no one questioned his new behavior. Recipients of his self-absorbed tune seemed to accept it with nodding heads and affirmative grunts. Even Daichi was indifferent to his new attitude.

The only person who had a difficult time with this new behavior was Yoshi. In his heart, he knew it really wasn't like him to be this way. While he learned from the experience that this particular manner did not suit his identity, it also proved to him that he was capable of acting in this fashion. He surmised that being a braggart was probably something he never needed to be, but should the situation call for it, he now possessed the confidence to pull it off. After a few days of this behavior, he shared the odd experiment with his old confidant. "I was surprised you did not call me out on it, Daichi-san. I must have come off like such a heel."

"Actually, you did such a good job at it, I really thought it was who you are," replied the old monk. He was checking out the gears on his two-wheeled apparatus, preparing it for another jaunt. "Besides, each person has a model of the world, a master has no need to violate it," Daichi explained.

"So I can be rude, and you'd let me get away with it?" Yoshi said laughing aloud at the idea.

"Who am I to judge another's way of being? Perhaps being a braggart fit into your identity. I can accept it as long as it does not pose a threat to my own identity." As the monk mounted his ride, he offered one more bit of advice. "Now you know what it is like to communicate in such a way, store it in your memory. I have no doubt you shall come across others who act similarly. You shall now have an understanding that will allow you to listen instead of just hear." A particular student at the school immediately came to Yoshi's mind.

As Yoshi sat in the tall grass watching Daichi ride his odd vehicle around the glen, he found himself fixated on the operation of the device, particularly the front wheel. Today it looked rounder than usual and gave Daichi a smoother ride. The wheel was similar to a watermill in that it had several beams protruding from the center. Yoshi counted ten such beams. These beams met up with the circle of iron that surrounded them. From his earlier encounters of watching the monk, he had noted that these beams were of varying length, thus causing the wheel to cave in on certain parts. When several beams were shorter than the others, it led to a very bumpy ride for the monk. But today, the beams were extended to nearly the same length thus making it far easier for Daichi to maneuver.

"I see you fixed it," Yoshi shouted to the circling monk. Daichi did not hear the young man, so Yoshi stood up from his comfortable position and intercepted the monk. "I can tell you fixed those beams on the wheel," Yoshi repeated pointing to the wheel. "You are struggling much less today."

Daichi stopped and studied the wheel in question. "Ah, yes. It seems I am much more in balance today. Perhaps I have you to thank for that."

"Me?" Yoshi asked stunned. "I haven't gone near your device, Daichi-san. I would not know the first thing to do with it."

"Here. It is time you ride it." The old monk dismounted and held it for Yoshi to get on.

"I have to say, it does look easier today than before," the young pupil observed as he got on top of the contraption. The old monk guided Yoshi's feet to sit properly on the pedals and provided him a brief overview of how to ride. He told him to pump his legs in an up-and-down fashion and steer with the bar that controls the front wheel. To Yoshi, it looked simple enough and, after a deep breath, he did as the monk instructed.

While he had never broken a wild horse, he had seen others do it on many occasions. After the first several feet of travel, he felt like he was breaking in an untamed steed. The vehicle bounced up and down and Yoshi furiously maneuvered it to keep it going straight. His fight would last all of ten seconds before he and the vehicle came crashing down. Fortunately for both, the deep grass cushioned their fall.

As Yoshi rose in embarrassment, he inspected the ride and noticed that the beams on the front wheel were now all different sizes. They had somehow morphed from the uniform size when Daichi rode it. "How can this be?" Yoshi exclaimed as he showed the old monk the change to the device. "When you were riding it, they were all level. What did I do to it?"

"You are out of balance."

"Well, it's hard to stay upright with all these beams of different sizes. It makes the wheel crooked and impossible to steer."

"I do not mean the wheel. I mean you are out of balance." The monk took the vehicle from Yoshi and mounted it. Yoshi stared in stunned disbelief as the beams on the wheel, defying all known laws of nature, grew to a more uniform length. The wheel was now much rounder and smoother, allowing Daichi to easily peddle away.

After shaking himself out of his trance, Yoshi ran after the monk. "How did you do that? What kind of black magic is it?"

Continuing his ride away from the glen, the monk shouted his explanation. "This gadget I ride is more than just a mode of transportation. As I built it, I prayed to the gods for guidance and they returned my prayers with a great gift, the wheel of balance. This great wheel reflects the life I am leading. If I am deficient in a particular area, a beam will shrink accordingly. The wheel becomes unstable, and the vehicle is hard to propel." The monk picked up his pace and Yoshi was forced to run faster to keep up.

"But when I got on it, the beams all changed sizes. Does that mean I am out of balance?" Yoshi asked with labored breath.

"It is a wonder you stayed upright as long as you do," the monk replied and sped faster.

"What?" Yoshi heard what the monk said but did not understand. Before he could press him for more information, he stumbled over a rock and fell shoulder-first into the gravel path. Rolling over onto his back, Yoshi gazed up at the sky above as he heaved in and out to refill his lungs. The sky held an abundance of clouds this afternoon and the sunlight forced its way through where it could. It broke through in beams of light, some long and some short. "Again, with the beams," Yoshi mused to himself. Yoshi lay there for a little while, expecting the old monk to come back and check on him.

As he waited, he thought about Daichi's observation that his life was out of balance. Yoshi fought this assessment as being ridiculous. He was more balanced now than at any other time he had been at the school. His lessons were going extremely well with many instructors offering compliments on his performance. The operations at the farm and his relations with the staff had never been better. Even, his friendship with Haru had been restored and they were once again engaging in spirited sparring sessions and informative discussions.

The old monk had been right about so much, but on this point, Yoshi had to disagree. *It's just some silly contraption*, he concluded. Since it became evident that the old monk would not be returning to check on him, Yoshi rose up and dusted himself off, chiding aloud, "I have no problem staying upright, it's that stupid machine." Mumbling to himself, he headed back to the school.

As he walked through the main courtyard, he spied Kira coming from the opposite direction. As they made eye contact, Yoshi instinctively allowed a smile to escape, which was returned by the young woman. He was shocked that he allowed this overt sign of affection to be revealed. Since their encounter after he sparred with Haru, Yoshi had steeled himself to remain cordial yet distant from Kira. While he did not seek to avoid her, he kept their conversations polite but short, always excusing himself for another appointment. His affection for her was still as strong as ever, but he concluded that it had no place in his life as a samurai in training. It was a sacrifice he begrudgingly forced himself to make. Now, the test of that sacrifice was rapidly approaching.

"Yoshi-san, I know you are rushing off to another duty so I will not keep you." Yoshi believed her tone revealed she knew his standard excuse was a ruse. "I wanted to return these scrolls I borrowed. I found them very enlightening, and I thank you so much for sharing them."

"You are very welcome, Kira-san, but you could have returned them to me during the evening workshop. It would give us time to discuss them with the group."

"I am not sure I will be able to attend those any longer, Yoshi-san." As Kira handed the scrolls over, she refrained from making eye contact. "I have... I have other appointments I need to tend to. You are not the only one so busy Yoshi-san." Regaining her composure, she smiled back at Yoshi, hesitating for a moment as if expecting a response from him.

Yoshi felt the air go out of his lungs. The workshop was the only time they spent together. Although he had imposed a moratorium on encounters with Kira, the workshop was an opportunity to *cheat* on his own vow. Now, his decision to avoid a closer relationship with Kira would be fully realized. The reality left him at a loss for words. All he could do was stay transfixed on the beautiful woman before him, praying the moment would dissolve into a bad dream. Finally, after deeming the moment all too real, he responded with a measly, "I see."

"Well, I knew you would understand. I am sure we will run into each other every now and then." She bowed and hastily walked off.

That evening's workshop was a blur to Yoshi. He heard sounds and saw images but none of it registered in his mind. His eyes constantly drifted toward the horizon; expecting, hoping, and praying she would arrive. He would look in vain. Many of the other students recognized Yoshi's lack of concentration and asked if anything was wrong. He responded that all was well and followed that up with a futile attempt to focus on the discussion at hand. It would continue like this for the next week's worth of workshops. His continued lack of concentration led to an embarrassingly easy defeat to Haru in one of their sparring sessions. "I should gloat," Haru said as he offered assistance to the fallen Yoshi. "However, I know I just defeated a man with half a mind. You should find the rest of it before you lose it completely."

Heading back to his room that night, Yoshi was completely perplexed by his current funk. *So what if I do not have her in my life, everything is going just fine*, he thought. *It is just one aspect of my life, it's not everything.* His protestations did not have the desired result. The emptiness he felt continued to gnaw inside him, eating away at everything he felt and thought. It had the cumulative effect of diminishing his level of performance in the classroom, in his sparring sessions, and at the farm. The pain was growing too great, begging for relief. The time had come to swallow his pride and seek help.

"It's a metaphor, isn't it?" Yoshi asked the old monk as he rode around the glen. Yoshi had found the old monk after searching across the school grounds and beyond. This was not their usual time to meet, but Yoshi needed guidance, and waiting was not an option. "The device you ride, it's a metaphor for how to navigate life, right?"

Daichi stopped in front of Yoshi. "Be careful Yoshi-san. You might be on to something." The monk offered a ride to Yoshi and he got on it. Slowly, almost imperceptibly, the beams that connected to the front wheel changed size, and with it, so did the shape of the wheel. Yoshi began to pedal but within moments the ride was out of control, and he just barely kept from falling completely down. Examining the wheel, Yoshi saw one of the beams was much smaller than the others, causing a huge indentation on the wheel.

"I believe I know what aspect of life this beam represents. But that aspect is not nearly as important as the others. I do not understand why it should give me so much trouble."

The old monk silently opened up his hands and extended all his fingers, beckoning Yoshi to do the same. When Yoshi obliged, the old monk grabbed hold of Yoshi's left pinkie finger and unsheathed a small sword from his belt. He quickly maneuvered himself to block Yoshi's attempt to retreat, grabbing tight on the captured finger.

"What the hell are you doing?" Yoshi screamed.

"It is the smallest finger on your least dominant hand. You will still be able to function and have a fairly normal life without it." The monk placed the blade's sharp edge on the crease where the finger met the palm.

"Are you crazy? It will hamper my ability to fight and work and many other things." Yoshi's brain fumbled for other reasons to defend his finger's importance but the fact he had to offer any defense blew his mind.

"But it's such a little thing," the monk said in an infant-like tone. The blade's edge was nearly piercing the skin.

"Okay, okay, I get the point." Yoshi felt a relaxation in the old monk's surprisingly tight grip. He yanked his hand to safety, shaking it out to restore blood flow. "Couldn't we have just visited the stream to get your point across?" Yoshi eyes were stuck wide in shock over the old monk's actions.

Daichi held out his hands again with the fingers extended just like he had.

"Oh, no. I am not falling for that again old man," Yoshi said shaking his head furiously.

Closing a finger as he read off each item, the old monk recited the following: "Physical, Mental, Emotional, Business, Community, Financial, Relationship, Family, Spiritual, and Health."

"They each represent a beam on the wheel," Yoshi acknowledged.

"No, they each represent an area of balance in life. Each is of equal importance, and each is vitally necessary to lead a complete life. You are right Yoshi-san; the device I ride is a metaphor. It represents one's ability to navigate an existence in harmony with oneself. As you see, when one of the wheel's beams is deficient, the ride becomes bumpy. As you have also seen, when one area of your life is deficient, your life becomes difficult to navigate."

"So, my issues with relationships affect everything else."

"How can it not? You are the same person in all these arenas of life. If you are unfit in one, it cannot help but cause you pain. The wheel keeps spinning. It might be smooth in a few areas, maybe most of the areas, but it only takes one dent in the wheel to cause the ride to go off track."

The old monk could see the puzzlement in Yoshi's eyes. He stepped close to the young student and put his hand on his shoulder, focusing his eyes on Yoshi's. "When you engage an opponent in arms, what is your first objective?"

Without missing a beat Yoshi responded, "Seek to strike when he is off balance." The light clicked in Yoshi's mind. "So, it's about staying balanced," he murmured under his breath.

"Just as it will save your life on the battlefield, it will save the life worth living. If there is one thing you should always hold in your mind, it is that."

The monk got back on his ride and began to pedal off.

"But how does one achieve balance?" Yoshi shouted after the departing monk.

"Attend the School of Aspen," the old monk hollered back in response.

"Very funny," he said to only himself. He had been studying at the school for well over a year now and there has never been any mention of balance in any of his studies or with any of the swords he had received. Lately, his focus had been on how the roles he played in various aspects of his life can change while not changing his identity. He thought he had mastered that lesson, but his current depressed mood coupled with the fact he had not graduated to the next sword told him otherwise.

Upon retiring to his quarters that evening, he wrote out the list of areas of balance just as the old monk had given him. Laid out before him, he spent time on each one, devising a plan of action on how he could improve on each. Some he found came to him easily; others he knew would be difficult. Thinking about the task ahead of him, he felt an enormous burden fall upon him. "How can I achieve this?" he asked.

"Attend the School of Aspen." The monk's cryptic reply came back to him. He looked over at the Sword of Roles hanging from his wall alongside his posted identity statement. The School of Aspen had thus far given him a great education, but more importantly, it had given him three Swords of Illumination. He racked his mind to discover how these swords aided him. Then it struck him.

"Attending the School of Aspen has given me the Swords of Illumination." He took out another sheet of paper. In the center he wrote, *Identity*, the first sword he received. Below it he wrote, *Mission and Purpose*, the second sword he received. He realized that these two swords helped mold who he was and who he wanted to be. "The center of the wheel," he whispered as he drew a larger circle around those words. Then, from the center, he drew ten equally separated lines linking his *Identity* and *Mission and Purpose* to the outside circle, or outside of the wheel. These beams he realized were the ten categories of balance. He wrote the names of each category along the lines emanating from the center. The lesson of the Sword of Roles teaches him the roles he had to play in order to achieve fulfillment in each area. The monk spoke as plainly as he ever had about this lesson. Balance was the key. Attending the School of Aspen had given him the tools to achieve balance. The roles he played were not just how to behave at work or school or anywhere else. Roles dictated how to behave in order to achieve balance in these ten areas, and thus in life.

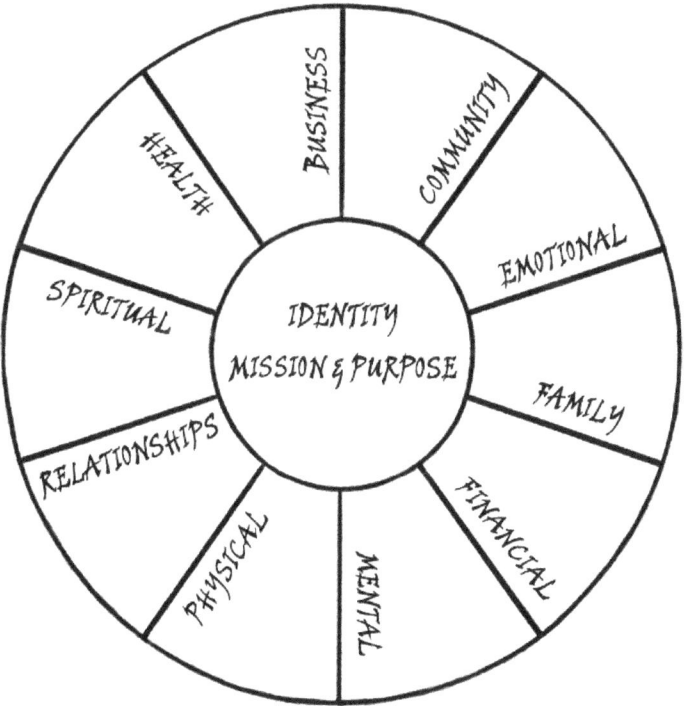

Then he recalled the sword ceremonies and the line spoken at each of them. *"You have been called here tonight to take one more step in the path of enlightenment and balance."* Balance. In his zeal to get his hands on the next sword, he never truly listened to the words being spoken. The answer was always there.

His mind raced with ways he could improve each aspect of his life. Ideas, plans, and actions were jotted down on parchment so he would not forget the flood of thoughts flowing out of him. He knew he did not have a surefire way of achieving complete balance in each area, but he was confident that he had taken the first, important steps necessary to succeed.

His first steps toward a life of balance were literally taking steps. Yoshi awoke a half hour before the morning bell. He slipped on his shoes and jogged off into the misty mountain air. While he thought of himself in good physical shape, he knew he could improve. Whenever he found himself chasing after Daichi as he rode his device, Yoshi quickly became out of breath. *If I don't keep up with that crazy old man, I might miss something important*, he thought as he picked up his pace through the woods. He returned in time to start the morning exercise session for all the students. There was many a cocked eye staring at the perspiring Yoshi as he joined his fellow students. While a little sore from the run, he found he had an unusual burst of energy and completed the exercise regime with great rigor. The burst of energy propelled him throughout the day as he looked for Kira. Her absence left a huge dent in his wheel, and he could not ride straight until it was filled. More importantly, he thought he might be in love with her.

The rotation of classes had changed a week earlier, and Yoshi and Kira no longer shared any instruction time. He decided he would approach her prior to her musical group's meeting and make his confession. He was confident in his feelings and the straightforward approach to take. Should she not return the same feelings, he felt that having a resolution would bring ease to his mind. His heart laughed at the notion that all would be fine; it knew it would break should Kira not feel the same. Building up courage with every step, his meeting with destiny hit an unexpected roadblock. As he turned on the path, he spied Togo walking straight toward him along with two of his usual mates. Yoshi wanted nothing to do with them, especially given the moment, but turning around would be an obvious sign of avoidance and one his pride could not take.

As the trio came closer, Yoshi could see they were all carrying bows and arrows. A sick feeling rose up in the pit of his stomach as he realized where they were headed and why. Togo stopped and mockingly bowed to Yoshi. "You should join us. We are going on a little expedition. I think the trip will do you good. There might even be fruit to pick."

Yoshi could feel the rage begin to boil up to the surface. He struggled to suppress the overwhelming desire to lash out at Togo, verbally and physically. The desire to strike was unlike any he had ever experienced. He could fight it no longer. His meeting with Kira would have to wait until his blade met Togo. Yoshi's brain ordered his right hand to grab his sword, but before the signal could reach its intended target, it was blocked by a thought.

Who am I in this moment?
What is my identity?
Who am I in the specific moment of now?

It was all the lessons of the Swords of Illumination cascading at once. An instinctive impulse washed over him as he felt his blood pressure drop. "Togo-san, while it would be my great honor and pleasure to join you, I have a great many things to attend. The exceptional mastery I have exhibited in combat class has led several senpai to request my leadership in their classes. Furthermore, the operations at the farm have achieved such a high profit margin that the senior monks honored me with a heavy bonus, which I plan on using to purchase some fine new robes. I need to purchase the new garments prior to my attending dinner with several elders this evening. They were kind enough to ask me to join their discussion of Buddhist philosophy. I am sure you can understand as someone else with a busy schedule, that leisure time is a luxury I cannot enjoy. I wish you a pleasant trip."

"Very well," were the only words the stunned Togo could muster. Yoshi did not lie about a single event on his schedule as he did have to attend to all those items. The deception was in the boastful manner he spoke. He employed a behavior that mirrored Togo's, and one his classmate would never expect from him. As Yoshi bowed and left the stunned silent group, he smiled at his achievement. He used a change in behavior to ease a potential conflict. He also realized how utilizing his knowledge of all three swords helped in the *emotional* area of his life. His rage nearly led him to a disastrous response, but by calmly analyzing who he was and who he was at the given moment, he prevented his emotions from controlling him. Now a different set of emotions were driving him on his way to Kira. *I hope they do not lead to a disastrous result.*

As he rose above the hill, he looked down on the bright green clearing where the music group met. Yoshi stared at the position of the sun to make sure it was the right time of day. He ran through his memory to make sure today was the day they normally met. As he descended from the hilltop, he spied a young woman he recognized as being part of the group. Reining in his emotions so as not to seem too excited, he casually inquired when the group would meet again.

"Not until Kira-san returns to the school. She is on a personal leave of absence," was the response from the young student as she hurried off.

Yoshi felt a tinge of guilt for his disappointment. While he felt bad that he could not tell Kira how he felt, he was sure it could not compare to whatever caused her to take a leave. He also felt helpless since there was nothing he could do to comfort or aid her. With the air taken out of his emotional balloon, Yoshi trudged to his appointment as a guest instructor for the combat class.

On the way to the dojo center, he passed the school's main Shinto shrine. He had visited the shrine before, but not frequently. He would enter it to pray on special observances, school events, and on the anniversary of the passing of his father. Yoshi paused before it and reflected. There was one thing he could do for Kira. After washing his hands at the entrance, Yoshi slid off his shoes, entered the shrine, and knelt before its kami. For the first time, he prayed for someone other than himself or a family member. Yoshi prayed for Kira.

The evening discussion with the group of elders went better than Yoshi could have dreamed. He felt like a sponge, absorbing the knowledge and debate between these learned men and women. He mostly refrained from talking in favor of listening but was satisfied that he added constructive and insightful thoughts to the proceeding when he did speak. While rewarding, the day had been a taxing one for Yoshi, both physically and mentally. Thoroughly exhausted, he was a few feet from the entrance of his lodging area when a voice stopped him.

"Yoshi-san, please follow me." It had been several months since he had last seen the senior senpai, but after a moment to regain his composure, he recognized the senpai as his escort to the sword ceremony. His heart began to beat in great anticipation as he followed his guide through the same path, hallways, and doors as the last time. As the chamber room was slowly illuminated, he caught from his periphery two other students standing beside him.

Just as before, twelve robed elders entered the chamber. The students knelt before them and, when directed, offered up the Sword of Roles they carried. A different elder from the previous two ceremonies spoke, the voice clearly from a female elder. "You three have been called here tonight to take one more step on the path of enlightenment and balance. By being here you have shown to yourselves that you understand the great gift of the Sword of Roles. In time, you will learn its true power. It is now time to receive the next level of enlightenment." Other elders knelt before the students and presented the encased new sword.

"Before you accept the next Sword of Illumination, you are permitted to ask one question of this council in order to gain additional knowledge."

Yoshi thought hard about what to ask during this rare occasion. He wished he had more time to prepare, but that was obviously not an option. At his turn to speak, Yoshi inquired, "Are there specific steps that can be taken to help engineer personal change?" Yoshi found each step of his evolution at the school required a high degree of struggle. He thought perhaps there was a process in which he could affect changes without the pain.

The elder spoke. "The specifics of change are unique to every man, woman, and child. No one person can offer a dynamic that can truly affect another. The one constant is that change begins in the general but happens in the specific. Thinking initiates; acting demonstrates."

At the conclusion of the inquiries, Yoshi felt the sheathed sword placed delicately into his outreached hands. When the elders departed, Yoshi withdrew the sword and read its inscription:

Sword of Outcomes

"I've ridden a lot of bicycles in my time, but never rode one that told me if my life was messed up," Tom sarcastically observed. "Do they sell those in Japan? Maybe we can open up a dealership here in the States?"

"I don't think there is a need for such bicycles," the old man calmly answered to diffuse Tom's annoyance. It failed.

"Oh, I disagree. I think it would be a huge seller. Think

about it. Who wouldn't want a bike with a magical wheel that shows them how their life is screwed up by making them crash. At least with the concussion they suffer, they won't remember half their problems. How else would someone know if their life is out of whack?"

The old man simply stared without responding, as if he was waiting for Tom to answer his own question.

Tom stared back in defiance, silently demanding an answer from the old man. He held this look even as his own mind answered. *They know they are out of balance because they end up lost in the middle of nowhere.* He finally broke the stare down by bowing his head in resignation.

"That wheel of balance that Daichi rides is really inside all of us," the old man explained after he saw Tom answered his own question. "But instead of riding on a bicycle, we feel it in our heart. When an area of our life does not support who we want to be, our life becomes unmanageable..."

"And we fall off the bike, so to speak." Tom finished the thought and the old man nodded in agreement.

Tom continued. "If I can only get set with the money area of my life, I know that everything will run smoothly. These other areas of so-called balance, they will all fall in line if I can just get financial security."

"There is no doubt that is one important area of your life, one of several important areas," the old man said. Tom started shaking his head, so the old man shared another example. "The car you prized. The one you bought and cared for in your youth. What was the most important part of it?"

"Well, I guess it'd had to be the engine," Tom answered somewhat bewildered why the old man would bring that back up. "I tell you I wish I had that engine right now for the car sitting up there."

"Good point," the old man smiled. "But what about the tires? If they were all flat, wouldn't the car be useless?"

Tom just nodded in agreement.

"I am not an expert in automotive issues, but I also understand the steering and brakes and lights and mirrors..."

"And transmission and air conditioning and radiator. I get the point. Every part of the car is important."

"And every part of your life is equally important. You can have the financial security you crave, but if you do not have the happy family and loving relationships to share it with, what good is it? If you do not have the mental and physical health to live a long and active life, how can you enjoy those relationships and wealth?" The old man paused to allow Tom to absorb the comment.

The wheels in his mind were turning, not unlike the wheel on Daichi's bicycle. In a revolving fashion, he recalled the times in his life when things went great and the times they seemed to fall apart. As he thought, he discovered a consistent pattern. The times when he was confident and secure with one or even several areas of his life, his life went along smoothly; but then suddenly and seemingly out of nowhere, something would pop up and send his life careening out of sorts. And it would always be in an area of his life he had neglected.

He thought things were going okay this morning during breakfast until his little girl spoke those fateful words. *"When I grow up, I want to be just like you."* His wheel of balance hit the area he had neglected tending to with the care and attention he should have—his family. This dent sent him flying completely off his bike, all the way to some remote wooded area miles from home.

CHAPTER 12

Sword of Outcomes: Part I

The fireplace's flames projected dancing beams of amber across Yoshi's bare chest as he stood in the center of his family home. Slowly and methodically, he dressed himself, deliberately applying each layer of his samurai armament. He slid the lacquered iron breastplate over his head and secured it firmly over his chest. In the middle of the plate, in shining silver, was the same symbol etched on the medallion his mother had worn for as long as he could remember.

At the entrance was his mother, holding in her hands the crimson helmet that would soon adorn his head. He took in her visage, backlit by the setting sun. Her face had a combined look of deep pride and grave concern. Taking the headgear from his mother, he bowed to her. "I thank you for all that I am," he whispered to her and exited the house.

Rising up on his steed, Yoshi hollered the command to go, and the horse sprinted into the forest to the north. Weaving in and out of the aspens at a harrowing and nauseating pace, the horse knew where he was going without any direction from his rider. Yoshi's eyes burned with focus and determination, widening as he saw the clearing ahead.

As soon as he entered the valley, the silence of the forest was broken by the explosion of the sound of battle. Samurai, both on foot and on horse, were engaged in fierce conflict. The sounds of victory and the last gasps of defeat blended together in a macabre symphony. Without hesitation, Yoshi drove headlong into the fray. In one fluid motion, Yoshi leapt off his horse and unsheathed his sword. Instantly, he struck down the first foe he faced and followed it up with five equally brutal victories. Yoshi saw fear in the eyes of the next several foes as they all succumbed to his lightning-fast moves and unmatched skills.

Just as suddenly as it started for Yoshi, it abruptly stopped. All the combatants froze in their tracks and looked to the center of the valley. Parting the way before him, Yoshi saw two combatants circling each other, swords raised and postures set for battle. As he walked closer to the duo, the light hit the breastplate of the combatant in red, illuminating the same symbol that adorned Yoshi's chest. The samurai's eyes met Yoshi's. Those eyes were all too familiar to him as they were the eyes of the man that raised him. Circling in front of his father was the samurai that struck him down at Hamasuka's farm, the infamous rōnin, Jaiko.

"I will not allow this," Yoshi yelled. Marching with purpose, he headed to engage the dark samurai. But as he marched, the distance between him and the pair only increased. His gait turned into a trot and then into a full sprint, but all his efforts could not shorten the distance between him and his father's slayer. Running until his heart was near explosion, Yoshi screamed from the depths of his soul, but to no avail. The dark samurai spun around and, in a flash, sliced Yoshi's father right through his midsection.

"No!" Yoshi sat straight up on his mat, cold sweat drenching his body. He could hear murmuring outside his room. A knock rapped on his door.

"Yoshi-san are you okay?" the unknown voice asked. Yoshi, still shaking could not find the voice to respond. His rice paper door slid open slightly and a head popped in. "Yoshi-san, do you need help?"

In a hoarse whisper, Yoshi finally responded. "I am fine, thank you. Must have been tonight's meal." He feigned a smile to his worried neighbor, who bowed and took his leave. Lying back down, Yoshi closed his eyes but did not sleep for the remainder of the night. He was too exhausted to dream again.

"I had the same dream last night." Yoshi and Daichi were sitting in silence inside the teahouse as the rattle of the falling rain echoed off the bamboo roof. Daichi poured his young pupil some hot tea.

"Did you reach your father this time?"

"No, I failed once again," Yoshi sighed. "It's as if my dreams are taunting me." Yoshi took out the sword given to him two weeks prior. Engraved on its shiny silver blade it read:

Sword of Outcomes
What do I desire in this moment?

"Ever since I received this sword, I have been focused on what I want," Yoshi continued. "I so want to be the samurai that my father dreamed I would become. I want to be great so I can avenge his death. More importantly, I wish to give purpose to his life, by living a life of purpose. I want this but I fear my dreams are telling me I shall never achieve it. Perhaps this is the last sword I shall receive at the school."

"Perhaps it is," the monk responded as he took a gentle sip of his hot beverage.

"I was hoping for guidance rather than validation, Daichi-san."

"I am sorry I failed you, but I honestly do not see your

predicament. You are getting exactly what you seek. You want to be a samurai."

Thinking the monk's statement to be a question, Yoshi yelped an answer. "Of course I want to be a samurai. Why do you think I am at the School of Aspen?"

"That is for you to answer." With that, the monk set down his tea and rose to exit. "I am at the School of Aspen to enjoy its beautiful surroundings." The old monk walked out to the porch, slipped on his shoes, and strolled right out into the pouring rain.

"But you are getting all wet!" Yoshi shouted at the smiling monk soaking in the rain.

"Why should I let that stop me?" His voice trailed off as he headed off the path and into the trees.

You have to give it to him, Yoshi thought. *He doesn't let anything stop him from what he wants to do.* That must be the wisdom of his words Yoshi surmised. He had overcome obstacles to get this far and shouldn't let anything stop him as he inched closer to his goals. Perseverance is one thing, but without direction he felt he'd be swimming up the mountain stream as it dragged him back down.

As the rain continued to pound outside, Yoshi met with his staff at the farm. With the approaching summer speeding up operations, it was the perfect time to start mapping out how they would proceed for the rest of the season. In the spirit of getting his staff more involved in the decision-making process, Yoshi encouraged input from his co-workers and jotted down their ideas and concerns. During this discussion, Yoshi's mind wandered to his time as a youth.

Peering through the slit in the sliding rice paper door,

Yoshi spied his father deep in thought as he stared at the pen and paper before him. Without turning his head, his father called out, "I smell a suspicious young boy in the room." Yoshi could not control his giggle. Gesturing for him to enter, Yoshi rushed in to sit beside his father.

The inquisitive young boy immediately asked, "What is it you are doing, father?"

"Making my list, Yoshi-kun," his father replied. "This is the list of things I desire to achieve in the upcoming year."

"Why do you need to write it? Don't you already know what you want to do?"

"For focus, son. By making this list and thinking about ways I can achieve these goals, I am clarifying what I want to accomplish and how I plan to do it."

"And what is this list for?" Young Yoshi reached over his father's lap and picked up a tattered sheet of paper. "And why are some items circled and some are not?"

"This was last year's list. The items circled were the things I was able to accomplish."

"But not everything is circled. If you did not achieve everything, aren't you sad?"

Kensi lifted his only son and placed him on his lap. "Why should I be sad when I have accomplished so much? I am proud of the things I did on this list. More importantly, I am proud we have a home, you and your mother are cared for properly, and we are all healthy and content. There is only one thing I am sad about."

"What is that?" a concerned Yoshi pleaded.

"That you have not finished your chores," his father responded with a claw-like grab of Yoshi's belly. Yoshi yelled with laughter as the tickle drove him off his father's *lap. He broke Kensi's grip and scurried off giggling to complete his tasks.*

"So now what?" Hideki asked from across the table, returning Yoshi to the present. From their group discussion, Yoshi had heard several great ideas and thoughts, but as he looked down at his sheet, he realized there was no order to them. He set out with the group's input to compose a set of specific goals to be accomplished in the coming year. Accompanying each goal was a discussion on how each would be achieved. Yoshi could feel the excited energy coming from his staff as they developed their objectives. After the meeting was over, several of the staff lauded Yoshi for providing a sense of direction and purpose to the farm's employees and making the process refreshing and invigorating.

The meeting also served the dual purpose of getting Yoshi on track. If it was good enough for the farm, Yoshi thought it would be useful to do the same tactic for himself. He made a written list of all the things he wanted to accomplish. He wrote a litany of 'I want' statements.

I want to be a great samurai.
I want to improve my relationship with Kira.
I want to become a stronger fighter.

He studied the areas of balance and created goals for each area and tasks he needed to do to achieve them. It took well into the morning hours, but Yoshi finally completed it. Exhausted, he looked at the list and thought its length to be daunting. "Have to finish my chores, Father," he said softly to himself. Tomorrow he would begin to tackle them, but tonight he needed sleep. Tonight, his sleep did not include images of battles and his father's death.

Yoshi found his new morning ritual was the perfect time to collect his thoughts and plan how he would achieve his list of goals. Just like he had for most mornings during the past couple of months, Yoshi rose before the morning bell and ran for thirty minutes. It began as a way to get in better shape, so as to keep up with the peddling Daichi. It evolved into a period of time he could focus on preparing for the tasks of the day and the things he wanted to accomplish. Lately, it provided an extra benefit, preparing him for the upcoming heralded race.

Every year, the School of Aspen transformed from an institute of study to a carnival of merriment. The Grand Summer Celebration was the largest festival the school held and commemorated the first day of summer. It was a joyous event and the students, senpai, monks, and elders enjoyed the pleasant weather. The schedule included activities such as special dedicated prayer services to the gods, music and dance performances, and demonstrations of combat techniques. The day culminated with a grand feast and bonfire attended by the entire campus. Prior to the feast's beginning, a cross-country race was run by students at the school. The route covered the entire circumference of the School of Aspen's vast campus and ended at the steps of the grand temple in the main courtyard. The race always enjoyed a sizable participation from the student body, both male and female. The first student to reach the temple steps was given the ceremonial title of Prince or Princess of Summer. He or she is said to be swifter than the wind and able to outrun Mother Summer herself. The prize included a crown of gold leaves and a seat alongside the elders at the grand feast.

As Yoshi raced alongside the creek on his return leg back to campus, he envisioned himself dining with the elders once again and joining in on their fascinating conversation. Since he began his daily run, he felt the physical benefits of the exercise as both his stamina and speed increased with each week. Never encountering another soul taking the same measures as he was, Yoshi did not think he was over-confident in believing he could, and should, win the race.

It seemed the entire school was in a jubilant mood on the day of the summer festival. Due to his comfort level and confidence, Yoshi enjoyed this year's festival far more than the first one he attended. He could not remember the last day he laughed as much and enjoyed the society of his fellow students. He found himself so enthralled with the proceedings that he was shocked when he realized he was not anxious about the impending race. When the bell rang out calling the participants to the starting line, it caught Yoshi as a bit of a surprise.

Yoshi surmised there were at least 100 students gathered at the starting line. Scanning through the crowd, he saw many familiar faces but not the one he most expected to see, Togo. His eyes turned to the crowd forming along the sides of the racers. From within this crowd, he finally spied his erstwhile adversary. It was obvious he was not participating, and Yoshi hurriedly buried his disappointment. Alongside Togo was an older gentleman he had never seen at the school. With the stature and dress of a warrior, he assumed him to be a samurai of some sort. Togo and the stranger stoically conversed while looking at the crowd of racers. Yoshi thought he detected eagerness in Togo to race but perhaps the old stranger was holding him back. *Maybe, Togo has found his own Daichi,* Yoshi mused to himself.

Turning his focus to the path before him, Yoshi stared at the official starter. In the tower above the grand temple, a single archer dipped his arrow in the flame, placed it on his bow, pulled the string back, and shot the lit arrow onto the pre-dusk sky. With a thunderous explosion, the stampede of racers shouted in unison a deafening cry and raced off down the path.

Yoshi deemed the best strategy was to pace himself early and allow his built-up endurance and speed to propel him toward the end of the race. The race path was as scenic as it was long. It took the racers along the creek that bordered the western edge of the campus, through the forest between the first and second gates, and across the bridge over the east river. It was after crossing the bridge that Yoshi decided to pick up his pace. He figured he was near the front of the middle pack and, with three-quarters of the race completed, this was the right time to make a run for the lead. The path would take them right past the hot springs then circle around the back of the women's quarters, eventually intersecting with the steps leading to the Temple of the Swords.

As Yoshi reached the steps and started his descent down toward the main campus, he saw only four other racers ahead of him and he could tell their strides were labored. One by one, he passed each runner, overtaking the last one just as they entered the main courtyard. There were about two hundred yards until the final turn to the steps of the grand temple. The enormous crowd lining these final yards cheered the racers on passionately. Yoshi assumed the crowd was loud but their yells were drowned out by his own heavy breathing and thumping chest. As he focused on making the turn and reaching the first step of the temple, he envisioned the gold laurel lying on his head, the delicious array of food before him, and the laughter of the elders at one of his delightful tales. Yoshi felt the sides of his lips turn upward as he reached the final turn. He thought a smiling sprinter might look funny, but he was so happy and too tired to care.

It took about a dozen steps after he made the turn for the smile to disappear. Standing on the steps of the temple receiving congratulatory handshakes and pats were not one, not two, but five other racers. His eyes wide and mouth agape, Yoshi's momentum pushed him to complete the race and reach the steps of the temple. Bent over at the waist and gasping for as much oxygen as the surrounding aspens would provide, Yoshi was shocked. The lead pack was obviously farther out than he suspected. The second-guessing of his strategy bombarded his mind, but he politely accepted the congratulations from the spectators on his fine finish.

"Coming in sixth in this race is nothing to be ashamed of Yoshi-san," Haru consoled as he escorted Yoshi to the grand banquet. "Heck, half the racers could not even finish and I, along with most of the school, wouldn't even attempt it. Besides, would you not prefer to dine with me tonight than those stodgy old elders?" His question brought a laugh out of Yoshi and eased the sting of his disappointment.

"I was impressed too." The voice startled him so much that his racing heart skipped a beat. He had heard that voice rattling in his head for weeks but hearing it outside the walls of his brain caught him off guard.

"Kira-san!" he blurted out in excitement. Slowly reining in his exhilaration, he continued. "How have you been? I heard you had to go on leave. I am so sorry. I hope all is well. Are you back for good?" Yoshi could hear the litany of questions come out of his mouth as if he was a third person in the conversation. While embarrassed with his schoolboy inquisition, he felt powerless to stop it.

"All is well. Thank you so much for the concern." She could not help but smile at the reaction she was receiving from her fellow student. "I have returned to complete my training after tending to some unfortunate family issues."

Sensing this moment did not require him, Haru found an escape. "I will run ahead and secure a spot for us in the dining area." He rushed off ahead leaving the two to stroll to the feast. As they walked, Kira told him the story of how her mother had suddenly taken ill and passed. The memory still fresh in her heart, her eyes welled up as she related her tale. Despite the obvious tragic nature of her story, Yoshi's heart was full just being in her presence. He had thought about seeing her since the day he had vowed to confess his feelings. Now that the moment was upon him, he was unsure how to proceed. He wanted so much to tell Kira how he desired her to be a bigger part of his life, about how much she meant to him. But he wouldn't get that chance.

"I know that each of us at the school has our issues and our own reasons to become samurai," Kira said. She spoke as if she had rehearsed this part and was concentrating on getting it right. "Because of this, our energies and time should be focused on accomplishing those goals. I will confess to you that in the past I looked forward to spending time with you, time that would have been more valuably spent in the pursuit of our endeavors. My mother's passing has reminded me that I need to focus on why I am at this school."

Yoshi could not stand to hear anymore and interrupted. "Kira-san, I would never consider the time we have spent together as a waste, but rather a blessing. These weeks since you have left, I have discovered how valuable our relationship is to me and I want to tell you..."

Before he could say aloud what his heart had been yearning to say for weeks, Kira cut him off. "Yoshi-san, I am flattered by your comments, and I am sure they are heartfelt. However, I also know it would be in both our best interests to keep our relationship as peers so as to avoid any unnecessary diversion. I am sure you agree."

He thought she was holding back but did not want to take the chance he was wrong. "Of course, Kira-san. You are wise to suggest this. Please know you are welcome to come to me for any advice or if you should ever want to... talk about anything." He fumbled for words he had not prepared. He was not sure if his chest ached from the stress of the race or from the moment at hand.

"And please know you can do the same. If you will excuse me, having just gotten back, I have much to do and I am afraid the feast will have to do without me." Kira bowed and hurried off as the sun dipped below the horizon.

The feast would have to do without Yoshi as well. *Haru will understand*, Yoshi thought as he walked off into the woods. He needed to *get out of his mind* more than ever. The day that started out with so much fun and laughter had ended with despair and defeat. The sting of disappointment from losing the race had been replaced with a more potent blow brought on by Kira's conversation.

As he reached the moonlit waterfall on the outskirts of campus, Yoshi felt all his self-doubt rear its ugly head. He wanted to win the race, and he failed. He wanted Kira, and he was denied. He wanted to be a samurai but spent more time as an apple farmer than as a warrior. He thought about how the Swords of Illumination had been a great source of wisdom and enlightenment, but what good is it if he does not achieve his goals?

Taking a seat at the waterfall's edge, he escaped into the sounds of nature around him. He listened to the cascading water from above meeting the water down below, the sound of the wolf howling to the stars, and the creaking of the trees from the blowing breeze. Soon the creaking became louder than any tree should emanate. Before he could recognize the true nature of the sound, the old monk wheeled behind him and kept peddling down the bank of the river. While Yoshi did not want the company of others, Daichi was the one person he desperately wanted to see.

Yelling out his name, Yoshi raced after the old monk. "Yoshi-san, whatever are you doing out here so late?" the old monk asked without slowing his pace.

Catching up to the old monk, Yoshi jogged alongside the still-peddling Daichi. "It's sort of a long story." He related the events of the afternoon. He detailed his disappointment with the race and his even greater disappointment over Kira.

"I never knew you were so interested... in running," the old monk observed.

"Actually, I have you to blame for that, Daichi-san. I took up running to get in better condition so I can keep up with you when you are on this contraption," Yoshi responded, slightly dismayed that the old monk would focus on that and not the story with Kira.

"Then let me be the first to congratulate you on your great achievement. I am very proud of you, Yoshi-san."

"Whatever are you talking about? I am sorry if I did not make it clear, but I lost the race."

The old monk smiled. "If you lost, how are we having this conversation?" It took a couple of seconds, but Yoshi finally comprehended what the old monk meant. Here was Yoshi, without breathing very hard, running alongside the monk and able to converse with him. This was the very reason he started his extra exercise routine in the first place.

The old monk slowed to a stop as he witnessed the comprehension wash over his young pupil's face. "You wanted to be able to keep up with me. And now you can. What magic did you conjure that made your wishes come true?"

"It was nothing like that. I just started running to build up my endurance and I guess it just sort of happened."

"Oh, Yoshi-san," the old monk responded with a real sense of disappointment. "If you really believe it just sort of happens, then I guess you still have a lot more running to do." With that, the old monk peddled off and disappeared around the turn in the creek, once again leaving Yoshi alone in the night.

"It did not just happen," Tom blurted out. "By jogging every day, he got fit and now can keep up with the old man on the bike. Please tell me he got the lesson."

The old man nodded his head. "Haven't you ever been told something, but in the heat of the moment when your thoughts and focus are elsewhere, you failed to see it?"

"I guess," he replied, not catching the old storyteller's implication to Tom's current situation.

"Yoshi would understand what his teacher meant as he lay awake that night. He realized that there was a step between wanting something and having something."

"Yeah, it's called hard work. There's not a thing I've ever achieved without working for it," Tom said.

"But I hazard to guess there might be some things you seek that you have not gotten, despite your hard work."

Tom had no response for this. The fact of the matter was he really believed he was working hard at all the aspects of his life, family job, and friends. Although he was loath to admit it to this old stranger, he was falling short in many of those areas despite his toiling. He had no answers and he thought neither did this man or his ancestor.

The old man had touched a raw nerve in Tom. The whole evening, he knew the old man was sensing his pain, trying to help. But no words of consolation could make his life okay. No amount of advice or some random story about an ancient ancestor could fix him. Yet the old man stoked the fire and prepared himself to continue the story, seemingly determined to give Tom some relief, and maybe a bit of camaraderie.

CHAPTER 13

Sword of Outcomes: Part II

"I guess sometimes when you lose, you really win," Haru replied as he gently eased himself into the hot spring.

It had been an especially demanding day of physical and combat training for Haru and Yoshi, and both relished the chance to ease their aching bodies in the natural hot springs behind the living quarters. On the way to the springs, Yoshi shared with Haru his disappointment in losing the race but the valuable lesson the old monk pointed out to him about achieving his goal.

"And when you win, you can really lose," Yoshi added. Without saying it, both knew Yoshi was referring to the infamous sparring session with Haru many months earlier. It was Yoshi's way of acknowledging that while the wounds might have healed, he was still aware of his fault.

Laying his head back and sighing into the evening sky, Haru took a moment to contemplate. "Perhaps that is the key. Do not set yourself up in a situation in which you can fail, but rather seek outcomes where you can only win."

Yoshi figured that was a simplistic answer to a complex problem. *How can one come up with only winning situations?* he asked rhetorically in his mind. The issue that really bothered him, and the one he dared not share with Haru, was his disappointment with how things worked out with Kira. He felt he lost her, and there was no winning in that. Yoshi quickly steered the conversation to other less hefty subjects. As his body limbered in the steamy mountain water, he needed his mind to join his body in relaxation. A petty conversation about the day's lunch would suit this goal, but before he could guide their conversation in that direction, Haru took the conversation down another path.

"So, are you going to put your name on the list?"

Haru was alluding to the upcoming school competitions and by 'the list' he specifically meant the sign-ups for the Kenjutsu fighting competition. While participating in the previous few school-wide assemblies, Yoshi had stayed away from the Kenjutsu trials. He did this not out of fear, but because he was working on new techniques such as enhancing his blending and balance. He wanted to be fully confident in his new methods before showing them for the whole school to see. This was the reason he had given to Haru and his other classmates when they queried him about not participating. Yoshi kept from his inquiring comrades the real reason he avoided the competition. He wanted to show off his skills to just one person—Togo.

Yoshi knew that if he signed up for the Kenjutsu competition, the senpai would pit him against Togo. Their previous sparring match was still talked about throughout campus. Haru had told Yoshi that a lively debate had engulfed the school on whether he could best the still-undefeated, stellar pupil. Yoshi had always shrugged his shoulders in a self-deprecating manner and mused aloud that it would be a difficult task.

But since the day after his defeat to Togo, Yoshi had been bent on achieving victory in their next encounter. He replayed in his mind's eye their battle repeatedly. He second- and third-guessed his decisions while remembering exactly the tactics Togo used. At every chance he got, he studied how Togo moved in sparring lessons, seeking ways he could emulate him as well as defeat him. *To beat him, I have to be him*, Yoshi surmised. *Not as a person, but as a fighter.* For as much as he disagreed with Togo, he had to admit what everyone at the school knew—Togo was the finest warrior in the School of Aspen. Yoshi concluded that defeating Togo in such a setting as the school-wide trials would vault him to that lofty and supreme position. *Is not my goal to become the best samurai I can be?* he thought. *Such a victory would surely lead to me becoming a great warrior.*

Before Haru asked his question, Yoshi had already concluded that the time was ripe for him to accept the challenge. He told Haru that he was indeed going to sign up, and the next afternoon he followed through on his word and inked his name on the list posted upon the learning center's main entrance. The ink was not dry on the paper before Yoshi, practice swords in hand, was marching to a remote area behind the apple farm to shadow spar. The match was in seven days, and he felt he needed every bit of that time to hone his skills. Stomping down the same path to the farm that he had taken hundreds of times, he paused to greet the two approaching monks with the obligatory bow. As he straightened back up, he noted something he had never seen in all his previous trips down this route.

Has this always been here? Yoshi asked himself as he looked down the small opening in the woods to the north. It was clearly a man-made opening and not one caused by the naturally random alignment of trees. Walking to its mouth, Yoshi peered down the pathway. Up ahead was the beginning of a column of stone steps that continued up beyond his sight.

His desire to get back to training stopped him from further investigating the steps, but his curiosity gnawed at him throughout the next day. He asked around the campus about this path and learned from a young monk that the steps led to an old shrine, but that shrine had not been maintained for years. This was the first time he had heard of this place and asked the young monk why it was never visited. "Why would we need to venture out of our way when the school built the beautiful one in our main courtyard," was the monk's response. It was true that all his and everyone else's religious observances exclusively took place at the splendid, and much newer shrine near the main entrance. Not that his observances were all that frequent. He would visit the shrine for all the important commemorations and events, but he never found the desire to visit during his own free time. Sure, he would seek guidance from the gods, but only in times of great need. Most other times in his life, Yoshi did not counsel the kami.

When he wrote out his plan of action for each of the areas of balance, he had nothing to write for *Spiritual*. Since the day his father passed, his focus was on becoming a samurai and the physical and mental preparation needed to accomplish it. The spiritual side was always considered a traditional, almost quaint, part of the samurai experience, but not one Yoshi placed with much importance.

That afternoon, as he walked to his usual private practice area, he paused before the newly discovered path. More out of curiosity than any real plan, Yoshi climbed the steps. Thick trees lined both sides of the path with branches meeting above to form a natural canopy. The stone steps were covered with overgrown foliage and more than several were cracked. The pathway was barely lit by the few beams of sunlight breaking through the branches. After twenty minutes of climbing, Yoshi began to wonder if the young monk was wrong, and if he would find nothing at the end of this path. His concerns were dispelled as the stone steps veered to the left and led to a small clearing.

The starkness from the dark path to the sunlit opening gave the clearing an unusually bright splendor. A single shrine stood at the center of the clearing. Time, weather, and neglect had obviously taken their toll on the modest-sized temple; however, it was not the condition of the temple, but rather the emotion of the temple that Yoshi found compelling. The temple looked sad. It was a very human trait to give to an inanimate object, but that is what Yoshi found at the center of the clearing—a very old, decrepit, and sad temple. The broken tiles on the pagoda roof gave the temple a furrowed brow. The snake-like vines that crept across its front gave a distinctly downturned mouth. The interior was dark, cold, and barren; all the adornments had long since been removed.

The lone relic from its days as a center of adoration was a single stone statue. Despite the disrepair all around it, this statue was in remarkably good condition. Yoshi immediately recognized it as the goddess Benzaiten. In the Shinto religion, she is considered one of the seven gods of fortune and represents everything that flows such as water, words, eloquence, and music. Many also pray to her for financial blessings; for money to literally flow to them. Yoshi's familiarity with Benzaiten came from his mother, who kept a shrine to the goddess in the family home for as long as he could remember. His mother's devotion extended to her son, compelling Yoshi to always join her in prayer. Even as a young child, he considered this goddess one for females to adore and not for the masculine gender.

But as he looked upon Benzaiten in this new light, he was forced to reconsider his position. Staring long at the idol's face, Yoshi detected in Benzaiten's smile the wry question: *What took you so long?* Something about this clearing and this shrine put Yoshi at ease. His heart had been racing since he inked his name on the list, but for the first time since that moment, his heart rate returned to its normal repetition.

Untying the practice swords strapped to his back, Yoshi closed his eyes, held out the bokken, and conducted a visual match against his upcoming foe. The serenity of the setting enhanced his focus like never before. He *saw* Togo standing before him. He *felt* the breeze of his foe's bokken as it nearly missed Yoshi's head. When he struck Togo with a series of blows, his sword vibrated from the impact. Finally, he saw the exasperated look of a retreating Togo, his eyes widening as Yoshi's final blow came cracking across his jaw. He stared with closed eyes at his foe curled up on the ground with an outstretched hand seeking mercy. Yoshi's eyes opened, returning him to reality.

Studying the shrine once more before departing, Yoshi thought he detected a brightening of the building's disposition. It seemed somehow less alone. "You're right, you are not alone," Yoshi said to the shrine. It would become his new personal refuge.

A light rainfall gave everything in sight a glowing shine as Yoshi and Daichi walked in the midafternoon. Yoshi agreed to follow the old man for a task that the old man would not explain. During the trek, the young pupil related his decision to enter the sparring contest and his expectations in facing Togo.

"What do you hope to accomplish?" Daichi asked the student.

"I want to win," Yoshi answered as if the answer was self-evident. "What else is there?"

"Why do you want to win?" The old monk took a right turn and ascended a steep yet small incline with his pupil in tow.

"I want to prove myself a superior warrior and student and to show I have the focus, commitment, and wisdom to achieve this outcome." Yoshi felt he was being tested by Daichi, so he made sure to give confident, powerful answers.

"How do you plan to accomplish this lofty goal?" The old monk had reached the top of the hill and walked directly to the mountain stream up ahead. Yoshi sprinted a bit to catch up.

After a moment's reflection, he responded, "By not accepting defeat." And with only two days before the competition, Yoshi was very confident in his plan and his abilities. He had put forth twice the effort to train and constantly visualized victory. He could not fathom defeat.

"I am impressed Yoshi-san. I have never heard you so confident. You have determined a very clear outcome and coupled it with an equally precise purpose and plan of action. Congratulations, you have already achieved your outcome."

"So, you think I can win?"

"No. I think you want to win," the old monk answered.

Yoshi laughed with an exaggerated, loud chuckle. "I

understand the semantics. Wanting. Having. The difference is just the degree of hard work you put into it."

Just as the old monk reached the bank of the stream, he turned to Yoshi. "Where are we going?"

"I don't know. You are the one leading the way."

"Do you want to know where we are going?" asked the old monk.

"Yes. I have since we started this walk."

"And so you are fulfilled? You have continued to want something. With every step we have taken, the strength of your want probably grew. The more you want, the stronger the want. And you will continue to want until...?"

"Until I ask you where we are going," Yoshi sheepishly replied. "But, while I was going to ask you, I got caught in telling you about the competition and Togo and the host of other things and I just neglected to ask you. So where are we going?"

"Just like you, I wanted something. In my case, it was to host an entertaining evening with some of the elders. I planned on offering a tea made of leaves only found on the other side of this stream. I've wanted to do this for several days as a matter of fact, but it never happened. Things only changed when I moved from wanting it to desiring it."

"What is the difference?" Yoshi asked.

"Wanting made me talk and think about it. Desiring got me to this stream."

Yoshi fell silent for a moment and reflected on his own experience. He thought about all the things he ever wanted in his life such as attending the School of Aspen, becoming a better warrior, and obtaining knowledge. He had never achieved anything without a focused and concerted effort.

As for those things he has failed to achieve, it was always lack of action—a lack of true desire—that had prevented him from getting it. He concluded he never got anything by just wanting, he had to desire it.

The realization became as crystal clear as the water before him. "To win," he uttered out of the blue.

"Excuse me, Yoshi-san?"

"My outcome for fighting Togo. It is no longer 'I want to win' but simply 'to win.'" The old monk nodded. Yoshi did not detect approval, but rather mere acknowledgment in the monk's gesture.

"You are getting close to understanding the power of outcomes," the old monk replied without enthusiasm.

The two stood in silence surveying the stream before them. Yoshi sensed Daichi was concerned on how he was going to cross the stream. Yoshi studied the pathway of rocks sprinkled across the stream, judging which ones to use to get across. The stream was about thirty feet wide with large rocks strewn throughout that could be used as steps. Being as far apart as they were and slippery, he thought the route to be a bit treacherous for the spry yet still elderly monk. "In thanks for the lesson, allow me to get the leaves for you Daichi-san."

The old monk thanked Yoshi for the gesture of gratitude. He told him exactly what the leaves looked like and where to find them. With a short three-step running start, Yoshi took his first leap off the bank and onto a large rock in the middle of the stream. Swinging his arms wildly, he was barely able to maintain his balance. He took the next three steps in rapid succession, each step landing on a different rock. Standing on top of a large boulder only three feet from the shore, Yoshi leapt and cleared the water with plenty of distance to spare. Following Daichi's precise instructions, Yoshi hiked fifty paces into the wooded area and found the leaves just as the monk described. He plucked several and placed them in the pouch the old monk provided. He tied the pouch to the belt around his waist and headed back to the stream.

When he got there, he found Daichi's appreciative face on the other side of the stream. "Perhaps you should look for another area of the stream to cross. It might be easier for you," the old monk shouted, barely audible above the rushing stream. Yoshi brushed off the suggestion quickly. This was the path he used the first time and had no reason to believe it would not work again. He easily reached the first large boulder and retraced the three steps he had made on the journey over the stream. He eventually landed on the large rock between him and the shore. The distance looked farther to him than before, but after taking a deep breath he made the final leap to the bank. The split second his foot left the rock, he recalled why the distance looked farther. On the first trip, he took a running start to build momentum to clear the water. This time he was starting from a dead stop. Faced with the shocking realization that his current momentum would not get him across, he frantically flailed his arms in hopes he could somehow give himself extra propulsion.

It failed.

Both his feet landed at the same time; a good two feet shy of the stream's edge. His eyes caught a shocked Daichi desperately grasping for him, but it was too late. The awkward manner in which he fell caused him to fall backward into the stream, submerging himself completely in the shockingly cold water. Underwater for merely a second, Yoshi shot up yelling with no sound. It felt like a thousand tiny pins simultaneously struck his body. The shock of the cold water along with the slippery rocks below conspired to keep Yoshi from reaching the shore. After what felt like an eternity, he grabbed a hold of the old monk's outstretched arm and pulled himself to land.

Lying on his back and panting to the sky, Yoshi exhibited an odd blend of paleness from the cold and redness from the embarrassment. His only comfort was that at least he fell on the return leg and was still able to deliver the leaves. As he reached for the pouch on his waist, the last bit of dignity escaped. The bag was soaked through and through; the leaves would be useless for tea.

The old monk smiled at the sight of the red-faced Yoshi, offering him another helping hand. "I am so sorry Daichi-san for ruining your gathering. I guess you'll have to postpone it," Yoshi spoke through chattering teeth.

The old monk removed the heavy blanket from off his back and put it over his freezing pupil's shoulders.

"Oh no. I was going to host it whether I got the leaves or not. The party is this evening, and I would like you to attend."

As he dried off and warmed up with new clothing, Yoshi was a bit perplexed and slightly perturbed with the old monk. Getting the tea leaves seemed so important to Daichi, but then he just dismissed it as inconsequential to his party. Yoshi felt he was made to look like a fool by making the efforts to get the leaves. Thinking that perhaps the old monk did it out of some sort of amusement, Yoshi's irritation helped warm him up as much as the fire before him. He would try to bottle up any antagonism during the evening. As he entered the teahouse to the room reserved for Daichi, he heard the laughter before the rice paper doors slid open for him.

Inside were Daichi and five elders whom he did not recognize. They were all men of advanced age, which gave them an air of wisdom. The group seemed to be responding to a comment made by their host when Yoshi's entrance interrupted them. As he joined the circle of men, Daichi introduced Yoshi to the group. They each responded with comments about how much they have heard about Yoshi and how it was a pleasure to meet "Daichi's great pupil." His feelings of embarrassment melted away with the effusive nature of the praise he received; it was clear the old monk held him in high esteem.

As the evening progressed, Yoshi became completely enthralled with the conversation and the exchange of ideas and philosophies. Sometimes with levity and sometimes with gravity, the old masters discussed topics ranging from battlefield theories to Buddhism to the politics of the day. While he would provide some commentary, Yoshi chose to remain quiet for the most part and soak in the knowledge being dispensed.

The conversation turned to the accomplishments of Japan's great shogun, Tokugawa Ieyasu. Early in the century, he unified Japan under a single shogunate that still ruled to this day. It had brought a great measure of peace, stability, and prosperity since it ended the continuing wars between rival factions that pocked Japan's history for centuries. Yoshi remembered his own father telling him tales of the great shogun's victories in such battles as the Battle of Sekigahara and the Siege of Osaka Castle. He was renowned for his ability to change tactics and allegiances in order to accomplish his goals. Many in the group agreed that his adaptability was his greatest attribute.

"And what do you think Yoshi-san?" Daichi asked the silent young man. "What led Ieyasu to greatness?" The old monk's question caught Yoshi off guard. He had allowed his mind to wander during the conversation to his mishaps earlier in the day at the stream. For some reason, the conversation about Ieyasu's decisions and tactics brought him back to the seemingly trivial task of crossing the stream. He realized the error in judgment he made in crossing the stream was not focusing on the ultimate outcome, which was to return safe and dry. He determined that if he had taken a moment before making his first leap and studied not only how to get across, but also how to return, he would have avoided his embarrassing failure. What puzzled him at that moment was why a conversation about Ieyasu would bring that to mind.

"He knew where he wanted to end up." Yoshi just blurted out the answer because it was the first thing that came to his mind. From the confused looks he received in response, Yoshi knew his answer was not as articulate as he had hoped. "Ieyasu always knew his ultimate outcome was to consolidate power under his own rule. All decisions he made and steps he took were done with achieving that one outcome. He never concerned himself with accomplishing secondary goals. By never wavering from that and never settling for less, he succeeded."

Silence greeted his response. The elders in the room

stared at Yoshi intently. He could not tell if they were contemplating what he said or expecting more from him. The elder named Nobuyasu broke the silence. "You are right, Daichi-san. He has a remarkable ability to see beyond the present." Yoshi realized he gave the response they all knew but wanted to see if Yoshi could grasp. He was being tested and he passed. Nobuyasu continued, "The secret to getting through the maze is to start at the end and work backward."

Two days later, Nobuyasu's words still rang in Yoshi's ears. Just as Yoshi had predicted, his name was printed alongside Togo's in the matchups that were posted in the morning. Sitting on his knees just outside the main courtyard, he visualized his fight, starting from his victory and thinking about each step in a backward fashion. He recalled the counter moves and patience Togo exhibited last time. He remembered the lightning-fast response to Yoshi's careless aggression. He saw his own hands lifted in victory and saw every step needed to get there. His confidence had never been higher. "To win!" He uttered it aloud when the senpai came to get him.

As opposed to last time, Yoshi heard the roar of the crowd. It was one of the largest he had seen since he had been at the school. He spotted Haru in the crowd and thought he recognized Daichi sitting with the elders high above. For a split second, he wondered if Kira was watching, then brushed that distraction quickly aside to focus on the moment at hand. His opponent entered the ring at the same time and never took his eyes off Yoshi. He had a focus and fury in his stare that Yoshi had never seen from him. *At least you know he respects you*, observed Yoshi about his foe. He returned the gaze to convey an air of calmness that belied his thumping heart. He thought about all the preparation, all the hours of sparring, and all the wisdom shared by Daichi and others. He felt the weight of being at the crossroads of a great moment on his journey, and he knew that victory today would lead him down the right path.

The two combatants bowed to the senior senpai officiating and then to each other. Yoshi knew his opponent would be Togo. What he did not know was the practice weapon the senpai would select. That was revealed when the senpai handed to each combatant the bokken, the far sturdier, and potentially lethal, selection—not the shinai used at their last engagement. They each took a step back and raised their bokken in a mirroring fashion as the crowd quieted to a murmur. The official yelled for them to engage. Instead of Yoshi taking the initiative like last time, he held back as did Togo. The two slowly circled each other while furiously studying the other. Yoshi sensed they both were waiting for the same thing, for the other to make the first move so he could swiftly counter.

In their first match and in every subsequent time Yoshi had witnessed Togo fight, he always met aggression with aggression. It is what made him so difficult to attack, and Yoshi had learned this lesson the hard way. Togo would step into attacks and force the fight to be conducted in tight proximity. There he could use his superior physical strength and unexpected blows to defeat his opponent. Yoshi had prepared for this type of fight. He had worked on his physical strength and close combat techniques. Yoshi was ready for the face-to-face encounter that would likely follow.

After an exaggerated time of circling, Yoshi decided he would start things off. He took two steps toward Togo as if to deliver a blow. Just as Yoshi had anticipated, Togo rushed headlong to close the distance between them; so instead of unleashing a sweeping blow, Yoshi cut it short and landed a sharp blow to Togo's ribs. Yoshi could hear the air forced out of Togo's lungs as the bokken crushed into him.

With bokken pressed tight against each other, Yoshi and Togo wrestled to gain the upper hand. As much as Yoshi prepared for this fight, he could not simulate Togo's abundant strength. He knew he was losing the pushing match and decided to take a step back to disengage. Togo seemed to sense this decision even before Yoshi made it. In the half-second Yoshi relaxed his muscles, Togo exerted tremendous force, pushing Yoshi back. Off balance and struggling to stay on his feet, Yoshi took several steps back while Togo unleashed his fury. One, two, three blows landed cleanly on Yoshi's midsection. A fourth blow came out of a spin move and clipped Yoshi on the side of his head. A last-second step back prevented the hit from landing directly, but the grazing blow did enough damage to open a cut on Yoshi's forehead. In an instant, blood poured from the cut and flowed into his left eye, blurring his vision. Yoshi spent the next several moments in full retreat and defense mode. He frantically relied on instinct to block the next three blows by Togo and wildly swung his bokken in a desperate attempt at an offense. One of those blows, by pure luck, found its target on the rib cage Yoshi had struck earlier. The blow was not strong but the damage from the previous hit had softened the area. Perhaps out of anticipation of

Yoshi's offense or in order to catch his breath, Togo decided to go back to his patient approach.

Yoshi could not have been happier for the reprieve. Wiping the blood from his brow, he focused to stop his head from spinning and cease the ringing in his ears. He knew he was lucky this match was not over yet. Most battles end rapidly and very few extend as long as this one had. As he circled Togo, he was rapidly gaining focus but was at a loss on how to proceed. He had prepared to defeat Togo by beating him with his own style, but that clearly was not going to happen. Frantically, he thought of his desired outcome, 'to win.' But now the very real possibility faced him that he would not achieve this and 'to lose' was becoming the more realistic outcome.

It took a split second for Yoshi to take in where he was and the moment at hand. *I am at the School of Aspen, studying to become the greatest samurai I can be*, he spoke to himself. *My role is that of a student. These competitions, my class, my sessions with Daichi—they are about acquiring knowledge that will lead to greater things.* He gripped the bokken in his hand. *These are not blades. This is not battle. I have seen men in battle, and this is not it. This is an opportunity to learn, to grow, to be the best I can be.* As all these thoughts ran in his mind, he could also sense the wheels turning in his opponent's mind and the anxiousness in his eyes. *I am here to be samurai, to master the Swords of Illumination, to achieve balance. I have a new outcome—to be the best I can be.*

It was as if his new outcome set out a starter's yell, but instead of racing, his heart and muscles relaxed. His facial muscles eased, and serenity overtook his entire aura.

It was obvious to Yoshi that Togo sensed the relaxation. He also sensed his opponent would see this as the perfect opportunity to strike. While Togo usually wanted his foe to strike first, Yoshi knew Togo could not pass up this great opening. With a deep exhalation of breath, Togo rushed upon Yoshi.

Yoshi realized that he could not fight Togo's fight, it was time for a different tactic and that was to do whatever his opponent does not want him to do. As Togo closed in, Yoshi quickly rushed to his right and took two quick strikes to Togo's sore ribs, then swung around Togo. Togo quickly spun around but by that time, Yoshi had taken two steps back. Extending his bokken as far in front of him as he could, Yoshi stood his ground. The blood from his cut had now effectively blinded him in one eye, but Yoshi refused to wipe at it. His focus stayed straight on his foe.

Clearly agitated at this turn of events, Togo rushed his foe again, launching his attack from Yoshi's blind side. While he never saw the actual blows coming, Yoshi knew they were imminent. He blocked the first blow and sprinted past Togo to get behind him. When he detected a hesitation in Togo to spin back around, Yoshi landed another quick crack to the injured ribs of Togo. The pain buckled him at his knees, but he quickly recovered, spun, and launched another direct assault at Yoshi that was met with the same result. Yoshi's blow to Togo's ribs was even harder than the last one and sent him stumbling. Togo took several elongated steps to maintain his balance, even having to reach his hand down to the ground to prevent from falling completely over. Yoshi thought there was something unnatural about the way Togo touched the ground, but quickly dispelled it to regain focus.

Togo took back his stance facing Yoshi. Beads of sweat covered Togo's face and his breathing was labored. His elbow hung lower than normal to protect his injured ribs. While he looked terribly vulnerable, Yoshi would not take the bait and launch an attack. As they circled each other again, the crowd was completely silent. The length of this battle was longer than any they had witnessed. The audience was afraid to make a sound, fearing it would affect the outcome.

Sensing Yoshi still will not charge him, Togo went on the offense again, but this time favoring his attack on Yoshi's 'good' side. Yoshi prepared to make the same evasive maneuver just as Togo raised his bokken. A thought flashed in his mind that it was strange that one of Togo's hands left the bokken just as he was raising it. Yoshi thought nothing of it and prepared to slide to his left when he realized why the hand left its place. The last thing he saw was particles of sand racing toward his eyes. He closed them as soon as he could, but it was too late. A fire broke out in his eyes and the only image he saw was the darkness of his squeezing lids.

With one eye blinded by blood and the other by sand, Yoshi raced backward and swung his bokken wildly to keep his opponent at bay. Fear gripped him as he knew in this condition Togo could inflict serious harm. He kept swinging at every sound he could hear but it was no use. Two explosions of pain emanated from both sides of his ribs. The pain of the blows was exacerbated by the fact he didn't know they were coming.

He sensed Togo was now toying with him and could put him down at any moment. He also now feared he would suffer the indignation of the official stopping the fight before its conclusion. As much as he did not want to suffer great harm to his body, he did not want to suffer this great injury to his pride. If the fight was to end, he would end it. Realizing the cause was lost and nothing more could be gained from this experience, Yoshi took two rapid steps back, dropped to one knee, bowed his head, and laid his bokken on the ground before him, a clear sign of surrender.

Half expecting to receive another blow, his fears were eased when he heard the yell of the senpai to cease and the roar of the crowd. Wiping the blood and sand out of his eyes, Yoshi was able to get a blurred image of Togo's raised arms in victory, although he took some pleasure in the fact that one arm was significantly lower than the other, still favoring the injured ribs. The senpai kneeled before him and examined his face. "Yoshi-san, I did not see the sand get blown into your face. I obviously have my suspicions on how it got there, but since I did not see it, I cannot rule on it. I suggest you make a formal complaint and attempt to get the fight declared a draw."

Sitting with Haru by the koi pond an hour after the match, Yoshi's face was covered with a macabre makeup of blood, sand, sweat, and tears. "While it was nice of the senpai to suggest it, I told him I would not seek any redress," he told Haru as he finished telling his side of the experience.

An angry and stunned Haru responded. "Why not Yoshi-san? What Togo-san did was without honor. You clearly had the advantage until he pulled that tactic. I feel if you do not, I must make a statement."

Grabbing his friend's arm, Yoshi calmed him down. "I realized something very important in the middle of that fight. That winning or losing had no bearing on who I am or what type of samurai I shall become. My outcome moved away from something as frivolous as victory to something greater. I learned. I grew. I saw for a moment during that fight that I can be the samurai I dream to be."

"You could have shown the school you are better than Togo," Haru protested.

"And instead, I showed myself something even more important. It is not about being better than someone else, but being the best that I can be."

After a moment's reflection, a smile crept onto Haru's face. "I guess sometimes when you lose, you really win. Who knew I was such a philosopher?"

"Haru, the great!" Yoshi responded. They broke out into a roaring laughter that attracted a host of koi to their side of the pond. It also attracted other visitors.

Daichi, Nobuyasu, and a few other elders walked past the pond when their conversation was interrupted but the young students' laughter. Making eye contact with Yoshi, they all stopped and silently bowed deeply to Yoshi. Stunned at the sign of respect, he slowly stood up and returned the bow. For the first time that afternoon, the water welling up in his eyes had nothing to do with blood or sand.

Later that night, the senior senpai visited Yoshi's room. Just as he had on three previous occasions, he escorted Yoshi to the sword ceremony chamber. As the room gradually received light, Yoshi saw there were three other students with him. The one standing to his left was Kira. This was the closest he had been to her in weeks and his heart raced at being near her again. It was the first time during one of these sword ceremonies that he was nervous about something other than what was about to happen.

After the twelve robed elders entered the chamber, the group of students each relinquished their Sword of Outcomes. A different elder from any previous time spoke. "You four have been called here tonight to take one more step on the path of enlightenment and balance. By being here, you have shown yourselves that you understand the great gift of the Sword of Outcomes. In time, you will learn its true power. It is now time to receive the next level of enlightenment." New swords were placed before each by kneeling elders.

"Before you accept the next Sword of Illumination, you are permitted to ask one question of this council in order to gain additional knowledge."

This time, Yoshi was asked to speak first. It took only a few seconds for him to come up with his question. "How does one really know which outcomes are the most important to achieve?"

It was a question he had prepared to ask ever since the battle with Togo. While he felt at ease with his decision to change his outcome, there was a lingering feeling of doubt about whether it was the right choice.

"It is determined by what value you place on each one of your outcomes," the elder responded.

Yoshi was disappointed. He found the elder's answer lacked the insight his previous questions received. It brought him no closer to grasping how outcomes are chosen. Those concerns were allayed when the ceremony concluded. After the elders departed, he unsheathed his new sword and its engraving.

Sword of Values
What values do I desire in order for me to fulfill the destiny of who I have chosen to be?

"I can relate to this Yoshi character. I feel like I get sand thrown in my eyes all the time," Tom said while fixated on the dancing fire. "But in my case, the blows keep coming and I feel powerless to stop them."

"What are the blows?" the old stranger asked.

"Oh, you know, life's little failures." Tom laughed it off but the concern in the old man's eyes encouraged him to open up. "I promised my wife I would own my own company by now. I promised her a home on both coasts and plenty of vacations and all sort of other things." Tom bowed his head and shook it, crushed by the knowledge he had failed to achieve any of what he promised. "Most importantly, I promised myself that I wouldn't be like my father, beaten down by life."

"You ever hear of a thing called New Year's resolutions?" the old man asked.

Tom shot him a look that said, *of course*. "Who hasn't heard of them? Heck, who hasn't made one... or twenty?"

"Do you make New Year's resolutions?"

"Used to, but not anymore. It got too frustrating and too disheartening not achieving any of the goals I set out to do. I said screw it; I've got too many other things to worry about than a stupid list."

"Those resolutions or goals become obligations, don't they? Like a burden."

"Exactly. Even if I do meet one or two of those goals, I just end up kicking myself over the ones I didn't get to. So, you agree that setting those goals is nonsense, huh?" Tom searched the old man for some camaraderie. All night he felt like he had little in common with the stranger. The old man had all the answers and Tom felt he had all the problems.

"No, setting goals can be a fine idea, but like with Yoshi, they should only be done to support your set of outcomes."

"I'll be honest; I'm not real clear how he sees goals and outcomes differently. Didn't he want to kick Togo's butt? How can he still feel victorious?"

"You spoke of all these things you wanted to provide your wife," the old man said in a soft tone to lower the anxiety in his guest's voice. "Why did you want to get all these things?"

"To make her happy. To give us a great life together. Why else?" The softer tone did nothing to sooth the irritation of bringing this point back to the fore.

"Is it possible to have acquired all those things, the company, the vacation homes, and still not be happy?"

Tom murmured in agreement.

"And is it not possible to have a happy life without acquiring those specific things?" the old man continued.

Tom had always assumed that joy and the acquisition of wealth went hand in hand; however, he begrudgingly admitted knowing families that were happy on relatively meager means.

"The point I am making, the point that Yoshi realized, is that you should put your desired outcome first. Set those outcomes to be what you truly want. You want your family to be happy. That's an admirable outcome and you have an obviously strong purpose behind it. Now, you can set up goals or action plans or steps or whatever you want to call it to achieve that outcome."

"What if I fail to achieve all the goals to support that outcome?" Tom asked earnestly.

"Does not matter. You may even fail to achieve any of those goals. But if you achieve the outcome, in your case a happy family, you have succeeded."

Tom thought about last summer's family vacation. He had hoped to take a week off and take them to Disney World in Orlando. Unfortunately, a busy work schedule and tight finances scaled back the big summer trip to a long weekend at the lake. Thinking back on it now, he recalled it being some of the happiest times his family had spent together. Returning his gaze to the flames, Tom thought back on that weekend. He saw his son and daughter splashing about in the lake. He heard the laughter as their canoe tipped over. He was awestruck by the beauty of his wife illuminated by the setting sun. As tears welled up in his eyes, he realized the reason was that they were simply together. His outcome was achieved.

CHAPTER 14

Sword of Values:
Part I

The force of the push sent Yoshi stumbling backward. He spun his body in time to bend down and push off the ground to keep his balance. Regaining his posture, he turned to face the hard-charging Togo. With no audience or fanfare, the two battled in the middle of the school arena. The only sounds were their grunts and the wind whipping around them. As his foe marched closer, Yoshi saw neither rage nor fear in his opponent's eyes. In fact, he saw no emotion at all.

As Togo's arms extended above his head to deliver another crushing blow, Yoshi's left hand flung away from his bokken and in the direction of Togo's face. As his hands opened, out flew thousands of tiny sand particles, racing into the eye sockets of his foe. Within a split second, Togo's eyes were completely covered in dirt. The blinded samurai let out a wail that shook the earth. It jolted Yoshi awake.

He found himself lying on the steps of the old hidden temple. Searching around to regain his bearings, he soon recalled trekking up the steps to his new refuge a few hours earlier to seek some rest. It had been two weeks since the fight and the ensuing sword ceremony, yet Yoshi's body still ached. As he shook himself awake, his eyes fixed on Benzaiten's weathered face. "What did that mean?" he asked the stone-faced kami. Her only response was her usual wry grin. Yoshi was distressed by this last dream. He despised what Togo did in their battle so why would his subconscious have him do the same terrible act? In the days since their encounter, he had been at an unusual peace with himself and his decision. Confident he made the right choices; he was still perplexed by his decision-making process. *It might feel right, but is it right?* he asked himself as he journeyed up to the shrine. Hoping to gain some insight by clearing his mind in this peaceful place, but he only ended up exasperating himself further.

He took out his new sword—the Sword of Values. Even in the overcast afternoon, the blade had a brilliant glow, as if it was attracting every bit of light it could find. On one side of the blade, a passage was etched.

What values do I desire in order for me to fulfill the destiny of who I have chosen to be?

He never thought of values being something he desired, but rather as something that was instilled. Yoshi felt comfortable with the values given to him by his parents and never sought to change them. Since he first read the sword's engraving, he wondered what the connection was to his values and destiny. "Another riddle to solve," he said to Benzaiten. Her smile seemed to agree with him.

The apple orchid was unusually quiet since many of the staff had departed to spend time with family during the upcoming winter months. While Yoshi really was not needed there, he still enjoyed stopping in for no other reason than to chat with his old friend Hideki.

As he approached the farm's entrance, he spotted an unfamiliar horse and wagon parked outside. Trudging closer, encumbered by the thick mud below him, he heard the yelling and laughter of two young boys. He could not see them, but it sounded to him like they were playing some sort of game. As he got very near, he could make out their dialogue.

"Let me do it!"

"Oh, you just missed!"

"Good shot!" It brought him back to his time as a child when he played all sorts of games and adventures with his friends. A smile firmly planted on his mouth, Yoshi walked around to the side of the farm to greet the young visitors.

As he quietly approached them, Yoshi looked on as the two boys, no more than ten years of age, tossed rocks at some object in the tall aspens. It was not until he was nearly upon them that he was able to detect their intended target. Nestled high and deep among the branches of a particularly impressive-sized aspen was a bird's nest. Barely poking out of the top of the twigs of the structure were the heads of three tiny eaglets. Yoshi immediately identified them as Japanese golden eagles. He was always captivated by these majestic birds with their huge wingspan and piercing eyes. Often, as he watched the eagles soar, he imagined being alongside them for their journey. He was instantly excited that there was a nest so near him and the opportunity to watch so close. His amazement instantly turned to anger as he realized what was happening. His initial joy delayed his comprehension that these boys were seeking to harm the eagles. In a voice born from the pit of his stomach, Yoshi erupted. "Drop those rocks!"

The boys were stunned frozen, both by the ferocity of the command and the surprise of the undetected intruder. After a moment, the two youths dropped the rocks and raced off in the direction of the farm. Yoshi paused to study the nest. Except for the animated chirping from the three eaglets, all else seemed fine. Seeing the boys run off toward the farm, Yoshi marched after them. Bursting through the barn's doors, Yoshi was not surprised to see the man the boys were cowering behind. It was the troublesome apple seller, Jungo.

"How dare you scare my boys like that," Jungo yelled as Yoshi neared. "I have half a mind to thrash you for your terrible manners." The seller reached into the pocket of his breast for some sort of blade, Yoshi presumed. Without breaking his stride, Yoshi was quickly upon Jungo and grabbed a tight hold on the wrist of Jungo's hidden hand. Yoshi could feel Jungo gripping something but continued to press the man's hand against his chest as he spoke.

"Jungo-san, I am sure you will be as alarmed as I was when I tell you what your children were doing." Yoshi used every bit of self-control to lower the volume of his speech. "They were attempting to destroy a nest of defenseless baby eagles. The respect of nature and all living things is something I am certain we both share and is incumbent upon us to instill in our youth." Yoshi's eyes never blinked, and he stared into Jungo's. He could see the fear in them as Jungo realized that he would be no match in physical confrontation against the young samurai. He also realized that, once again, Yoshi had given him a way out of confrontation.

"Thank you, Yoshi-san, for sharing this information with me," Jungo said as he released his grip on the blade. "I shall deal with my sons in an appropriately strict manner over these terrible deeds." Turning on his sons, the young boys scurried off back to their wagon to prepare for the punishment, although Yoshi had his doubts about its severity.

Jungo explained to Yoshi and the skeleton staff that

he was passing through with an offer for them to purchase some fine, thick hides. "When did you move from produce to hunter?" one of the staff asked.

Taking a longer pause than was necessary, Jungo explained, "My wife's family has some connections with fur traders, and I am doing this as a favor for them. They really are of high quality and should keep you warm through this bitter season."

Examining the hides, Yoshi did find them to be of great condition, but his still simmering rage could not bring him to purchase anything from this man. Hideki and the others did not share Yoshi's disposition and were eager to make the purchases. The group gobbled up about a dozen of the large pelts from a delighted Jungo. After the transactions were complete, he stepped up onto his wagon and took the reins of his horses. "I will see you again next harvest."

Yoshi watched as the trio, laughing raucously, departed past the horizon.

Yoshi told the story to Daichi as the two combed the forest outside the school for firewood.

"I see a trend with you Yoshi-san as a defender of life," Daichi opined. "First the doe. Now the eagles. What makes you care so much?"

Yoshi had joined Daichi on his firewood collection expedition through the forest near the school. While the school has younger students collect for the entire campus, the old monk demanded that he take on as much responsibility for his own care as possible. This also meant Yoshi taking on those tasks.

"Wouldn't you have stopped those boys from throwing the stones?" Yoshi asked.

"Probably yes, but you were clearly offended more than most would be. The question for you is why?"

Yoshi took in the question as he cracked a branch into smaller pieces. He recalled many values instilled by his parents throughout his upbringing such as a strong work ethic, personal honor, and a deep commitment toward expanding one's knowledge and ability. He could not remember any specific moments in which his father or mother shared a specific lesson toward protecting nature.

As he raised his head to tell his old master that he hadn't a clue why he respected nature, a sudden brisk breeze blew from the north, rustling the trees and Yoshi's robes. The feeling of the cool air on his face instantly took him back to the autumn afternoon he witnessed his father mount a horse for the last time. Kensi rode off to his tragic fate to protect and preserve... life.

"My father gave it to me I suppose," Yoshi finally responded. "But not by telling me, but rather in the way he behaved." Yoshi continued to explain how his father's sacrifice always inspired him and confounded him. "I have often asked myself why he would have given up everything to save someone else. I never put the two together, but I believe I share his passionate regard for life, in any form."

The old monk sat down on a tree stump to take a break, rubbing his tender back. "That is a very interesting explanation Yoshi-san. We have spent much time together these past months and shared many adventures. Would you say you have adopted some of my values?"

"Yes, most assuredly," Yoshi claimed. "I believe I have shared your value of knowledge and balance and so many other things."

"I enjoy being self-sufficient to the point I collect my own firewood, cook my own food, and make my own clothes. I strongly value self-reliance, as you know. Have you adopted this too?"

Yoshi knew the answer to be no. While he admired Daichi for the effort he took to care for himself, he did find it to be too much for him to do. He was quite content allowing the school to provide the basic necessities he needed; however, the old monk's question gave him pause about this position. It occurred to him that the monk had been a surrogate father figure to him since they began meeting and perhaps, he should be adopting more of the monk's values. "Honestly, Daichi-san, I have not shared that value as strongly as I should have. It is something I shall endeavor to undertake."

"And you would be wrong to do so." The old monk rose from his respite and continued back to the school with his armful of wood.

Following right behind, Yoshi found his master's response puzzling. "Why not? I think it is an admirable trait to have and I should adopt it."

"Because it's mine and you can't have it. People can have the same values, but they cannot share or exchange or lend them out like an old scroll. Values are quite personal and unique, only you can develop your own."

"But what of the values my family has provided me? Don't they influence what I hold important?"

"The biggest influence there is; however, whatever they taught you, you were the one who had to accept or reject it. I find it fascinating that your parents never forced this value of life on you, but that you adopted it on your own."

Yoshi was taking in all the monk had to say and did not pay attention to the direction they were heading. Suddenly, the monk stopped and looked up at one of the aspens. It took a moment for Yoshi to see what the monk was studying. Getting his bearings, Yoshi recognized he was on the outskirts of the farm and the monk was looking up at the same eagle's nest he protected earlier in the week. Together in silence, the two stared at the nest. Yoshi was fascinated at the peculiar activity of the mother eagle perched along the edge. She was carefully and deliberately plucking out the contents of the nest and spitting them to the ground below. In essence, she was deconstructing the nest as her young loudly chirped in agitation. When his curiosity could no longer be contained, Yoshi spoke. "Why is she doing that? She is clearly making her children uncomfortable."

"That is her intention," the monk went on to explain. "Eaglets, not unlike human children, hesitate to leave the comfort of their nest. They fear leaving that place of security. The parents have made the nest very safe and comfortable for the eggs and eventually the eaglets that they hatch. When the time comes for those babies to fly away, the parents start removing the smooth items that gave the nest a pillow-like feel. They want the inside to be spiny and uncomfortable, forcing the eaglets to want to depart. Their comfort zone removed; the eaglets are forced to take action. They must learn to fly and feed and care for themselves in order to survive."

The monk turned to Yoshi and grabbed a hold of the blanket lying on his shoulders, admiring the feel of it. "Your mother made this for you?"

Flustered by the sudden change of subject, Yoshi just nodded his head.

"It looks and feels nice on you, but I notice you are shivering a bit. It is not keeping you as warm as you need."

Yoshi knew the blanket was not thick enough for the weather today, but it was woven by his mother, and she gave it to him as a gift right before he set off for the School of Aspen. Although never directed to do so, he always felt an obligation to wear it despite its ineffectiveness. After studying the blanket one last time, Daichi released it and trudged back to the campus with his booty of wood. Yoshi remained behind, staring up at the mother eagle's continuing deconstruction. Warding off a sudden gust of wind, Yoshi bundled up with the blanket, but it provided little protection from the sharp blast of cold wind piercing his body. At that moment, the eagle stopped her work and returned Yoshi's gaze. Looking down at the human observer, the eagle's head cocked side to side in a quizzical manner. *Why are you wearing such a flimsy blanket?* was the response Yoshi heard from the bird.

"My nest is too comfortable. I need to prune it." Yoshi responded.

He trekked back to the campus with the old monk several yards ahead and caught up with him as they reached the monk's lodging. Yoshi laid down the firewood he was carrying and turned to leave but stopped in his tracks.

"This blanket was fine in the warmer climate of my home village, but not here. It is no longer... comfortable." Yoshi spun to face his master. "It is not unlike values, is it? A person's values can change as they move on in life. When they hold on to values that no longer suit them, they suffer and feel discomfort. But here I am, still shivering in this thin cloth." Yoshi smiled at his observation. "I choose to care more about wearing my mother's blanket than actually staying warm."

"And therein lies the choice every one of us possesses, but does not realize, Yoshi-san. You can choose your values." The old monk opened up a chest near his fireplace and took out a very thick blanket. While it was obviously old, it was in remarkably good condition. The monk handed it to Yoshi who accepted it with two open arms. "It would not offend me if you do not wear it."

Halfway back to his lodging, Yoshi draped the new gift around his shoulders. It instantly provided a shield from the cold autumn air. The blanket provided him warmth, but more importantly, it taught a lesson. The values he held in the past, even when he first walked through the gates of the school, needed to be evaluated. His life, just like the weather, had changed. While his aspirations to be a great samurai remained the same, Yoshi found the road to get there was full of turns and obstacles.

As he neared his room, he heard the whispered scolding of a man. He instantly knew the voice to be of an older gentleman but did not recognize it as anyone he knew. As he came around a bend in the path, he spied two figures lit by the moonlight. The stature and posture of one clearly identified him as Togo. Yoshi recognized the older gentleman with him as the same one who was with Togo during the campus race a few months back. Yoshi never broke stride and kept his gaze straight. He could not make out specific words, but clearly from the tone and gestures of the old man, he was scolding the young Togo. He had never seen Togo in such a submissive role. He found a slight degree of enjoyment from it but also found it quite uncomfortable. He picked up his pace to avoid recognition, or worse, entanglement.

Having succeeded in his elusion, he settled into his room for the evening. Placing the Sword of Values up on his wall, he read the inscription once again.

What values do I desire in order for me to fulfill the destiny of who I have chosen to be?

With Togo still on his mind, Yoshi thought about what values his fellow student must possess to reach his destiny. He clearly had no regard for honor and less regard for taking life. *Are those the values necessary to achieve success?* he asked himself. He thought about the dream he had at the shrine in which he took up Togo's tactics. Even though it was a dream, he felt disgusted with himself for even thinking it. He knew as much as he might act that way, it was not a role he could personally sustain. *Too prickly for me*, as he thought of the eaglets' nests. As he laid his head in an attempt to slumber away his mind's cares, he was jarred upright by a sudden slam on the outside wall of his room. After the slam, he thought he heard a slight whimper come from the outside. Clearly not natural, Yoshi grabbed his sword and raced outside to investigate.

When he turned the corner of the lodge, all he could make out in the night was a ball of a figure on the ground ahead, leaning against the wall of the barracks. As he slowly moved toward it, he held the grip of his sword tight, ready to unsheathe it in a second. A guttural moan came from the figure as it struggled to rise. Using the wall as support, it inched its way up to a hunched posture.

Determining it was an injured person, Yoshi released the grip on his sword and raced to the struggling stranger. "What happened to you? Can I help?"

Just a few feet from the stranger, his query was answered by the lightning-fast appearance of a sword, the tip of its blade mere inches from Yoshi's exposed throat. The injured man held the blade incredibly steady which was incongruent with his terrible physical condition.

"One step closer will be your last." Despite the hoarseness of the voice, Yoshi knew exactly who it was.

"Togo-san?"

Togo limped forward forcing Yoshi to step backward to avoid the blade. "How dare you leave yourself so easily exposed? I could slit your throat and you'd be dead before you hit the ground."

Despite the fierceness in his voice and actions, Yoshi saw a version of Togo he never expected to see; a scared little boy. He was clearly in physical pain that was compounded by the embarrassment of being discovered in his current state. Yoshi thought it must be worse for Togo that his rival was the one who found him. Yoshi was surprised at the empathy he felt for the young man before him. In a calm and soothing voice, he offered aid. "Togo-san, you are injured. Please allow me to get you some help."

"You will do nothing of the kind you impertinent little boy. You have exactly two choices. You can walk away, never to speak of this with anyone, or I can arrange for you to visit all the ancient samurai you read about in those silly little scrolls of yours." Togo quickly shot his hand out to brace himself against the wall to keep upright. "Choose!" he yelled in a whisper.

If this fool did not want any help, why should I give it to him? Yoshi thought as he took a single step back, arms held high. *If he should be crippled or die from whatever ails him, wouldn't the school be better off?* he mused as he took another step. *I bet not one person, even among the elders, would lose a night's sleep if Togo was no longer with us,* his mind still racing as he took another step back.

Well, maybe one person.

Yoshi detected unsteadiness in the blade held at his neck and knew this was his moment to strike. The three steps back provided enough separation for safety. In what must have been a blur to Togo, Yoshi unsheathed his sword and slapped it against Togo's, sending his ailing foe's blade flying off to the side.

With a look that combined shock and exhaustion, Togo dropped to his knees. "Make it quick," he uttered. Then he mumbled something that brought a chill down Yoshi's spine. "I am sorry I failed you, Father." Yoshi just stared at Togo for an exaggerated moment. For the first time, he saw himself in Togo and was not embarrassed. They were the same, two young men, each wanting to make his father proud. The moment so punctuated Yoshi's journey in life thus far, he was forced to bite his lower lip to keep it from quivering.

Togo looked up gloomily as Yoshi sheathed his sword and helped him up. As Yoshi slung Togo's arm around his neck, he first felt, then saw the blood-soaked back of Togo's robes. Togo let out a muted yelp when Yoshi grazed it with his hand. Careful not to touch it again and seeing that Togo could barely walk, Yoshi hoisted him on his shoulders and trudged off toward the main compound. He called out for aid as he approached the elders' living quarters and several came rushing out to give care.

Yoshi stood out of sight as the elders and senior senpai tended to Togo's wounds. There were dozens of gashes on his back that looked to be made by a blunt instrument or whip. As he watched them drape Togo's wounds with herb-soaked clothes and served him hot tea, Yoshi was still shaken by the episode. He thought about the conversation with Daichi earlier in the day regarding his respect for life. It was easy to stop little kids from throwing rocks, but quite another to put his life at risk to help someone who regards him as an enemy. It was as if that value was being tested for its strength, to the limits it would be followed. While he thought he passed, he wasn't sure what it all really meant.

As Togo's head began to clear, he told them the tale of his injuries. He was returning from a berry gathering expedition outside the main wall when he came upon a marauding gang of rōnin. The group of ten samurai was attacking a helpless fur trader with a full wagon of pelts. Togo said he felt a responsibility as instilled in him by the School of Aspen to defend the defenseless. "While the savages clearly did some damage, I was able to engage them long enough to allow the trader to flee safely away. Once I knew he was safe, I too retreated as ten samurai are even too much for me to take on." His forced chuckle caused him to wince in pain.

Yoshi knew this to all be an elaborate lie as he just saw Togo with the angry old man. He wondered if it was that man who inflicted such a beating on Togo. If it was a battle with the old man, then Yoshi found it strange that Togo's sword had no sign of wear or blood. Togo was clearly good enough to get some blows in any fight... unless... *It was not a fight; it was a beating... by his father.* The pit of Yoshi's stomach felt empty at the thought of the angst Togo must feel. To receive such a punishment from one's father had to be more embarrassing than painful. He fully understood the reason for the lie Togo told and believed he might have done the same in a similar circumstance.

As he walked outside to return to his room, two elders were standing outside talking. "Yoshi-san, thank you for helping Togo-san in his hour of need," said one of the elders. "Your compassion and thoughtfulness are impressive."

"Also, please make sure to tell your fellow students that no one is to travel outside the campus wall in a group fewer than four," the oldest one added.

"I am sure this was an isolated incident," Yoshi smirked, knowing the truth of Togo's story.

"I assure you it is not," said the first one. "We received reports of a fur trader found killed just six days ago in the woods to the east of the farm."

Yoshi stopped in his tracks. "What happened to the trader's pelts?" he asked already knowing the answer.

"They were all gone of course," answered the elder.

"Jungo," Yoshi whispered under his breath.

"I never knew that about eagles; that the parents deconstruct the nest to encourage the young to fly off. Is that really true?" Tom asked the old man.

"It is," the old man answered. "The nest is a comfort zone for the eaglets. By making it uncomfortable, it forces them to take action. To find a new comfort zone."

"I will tell you one thing; I didn't need my parents to take apart my room. I couldn't wait to get the hell out of there." Tom felt a bit of remorse hearing those words come out of his mouth and quickly addressed it. "I'm not saying I didn't love my parents and I truly appreciated all that they did for me. It's just that... I saw the way they had to sacrifice and give up on everything just to make ends meet. I was not going to take that value with me."

"Perhaps unwittingly, I suppose, they instilled the value of obtaining material wealth in order to gain security," the old man observed.

"Touché."

"So, you have developed your values completely on your own. I am impressed. I have found that I am influenced not just by my family, but also by my friends and the world around me. Sometimes I have been guilty of adopting their values and found they run different from who I am."

Tom knew the old man was being a bit sarcastic in his compliment, but he had no real argument against him. He was right, of course. He might have shunned the toiling nature of his parents, but he substituted it with the standards held by many in his professional and social circles—the belief that material wealth equaled success.

The inoperative car that currently sat at the side of the road was a prime example of this. His old car was paid off and still ran effectively, so the need for a new car was not immediate. At an after-work gathering several months ago, a few of the associates were crowding around their new cars. Tom sensed from the reaction of others the esteem and worth they placed on having impressive cars. If it were up to him, he mused, he would still have the car his folks made him buy as a teenager. It was not the prettiest or the fastest, but all the hard work and care he put into it made it the most valuable car he had ever owned. In the world now, he felt the appearance of wealth would help in his ascension up the proverbial corporate ladder. After a few serious discussions with his wife about taking on the extra expense, Tom won the argument, and two weeks after that gathering, Tom pulled into his office's parking lot in a brand new Audi.

Tom leaned back and stared up at the sky. He was amazed at the number of stars. Living in the city all his life, the night skies were clouded by the reflected light all around him. But here, wherever it was, he could see literally thousands of sparkling bits of light.

Away from the lights of his life, he was getting a new perspective not just of the heavens, but of himself. Away from his world, this night had given him a new viewpoint. Thinking about the new Audi, he realized that the adulation he received for the new car was nice, but all too fleeting. He never really wanted it, yet he felt compelled to get it. He adopted someone else's values and now those values have him stuck in the middle of nowhere.

"When I'm in the city, I see only a handful of stars," Tom observed. "But here, away from the glow emitted from everything else, I see so much more. So many more stars. So many more lights. So many more choices."

Tom was making an important discovery. An individual's answers are often found far from the influence of others— by seeking his or her own light. Tom was really starting to see that now and even felt a bit like one of the students at the School of Aspen. As he brought his gaze back down from the night sky, the old stranger was smiling at him as if he agreed with Tom's thoughts.

CHAPTER 15

Sword of Values:
Part II

The farm staff was shocked when they heard the tale shared by their samurai superior, but they also moaned in hesitation at the suggestion that followed. "The slain fur trader was found a week ago and Jungo arrived here only two days ago. Since these pelts were obviously acquired by him via questionable means, I think the right thing to do would be to give them up and have them sent to those in need," Yoshi concluded to the men circled around him.

Silence and blank stares greeted this last comment. They all agreed Yoshi was right that their purchase was tainted, but they were all conflicted about the appropriate response. They found it hard to relinquish these thick and lush pelts that would provide warmth for the next several winters.

Yoshi could see the debate raging in his staff's minds. It was easy for him to suggest the sacrifice when he had not purchased any of the pelts. After some reflection, he found himself agreeing with them. "You are right," he concurred without them saying anything. "Why should I ask of you something that I am not willing to endure? I will personally reimburse each of you for the cost of the pelts. While you will surrender the high quality and warmth they provide, I will sacrifice the price you have paid."

The staff made half-hearted objections to Yoshi's generous offer, but the young samurai would not hear any of it. There were six people he would have to reimburse.

Doing the math quickly in his head, he knew this would nearly wipe out his meager savings; but his resolve was strong and he knew it to be the right thing to do. Two days later, Yoshi collected each one of the pelts and reimbursed the staff for their loss. He had learned that a group of monks would be traveling to several nearby villages, and he gave them the pelts to distribute to those they deemed in need.

Traveling with four senior senpai as guards, the monks waved to the on-looking Yoshi as they departed the School of Aspen. Watching the large wooden gate slowly close behind the monks, he reflected on the values that made him take such action. Fairness and justice ranked high on his list of important values and his actions were thoroughly consistent with his standards. He also felt strongly about financial self-sufficiency. He prided himself on his ability to build up his savings in preparation for the day he would graduate from the School of Aspen. His savings would provide the means for him to pursue his goals and ambitions, in particular hunting his father's killer. Now, his reimbursement for the pelts had severely crippled his savings and would impede his future goals. He wondered if and why one set of values is more important than another.

"I would ask to borrow some money, but I understand you are a little low." Daichi's voice snapped Yoshi out of his trance. "I heard what you did. Both for Togo and with the pelts. You never cease to surprise, Yoshi-san."

"Do you think I did the right thing?" Yoshi asked his mentor.

"No." The monk gave a simple and direct response and turned to walk back to the main campus. Yoshi did not want to follow after Daichi. The old monk always seemed to give these obscure and contrarian answers, leaving Yoshi chasing after him for clarification. The young samurai resolved that this time he would not fall into the trap.

If that is what the monk believed, then so be it. I should have confidence enough in myself to not be swayed by the opinions of others, he resolved in his mind.

The resolve lasted almost three minutes before Yoshi surrendered to his curiosity and chased after the old monk. "Do you disagree with what I did with Togo or is it what I did with the pelts?" Yoshi asked as he caught up with the monk near the main shrine.

The monk spun on Yoshi sharply. There was a passion mixed with annoyance on the old monk's face that gave him a surprisingly youthful appearance. "I think both of them were incredibly foolish things for you to do," he said with a forceful yet soft voice. "I cannot understand why you would put yourself at risk to help someone who cheated you so blatantly and who obviously thinks very little of you, both as a samurai and as a person. Mark my words; he will continue to be a great obstacle for you, Yoshi-san. As for paying back your staff, you have put yourself in a difficult position for no good reason. You had nothing to do with the stealing of those pelts and now the hopes and aspirations you had for your future are temporarily, if not permanently, derailed. The question I have for you is why do you agree with what you did?"

Yoshi was left dumbfounded. His advisor had always spoken to him in a supportive manner, so the harshness of the tone completely caught him off guard. The old monk looked back at Yoshi seeking an answer to his query but never received one. Determining Yoshi had no response, Daichi quietly turned and entered the shrine.

During the next three days, Yoshi avoided the old monk, along with most people. The dressing down he took from Daichi had shaken him to his core. When he was not in class or work, he trekked up to the abandoned shrine. Sitting under the fixed stare of Benzaiten, he spent hours contemplating the meaning of the old monk's criticism. He had felt so sure of himself of late, but that security had come crashing down. The old monk had always preached that each person had his own unique way—in identity, purpose, and roles. But now, Yoshi thought perhaps the monk was just being accommodating when he made such comments. "Maybe there is a right way and a wrong way of doing things," he said to the stoned-faced god. As he spoke to the statue, he took the time to really study it. The structure was in remarkably good shape for the years of neglect it endured. The only reason it looked beat up was the dust and mold growing all over it. Yoshi took the edge of the blanket around his shoulders, the same blanket the old monk had given him, and wiped clean the eyes and forehead of the statue. As he was doing it, he believed Benzaiten's eyes sparkled, as if she was expressing gratitude for his aid.

Yoshi stood up and surveyed the entire shrine, but this time studying its structure and condition. Just like the stone statue, it was in remarkably solid condition. While it needed an intense cleaning and several of the wooden planks needed repair, it was not beyond reason to do so. Yoshi wondered what Daichi would think about him wasting time and energy fixing up this shrine. "How about if I don't tell him," he whispered to Benzaiten. "We'll keep this our little secret." The kami smiled back in agreement.

"Good afternoon, Yoshi-san." Kira clearly sought Yoshi out and he couldn't help being excited by that fact. It had been several weeks since their last conversation, save the short greetings they would share as they crossed paths around campus. After several moments of idle talk, Kira cut to her point. "I have a favor to ask of you. If you have some time available, would you mind aiding me with my combat techniques?"

Kira went on to explain her plight. She had advanced to a level of Kenjutsu rarely achieved by any of the female samurai. Most women are taught to defend themselves with the wakizashi, or short sword, and have limited experience in katana combat. Her skill and achievement had been on par, if not exceeding, many of the male students; thus, the senpai agreed to waive the usual gender restrictions and allowed her to attend senior Kenjutsu class. Unfortunately for Kira, she felt she had run into a roadblock in her development and was unable to compete effectively with her classmates. "I fear the senpai will soon lose patience with me and request my demotion from the class," Kira explained. "He would not be without cause in doing so. It is not the shame of the demotion I seek to avoid, but the shame of not doing all I could to succeed."

Yoshi looked up at the position of the sun in the west. There would still be some hours until it descended behind the mountains. "If you have some time right now, I would be pleased to offer whatever advice I can." Yoshi was elated at this opportunity to share time with Kira once again. He had terribly missed her participation in the evening workshops and, more importantly, their lengthy discussions afterward. As they chatted on the way to the training center, it was as if they were slipping into that same, comfortable routine they once enjoyed.

The familiarity ended when he found himself standing face-to-face with the shinai-wielding Kira. This was not a situation he ever envisioned himself being with her. It was the first time he had ever sparred with a woman, much less a woman he cared for, and he found it a bit unsettling. He forced himself to remove the gender of his pupil from his mind and concentrated on giving the best advice. While he wished she thought of him as more than just a teacher, he would show her respect by giving her the best advice possible.

Yoshi gave the command to begin and the two circled each other. He shouted basic tips such as reminding her to keep her balance and focus on her opponent's movements. Acknowledging him with silent head nods, Kira continued to circle but not initiate the attack. Yoshi felt she was deferring to him as the master, so he stepped toward her to attack. Just as he began his advance, Kira quickly stepped into him to meet his attack. She was able to block his first two blows and launch two of her own that were easily parried by Yoshi. Yoshi stepped back for a moment then began another assault. Kira made the same maneuver as earlier and engaged Yoshi in close quarters. This time Yoshi was able to use his superior strength to push her back when their shinai met. As she stumbled back, she was vulnerable to Yoshi's blows, but he held back in striking her.

"I've been hit before Yoshi-san," she said in response to his halted attack. "Better to be hit by your bamboo sword than the sharp blade of a real foe." He bowed slightly in acknowledgement. He engaged her again and she made the same tactical moves of quickly closing on him. Again, he was able to push her back and land a solid blow on her left arm. Undeterred, Kira continued to fight Yoshi in the same manner each time. After a couple more similar engagements, Yoshi finally recognized where he had previously encountered this type of fighting. It was the same style as Togo's.

He felt the skin on his face reddened at the thought that she would emulate his adversary. As she engaged him in the same manner once again, he abruptly stopped the sparring session. "Why are you fighting in this manner?" he said in a voice louder than he or she expected. "It is foolish and self-defeating. I can see why the senpai would want to remove you from the class." Yoshi was stunned that he allowed his anger to spill out like this but could do nothing to stop it.

Kira was equally shocked at the explosion, but quickly responded. "Am I not doing exactly what you did in your fight with Togo? I watched you during the fight and in the training leading up to it. You mirrored your opponent in order to counter him." Kira's irritation grew to match Yoshi's. "Why are you angry that I should take the same tactic?"

Yoshi realized she was right. He had done the same thing in preparing for Togo and met with the same result Kira was enduring at his hands. The reason he was enraged was not because Kira was adopting Togo's tactics, but because she was adopting Yoshi's. She was making the same mistakes he made in preparing for Togo. It was as if a mirror was placed in front of Yoshi. He did not care for its reflection, so he shattered it.

"I am angry at the parts of me I see in you," Yoshi blurted out. Taken aback at his honesty, Kira fell silent as Yoshi continued. "Since I can remember, I have been adopting ways and beliefs of others. My father's. My mentor's. Even my enemy's. As a boy, I dreamed of being just like the warriors I read about in those scrolls I shared. I tell you and others that I have come to the School of Aspen to be the best samurai I can be. In reality, I have come to be the best samurai in the eyes of others. I have been a fool."

Yoshi's voice quivered as the emotion poured out. He did not know if it was the release of all the pent-up energy since his encounter with Togo or being in the presence of someone he adored; but it was as if the levee was breached, and the river waters flowed unabated.

"Kira-san, you have asked me to give you a lesson in Kenjutsu, but what I have to tell you is much more important. Do not be like me. Do not be like anyone else. Choose what is most important to you, what makes you feel right, in here." Yoshi placed his hand on his chest. "Live that way, fight that way, and you will succeed."

Yoshi raised his shinai, and Kira did the same. "Now fight me in the way that best suits you." Yoshi stepped up to attack Kira, but this time instead of meeting him head-on, she squatted down, almost making herself into a ball, and somersaulted out of the way. She stayed low as Yoshi chased her, bolting from side to side, never getting close enough for Yoshi to do harm. In his zeal to catch up to her, Yoshi rushed at her. As she rolled away, she struck him twice rapidly in the right thigh. Yoshi stopped his pursuit and rubbed the area that would soon form a bruise. Breathing heavily and still in a crouched position, Kira warily stared at her mentor and foe.

Yoshi smiled, lowered his shinai, and bowed in deference to her. Kira stood up and returned the bow. A smile of revelation and pride slowly crept on her face. She seemed to realize that she did not have to fight the way of the *men*. Yoshi succeeded in showing her that her way could be just as effective, albeit unorthodox. "Thank you for sharing with me," she mustered a response. He knew she meant more than just the fighting lesson.

"I am always... available to you, Kira-san." He paused halting a thought from escaping his lips, closing them tight so as not to let it free.

Kira's smile melted away as she stepped forward to within a pace of Yoshi, her eyes locked on his. As she did so, she shared her own revelation. "At this moment, I, too, am angry with you. Because in you, in your hesitation to express your feelings, I see a reflection of me. My image of the samurai I am to become was one of complete dedication to learning and servitude. In that vision, I had no use for my heart. But I was wrong. I found a place for it. If you shall have it, my heart is with you."

Kira stood before Yoshi, both frozen by the chill in the air and the resolve of this moment. She spoke so eloquently that Yoshi knew he did not have the words to match her emotions, yet he did share in the passion. Words would not serve him. Silently, Yoshi got down on both knees and bowed down before her. His heart was hers.

Yoshi had not seen the old monk in nearly a week but stormed right to his cabin after escorting Kira home. "Because it was important to me. It felt right in my heart. You above all people should know that no one has to justify their belief or values to anyone else." Filled with confidence from his new bond in life, Yoshi was eager to address

Daichi's prior criticism. The incident with Kira clarified to Yoshi that he needed to embrace the values he held. He also needed to stop seeking the approval of Daichi and others regarding his belief system. Just as the old monk had done before, Yoshi did not yell or raise his voice but spoke in a very measured and firm tone. "The rightness or wrongness of what I do can only be judged by me."

Yoshi encountered Daichi just as the monk was walking out his door. The old monk seemed slightly taken aback by Yoshi's outspokenness, but in a split second recovered and continued the journey he was about to undertake. "Then how do you know if your values are right for you?" the monk asked as he continued on his way. "Since you are the only one who can judge them, how do you judge them?"

From the direction he was heading, and the extra blanket draped on his shoulders, Yoshi determined the old monk was heading to the hot springs. He followed behind, thinking for a moment about the proper answer. He wanted to reply, *Because my heart tells me so*, but feared it was too simple and trite of an answer.

Seizing on Yoshi's hesitation, the monk goaded him. "You had much to say a moment ago. Perhaps your fortitude is lacking in confidence." The monk stopped on the path and turned to Yoshi, awaiting his response.

"Because my heart tells me so," Yoshi finally blurted out.

"Take out your sword and read me the inscription," the monk commanded more than asked.

Yoshi unsheathed the Sword of Values and read aloud the quote engraved on the blade.

"What values do I desire in order for me to fulfill the destiny of who I have chosen to be?" Yoshi read.

"So, the answer is I know the values are right because it is what I desire it to be?" He made the observation more of a question than a statement but saw from the monk's expression it was an incorrect analysis. Without the monk saying another word, Yoshi studied the inscription again, reading it over and over again, as if new insight would suddenly emerge. The sunlight was beginning to slip behind the mountains and the inscription was a little hard to read. Yoshi tilted the sword to attract more light as he read it. As he turned it toward the escaping sunlight, he thought he spotted something new. Initially he believed it was a scratch, but on closer inspection, he saw an additional engraving, etched in small characters just below the main quote. Straining to make it out, he read his new discovery aloud:

"What is most important to me in ...?"

Yoshi looked up at the monk in confusion and embarrassment. "I've read the sword a hundred times, but I never saw this new engraving before," he confessed.

"The Swords of Illumination are more than some trophy pieces that possess single seeds of wisdom. They are a manifestation of the lessons they seek to teach. The sword in your hands is not unlike values themselves, Yoshi-san. Instead of merely reading or feeling values, they must be examined closely enough to get to their true significance and meaning."

The monk continued on his way to the hot springs with Yoshi in tow and examining the sword again. "What is most important to me in ...?" He struggled to make out the last word in the question. Spinning the sword frantically, he concluded there were no more words engraved. "There seems to be something missing from the new question on the sword."

"Life is full of blanks for you to fill in." The monk had reached the hot springs behind the men's lodging, slipped off his robes, and slid into the steaming pool. He closed his eyes, leaned back, and seemed to appreciate the healing warmth over his aged body.

Yoshi examined the sword once more, mulling over the monk's response. He sheathed it and turned to leave but returned back to the monk with one last observation. "I was wrong to even ask your opinion of my values. Your harsh criticism was your way of showing me the error of my ways."

The monk's eyes opened, and he smiled at his young pupil. "I find the best bits of advice are the ones shown rather than said."

He sat alone with his thoughts during dinner, barely looking up from his food, as if the answer lay somewhere in the rice and fish in his bowl. He pondered the new question on his sword and thought about the answer his master gave him, the answer with another cryptic meaning. He could not argue with the monk's conclusion that lessons learned are better than lessons told, and he knew this was yet another example of that. "What is most important to me in... life?" Yoshi thought that seemed like too broad of an answer for such a question.

As he stepped onto the path leading out of the dining hall, he saw Togo coming toward him. Walking quite gingerly, he had a young monk alongside him but not touching him. Yoshi imagined the monk was there to help the injured student, but the student's pride would never allow him to receive aid, especially in public. Because of their recent history, Yoshi saw an opportunity to thaw their frozen relationship and was anxious to test his theory. "Good evening, Togo-san. You seem to be healing well."

The young monk interrupted before Togo could speak. "He has healed remarkably fast despite the extent of his injuries. If it was not for your quick thinking and help, I am sure his recovery time would have been much longer." Togo shot a look to the young monk that, if it were a blade, would have eviscerated him. This had the desired result of silencing the chatter. Togo acknowledged Yoshi with a grunt of a thank you and an ever-so-slight nod. He then continued to the dining area, with the young monk behind but decidedly further back.

What is most important to Togo in dealing with me is maintaining his pride, Yoshi joked to himself as he strolled away. He cut his laughter short when he was hit with a realization. The question on the sword does not ask what is most important to Yoshi in life, but rather, in every aspect of life.

His revelation got the wheels turning in his head, specifically the wheel symbolizing the areas of balance. He chastised himself for not remembering that each Sword of Illumination built on the lessons of the ones before it. *Of course, the answers to this puzzle were given to me from the previous swords,* Yoshi said to himself.

That evening, he examined the sheet of paper where he wrote out the ten categories of balance. As he studied the sheet and what he personally wanted to achieve, he determined he needed to ask the question for each area. *What is most important to me in Physical, Mental, Emotional, Business, Community, Financial, Relationship, Family, Spiritual, and Health?* He spent the night feverishly examining each area and jotting notes on what was most important. He discovered that in many areas there was a whole host of things that qualified as important.

Culling through all the things he considered important and determining the most important value was not as easy an exercise as he had hoped.

Frustrated, Yoshi read the engraving on his sword again, only this time aloud:

"Sword of Values.
What values do I desire in order for me to fulfill the
destiny of who I have chosen to be?"

Something odd tickled his ear as he heard his voice recite the engraving. It was a particular phrasing he thought. "What values do I desire in order...," Yoshi paused mid-sentence. "In order," he sighed. Shaking his head, he realized the instructions were there the whole time. "I need to take these values in each area and order them."

For each category of balance, he went about reorganizing the list of values he held in that area. This proved to be a frustrating activity. He felt each area had more than one value that should be in the top spot. With the ink running out and his eyelids closing shut, Yoshi set it aside for another day.

The following day, Yoshi eagerly explained to Daichi how he figured out the lesson of the new question and how he applied it. "When it came to assisting Togo, I learned the most important thing to me was to come to the aid of another human being. I did not think about who he was or what the consequences or rewards might be. I was pleasantly shocked at the lack of offense I felt when he ignored me yesterday, but realized it was because I did not do it for the glory or recognition but because it is what I had to do."

The old monk had approached Yoshi as he left his class

and asked him to join him on a hike. Yoshi was excited since he had been looking forward to sharing with the monk his newfound insight. Daichi led the way through the freshly fallen snow. "I am impressed by your insight and self-discovery. Have you applied this examination to all the areas of your life?"

"That is why I need some guidance. In some areas of my life, I have a hard time determining what is really most important to me. I honestly think that several values are the most important in, say, my emotional life or my spiritual life. And what happens when one value contradicts another? When I paid back the staff for the pelts, it satisfied my value for the community to the detriment of my financial value of saving money." Yoshi paused and shook his head to clear out the confusion.

The old monk stopped and turned to Yoshi, looking him straight in the eyes. Yoshi was prepared for a revelation from the monk that would shine a light on the darkness of his uncertainty. Instead, the monk slowly bent down, scooped a handful of snow, and threw it directly into Yoshi's chest. The blow was not hard enough to actually hurt Yoshi, but the utter surprise of the monk's action sent Yoshi stumbling back and falling on his behind. Too stunned to even ask for an explanation, Yoshi stood and brushed the snow off his robes. As he looked down to remove the rest of the snow, another snowball hit him smack in the back. He turned to find the old monk standing several paces away with yet another snowball in hand. Before he could respond, that snowball ended up right in Yoshi's chest.

With the agility of a man many years younger, the old monk kept scooping up balls of snow and firing them at Yoshi, leaping in and out and side to side for different angles. The absurdity of it left Yoshi dumb, then busting out in laughter. After the sixth hit, he came to his senses enough to begin attempting to dodge the monk's projectiles. Although much younger and in better condition, he could not avoid the pelting from the quicker and sharper assailant.

The silliness of the moment grew into a bit of frustration, as Yoshi's robes and body were getting damp from the rain of snowballs. "Okay, Daichi-san, you have made your point," Yoshi cried out, hoping to end the barrage.

"And what point is that?" the old monk said as he hurled another snowball into Yoshi's midsection.

Yoshi had no idea what lesson the madman could be giving him with this snowball fight. "That you have great aim?" His feeble response was greeted first with a pause and then followed by a snowball careening off his head.

Yoshi had enough. He could not dodge the barrage, so he did the first thing that came to his mind. He scooped up his own handful of snow and threw it at Daichi. The first shot glanced off his shoulder, but the second shot landed in the middle of his chest, almost causing him to lose his balance. Yoshi then fired five more balls in rapid secession. Yoshi's barrage achieved its intended result of stopping the old monk from launching any more assaults. The old monk finally dropped the snowball in his hand, bringing an end to the exchange.

His breathing slightly labored, the old monk approached Yoshi. "There is always one value that is most important in any given situation. Sometimes it is clear, and sometimes it can be buried in your subconscious." Before Yoshi could interrupt and ask what this had to do with snowballs, the monk continued. "When I started throwing the snow at you, what was most important to you?"

"To avoid getting hit," Yoshi replied.

"Wrong. If that really were your most important thing, you would have simply run away. As fit as you are, there would be no way I could have managed to keep up with you. What was most important to you?"

Without hesitation, Yoshi answered, "To have you stop throwing the snowballs at me."

"Exactly. And your actions manifested what was most important to you when you started throwing the snow back at me. In the heat and stress of the moment, your true value was revealed."

"What values do I desire IN ORDER... meaning my prioritization of values in the order of most important to least important," Yoshi moaned as he realized the lesson of the sword.

"Ah, someone finally really read the Sword of Values," Daichi laughed.

Yoshi took in the words the monk was sharing and reflected on how they affected him. "If you had presented me with the hypothetical situation of saving an injured Togo, my replies would have varied between saving him and leaving him. But when I was face-to-face with the actual situation, I could not help but to act according to a value set I didn't consciously know existed."

Daichi nodded in agreement. "There might be plenty of values you possess, but the most important always rises to the surface at the moment you make a choice."

"Just now, would it have been wrong of me if I fled to avoid the attack?"

"Ah, Yoshi-san, I thought we crossed that bridge of judgment. There is no right, no wrong, just true. When you stopped me from throwing the snow, you were exhibiting a *moving toward* value. Your value dictated taking proactive measures. If you had fled to avoid my assault, you would have been employing a *moving away* value. Your actions would have had the same results by keeping you from getting hit with snow. A *moving away* value can be just as viable as a *moving toward* value. Not right. Not wrong. Just true."

They walked in silence as Daichi led the way and Yoshi contemplated the lesson learned. The last several days had really impressed on him the importance of values, of the self-discoveries that they revealed. He also realized that although he had received much knowledge thus far at the School of Aspen, there were so many more lessons yet to learn. So deep in thought, he paid no attention to the path the old monk was taking. When the monk finally stopped, Yoshi was stunned to see what lay in front of him.

Stacked out before him were the remnants of a cedar tree, the branches and base chopped up into long planks. Cedar was the wood used in the old shrine and these pieces would, once shaved down, serve as perfect replacements for the rotting boards now on the shrine. It took him a second to realize that this was not some odd coincidence. The old monk had found this tree and cut it up for him.

"Yoshi-san. I believe this wood would serve you well in repairing Benzaiten's shrine. Unfortunately, I cannot carry this all by myself, would you mind helping me?"

"I... I can't thank you enough," Yoshi stammered out. "But how did you know?"

The rustling sound coming from the woods interrupted his thoughts. Emerging from the tree line was a bundled-up figure, laboring as he dragged a large piece of cedar along the ground. Dropping the piece with the others, the cedar gatherer slid the scarf down from his face that was protecting him from the cold. Yoshi thought it odd because most men he knew would not think this weather was cold enough to protect one's face. His confusion was cleared up when the man's face had decidedly more feminine features than he expected.

"You should never tell a woman what you are up to," Kira said with a glowing smile. "She'll only want to help."

Two days later, Yoshi was visited by the familiar senior senpai to take him to the sword ceremony. Intercepting him on his way home for an evening workshop, the senpai bowed deeply to Yoshi, a sign of great respect that he had never shown to Yoshi. Although not a word was spoken, the senpai's respect remained palpable throughout the time he escorted Yoshi to the sword ceremony chamber. Before leaving him, the senpai again bowed deeply.

The ceremony was conducted just as the others had been, with the twelve elders filing into the dimly lit chamber. This time Yoshi could only detect two other students in the chamber but could not discern their identity. A different elder from the previous ceremonies spoke. "You three have been called here tonight to take one more step on the path of enlightenment and balance. By being here, you have shown to yourselves that you understand the great gift of the Sword of Values. In time, you will learn its true power. It is now time to receive the next level of enlightenment."

Yoshi and the others each ceded their Sword of Values, and a new sword was placed before each of them.

"Before you accept the next Sword of Illumination, you are permitted to ask one question of this council in order to gain additional knowledge."

The extra respect he was shown earlier by the senior senpai made Yoshi feel he had reached a stage few others accomplished. During his time at the School of Aspen, he had witnessed many students leave the school, including students from his initial class. Fanfare and well wishes were given to those students as if they had graduated; however, it was understood that those students had simply reached the level of development that suited them. Yoshi knew there was more the school had to offer and yearned to absorb it.

To the elders, Yoshi asked, "I understand that my values determine my destiny and that my actions are determined by the roles I play, but I feel there must be a bridge connecting the two. Is there such a bridge?"

The elder replied, "It is not a bridge but rather a core you seek. Nourishing fruit surrounds an apple's center but at its core are the seedlings that will produce another apple. At your core is your identity, which will produce the life you are destined to lead."

Yoshi's thoughts drifted to when he first discovered the Sword of Identity in his father's chest. The first person to see him with the sword was not his mother or another samurai, but rather Hideki, the irate farmer in the marketplace. Not realizing it until now, but his most important value then was to avoid conflict, so he retreated. It was a *moving away* value that suited his identity. Even then, his value structure was driving his actions. "It all goes back to the beginning, doesn't it? It is about serving who you really are," Yoshi replied to the elder who nodded in agreement.

When the elders departed, Yoshi did not quickly unsheathe the sword but rather returned to his room and stared at the covered sword. Instead of leaping into the next lesson, he wanted to take time to contemplate what he had learned. He thought about all the knowledge he acquired from the previous five swords and his understanding of how his value structure fit into creating balance. He felt like he was proceeding toward his desired destiny and making the right choices in doing so.

What gnawed at him was a feeling that he did not have a clear handle on how he made those choices. *There must be a way for me to make the choices in my life in a fluid and natural manner.* After a couple of hours of hammering his mind for an answer, he gave in to the hope he will gain insight in the future. Before he went to sleep, he picked up his new sword and slowly unsheathed it. It took all the energy he could muster to keep his laughter from waking the whole campus. The sword's inscription read:

Sword of Decisions
What decision that I do at this moment will create my life's path.

"So basically, the lesson this Yoshi learned was to follow your gut," Tom opined with dripping sarcasm. "Seems like a shaky philosophy to me."

"Perhaps a better way to say it is that your gut leads you whether you know it or not." The old man reached into his pocket and took out a nickel-sized object. Without looking at it, he tossed it over to Tom. Once in his hands, he instantly recognized it as a little compass, like you would find in a kid's cereal box. "Think of values as a compass," the old man explained. "No matter where you stand and face, your values always point to your own true self, your own true north. But unlike the Earth which has its true north set by a mysterious source, you have the choice to create your own true north by selecting the values that mean the most to you."

Tom twirled the small device in his fingers. As he turned it from side to side, the tiny arrow always bobbed in the same direction. Tom mused that no matter where he was in the world or how he held this little compass, the arrow was going to move to north. He then took a moment to look around him. "So, my values have sent me here, in the middle of nowhere, far from my wife and family? You'll excuse me if I say that makes no sense."

"Do you believe that being here tonight is the right place for you?"

"Then why am I here?!" Tom's aggravation launched him up on his feet. He paced between the fire and the edge of the trees. "It's just stupid that I am here. Stupid I just drove off. I should get back there." He headed back into the woods and to his car near the side of the road. Jumping into the driver's side, Tom popped the key into the ignition and turned. Nothing but clicking sounds responded. He pumped the gas pedal and turned the ignition again but received the same response. A third, fourth, and fifth attempt followed. Tom pounded on the steering wheel and screamed out of frustration from the deepest regions of his soul.

Tom opened his hand and stared at the tiny compass. The arrow pointed straight toward him. In his clouded state of mind, he could not tell if it meant that north was behind him or that the compass was validating the old man's advice. *No, being here is not the right place for me. Then why am I here? How did I get here?* These were the questions that ate at him from the moment he pulled off the side of the road to avoid certain death.

Emerging from the darkness of the trees off the side of the road, the old man ambled up to Tom's car. Tom opened up his car door and just sat there as the old stranger walked up and offered a drink out of his canteen. Tom ignored the offer, not taking his gaze off the device in his hand. "It's pointing back from which I came, where I obviously belong. How did I get here?" He looked up to the old man in desperation, waiting for a response.

"I'm allergic to shellfish. Gives me a terrible reaction. Makes me break out in hives. I know this because after eating shellfish a few times and suffering the consequence, I figured out that it was not for me. Like me eating lobster, you were living a life that did not suit you. I believe, while your intentions might have been right, you were behaving in a way that ran counter to what you really believe and value."

"Ending up here is my allergic reaction?" Tom asked.

The old man nodded. He offered the canteen once more and this time Tom took a swallow. In silence, the duo walked back down the hill to this campsite.

"So just don't eat shellfish, so to speak," Tom finally said breaking the silence.

"So to speak."

It couldn't be that simple. It was a matter of decisions. Some decisions are small while others are immensely significant. Hopefully, the old man's story about his ancestor would provide more insight, and perhaps even a little enlightenment for Tom.

CHAPTER 16

Sword of Decisions: Part I

No student at the School of Aspen held a sword beyond the Sword of Decisions. He had no idea if students held this sword indefinitely or if there was some later graduation to... something. While initially these thoughts brought up trepidation and anxiety, it soon faded away as he immersed himself in his daily life at the school.

The restoration of the old temple became a shared cause during the next several weeks. On days when the blistery winter was mellow enough, Kira, Daichi, and Yoshi scrubbed clean the worn statues, replaced the rotted wood panels, and returned emblems and statues of adoration to the shrine. Haru's inquisition on where his friend was spending all his free time led to the drafting of another soldier in the great restoration efforts.

When the four would work in unison at the shrine, it was often in silence. Part of the reason was due to focusing on their assigned tasks; however, a large measure of their collective silence was brought on by merely being in the presence of the shrine. There was an unmistakable energy emitted from Benzaiten's gaze and each of them felt it. Even Daichi, who had never been at a loss for words, remained silently humble in the company of Benzaiten. Although they never discussed it with each other, they felt the absorption of the energy helped enlighten them and give them focus, not just with the task at hand, but with every part of their lives. Each concluded that speaking, even idle chatter, would diffuse the energy, and so they hammered and cleaned without a word.

Yoshi had never been happier during his time at the School of Aspen. He embraced every dawn with renewed vigor and excitement. It was not just the communal effort on the shrine that elevated his mood. He felt a sense of purpose in everything he was doing at the school. Whether it was working on a menial task at the farm or absorbing a lesson in class or spending time with Kira, Yoshi felt his actions and behaviors fell in line with who he was and who he wanted to be. In no area was this more evident than his desire to teach others.

Now that he was one of the most senior students at the academy, he was given increased responsibility for teaching the lower-level students and he relished every opportunity. When lecturing, he spoke with an infectious passion. When supervising sparring sessions, he did more than criticize. He took the time to show the students what they were doing wrong and, just as importantly, to congratulate them on what they were doing right.

The attendance at his evening study sessions had never been larger or more engaging. The exchange of ideas and thoughts exceeded Yoshi's wildest imagination. When he started these sessions long ago with Haru, he hoped it would provide some assistance to others at the school. These sessions grew to such size and scope that they had to be held in the large dining area to accommodate all that attended. Several of the elders remarked to Yoshi that these workshops brought a vitality to the School of Aspen they had never witnessed. Students were more prepared and engaged in lessons than ever before.

Even Daichi was effusive with his praise. "Yoshi-san, I wonder if it is I who should be coming to you for advice," the old monk remarked during their return from working on the old shrine. There was some truth in his comments. Since he had received the Sword of Decisions, he had not had a single session with the old monk involving a lesson. The time they spent together was almost exclusively on fixing the shrine or helping the old monk with his chores.

It was after a particularly rousing workshop that it seemed everything came into focus for Yoshi. Still engaged in a lively debate with Kira as they departed, Yoshi spotted a young man sitting alone by the koi pond. He glanced over while remaining engaged in the conversation, however something about that young man would not leave his mind. After escorting Kira to her quarters, Yoshi swung back to the pond to find the young man sitting just as he was. For Yoshi, it was as if he was looking at himself almost two years earlier, sitting alone, reflecting on his place at the school and in the world. It was obvious he was an entry-level student, with the Sword of Identity hanging from his waist.

The young man had not realized someone was watching him and Yoshi pondered whether he should interfere. He had come to his realizations on his own and knew that made them more rewarding. Conversely, there was a part of him that cried out to guide the young man and explain to him the lessons of the Sword of Identity. He wanted to grab him by the shoulders and tell him to act as he sees himself to be, and in turn, the world will see him that way. As the debate in his mind raged on, a smile slipped over his face. *Who needs the advice now?* he mused to himself. The relaxation of the smile opened another option in his mind. "Why not do both?" he said under his breath and stepped out of the shadows.

The young man was so startled by the approaching senior senpai he nearly stepped into the pond. "Sir, I am sorry. I really should have retired by now," was the only response the shocked student could muster.

"No need to apologize. I often find the koi to be stimulating conversationalists." Yoshi smiled to ease the young man's nerves. "Are they giving you good advice?"

"It has been a decidedly one-sided conversation, sir," the young man sighed.

Yoshi took a moment to size up the boy. He looked not more than seventeen years of age. Already taller than Yoshi, he expected he would still grow some more. His frame was large but lacked the muscle that years of training at the School of Aspen will supply. In his eyes, he saw a tinge of sadness to accompany the despair he felt. Yoshi assumed the source of the sadness came from the young man's confusion and bewilderment, a place he knew all too well. "Who are you?" Yoshi inquired.

"Takeshi, sir. I am new to the school. Only been here two months," the boy fumbled out.

"I knew a Takeshi. He is a carpenter in the village where I grew up. He was a fine maker of wooden products; we often used his services. Are you a carpenter?"

The boy wrinkled his brow and shook his head no.

"Who are you?"

"I am Takeshi. I am new to the school." He repeated it slowly and slightly louder. He thought perhaps the senpai did not understand him the first time.

"There is a Takeshi that worked on the farm I supervise. He is the quiet sort but one of the hardest workers we ever had. He could pluck the apples off three dozen trees before the sun reached the top of the sky. Are you a farmer?"

"No sir, I am Takeshi. I am sorry if I am not clear."

"Takeshi, you say. Are you the Takeshi that bakes in the school's kitchen?"

"No sir."

"So," Yoshi said. "You are not the carpenter, or the farmer or the baker," Yoshi paused in thought as if he was recalling where he had seen the boy before. "Who are you again?"

"I am Takeshi. I am a samurai." The young samurai broke the silence of the night. He could hear woodland creatures scurry off because of the sudden burst of noise. Resolute, he repeated to Yoshi. "I am Takeshi. I am a samurai."

Yoshi met the stern gaze of the young student. "And don't you forget it." They held eye contact until Yoshi detected the light go on in the young's man mind. As the point became clearer to him, a slight smile crept across his face.

In a softer voice, he repeated, "I am Takeshi. I am a samurai." Takeshi bowed deeply to the senior senpai and retired to his room. As he watched him disappear into the darkness, Yoshi once again recognized himself in the young student. This time the resemblance came from the spring in his step and the confidence of his posture.

"In the end, I decided not to choose one way or another, but decided to do both." Yoshi had finished relating his tale of helping the young Takeshi. A light snow was falling, slowly blanketing the campus in a sheet of white.

The old monk and Yoshi shared a pot of tea on the deck outside of Daichi's cabin. The chilly climate and gradually worsening conditions made it a suitable location for their mid-afternoon session.

"For that moment, you were living in the world of *and* instead of *or.*" Daichi poured some tea into Yoshi's cup, and then into his own.

"The world of *and*? That is an interesting way of putting it." Yoshi blew on his tea to cool it down before sipping it.

"It is the world a samurai travels in. A world of possibilities instead of dilemmas. A world of expansion instead of contraction." The old monk stared up toward the sky. "I love the snow."

"Yes. Yes. It sure is... white." Yoshi thought the turn in the conversation was odd but thought he should go along. "I like it when it... falls."

"Did you know that no two snowflakes are exactly alike? Of the countless snowflakes nature creates, she is still able to come up with an absolutely unique design for each flake."

"My father told me that when I was just a young boy," Yoshi answered. He joined Daichi's examination of the falling snow. It momentarily took him back to the day his father told him this fact, a day not unlike the one he was enjoying now.

During that day with his father, young Yoshi was pouting that he could not figure out how to saddle his pony. Every time he attempted to tie it around the pony's back, it would bray up and scurry off. He had watched his father do it hundreds of times on the other horses and made sure to carefully repeat those steps. Frustrated and teary-eyed, Yoshi sulked outside his family home, watching the snowfall.

Standing behind him, his father explained that every snowflake was unique. Yoshi found it an odd comment to make given his situation, but it became clear once his father expanded on the point. "Yoshi, just as there are endless types of flakes, there are endless ways to accomplish what you seek. Don't make the mistake of getting mired down by one approach." The young Yoshi slept on his father's wisdom and the next morning went about his task with a completely new approach. He fed the pony pieces of apple. As he contently chewed, the pony remained still as Yoshi tied on the saddle.

"It is about possibilities, isn't it?" Yoshi blurted it out to the present-day Daichi. "As with the snow, so is it with our choices. There are always options."

Daichi seemed pleasantly surprised by the sudden revelation of his young pupil. "And what does that mean for the samurai faced with a choice?" the old monk pressed.

"It means having the vision to see beyond the two choices presented. I could have directly helped the young man, or I could have walked away from him thus letting him learn on his own. But I chose an *and* option. Both of my goals were achieved, I helped, and Takeshi-san was able to make the discovery on his own."

"Remember it is the outcome you are really seeking, not the choice," the old monk added. "Take out your sword and read it again."

Obeying, Yoshi read aloud, "'*Sword of Decisions. What decision that I do at this moment will create my life's path.*' Now that I read it aloud again, it sounds like an odd phrase. Shouldn't it read, 'What decision that I *make* at this moment?'"

"When you looked upon the struggling young student, what did you decide?"

"I decided to engage him, just as I explained."

"After you decided to engage him, what happened?"

"I walked over to him and sat down..." Realization overtook Yoshi as he continued. "I took action, didn't I? I acted upon the decision."

"Hence, you 'do' decisions," the old monk summarized.

"I've been reading this sword all wrong. I believed decisions were purely a mental act. In reality, a decision is made manifest by the action that follows."

"Yes, Yoshi-san. It is perfect you say 'manifest.' The Sword of Decisions is about living proactively rather than reactively. Every decision you do creates the pathway of your life."

Yoshi leaned back as his mind took him to an embarrassing memory. The day he fell into the stream while helping Daichi collect tea leaves. Every decision he took in deciding which rock to leap upon as he crossed the creek led to his ultimate failure.

"I've always thought life was about discovering your path, your destiny." Yoshi stared at the Sword of Decisions as if it were channeling this newfound insight. "You don't discover your path in life. You create it with the decisions you make." Yoshi looked up, waiting for Daichi to respond. But all Yoshi could decipher from the old monk was a slight smile of pride and the almost imperceptible nod of confidence.

A few days later, Yoshi, Daichi, and Haru trekked up the pathway to the old shrine. The snow had ceased for several days and began to melt; making it easier to work on their project. Today, they would replace the warped boards used for kneeling before the shrine. As they walked up the final steps, they vowed to complete it all before dusk. The usual fourth person on the team, Kira, was leading a music lesson for the new samurai and begged forgiveness for not being able to help. When Haru explained they would just be doing construction and not cleaning, she shot him a look that could have drawn blood.

Working on the shrine, Yoshi thought Haru looked a bit distant and his gait was sullen. He quickly dismissed it to keep with their unspoken code of silence and reverence of Benzaiten's shrine. With the sun rapidly slipping below the mountains, the three men put the finishing touches to the new boards. Beholding their handiwork, they knelt on the boards and bowed before Benzaiten, each making their own silent prayer and offering of gratitude. Yoshi, then Daichi, rose and bowed to the shrine, then collected their tools. Haru stayed several moments longer deep in mediation. *It seems mine is not the only spirituality being fulfilled by this shrine*, Yoshi thought as he patiently waited for his friend to finish.

The three descended the stairs discussing the progress they made on the shrine and how much they enjoyed finishing the tasks of the day on time. When they reached the main campus, Daichi bid them farewell while Yoshi and Haru headed for the evening meal. On the way, Yoshi excitedly told him about his encounter with the new student and the pride he felt not just in helping him, but with the workshop they had started. "To think, what you and I started together has grown into such a wonderful orchard.

Perhaps, you should join me at the farm," Yoshi said in jest, his laughter exceeding the din of the dining students.

"I am leaving the school," Haru said in reply to Yoshi's joke. He said it in a hushed tone, almost as an aside, and Yoshi was not sure he heard him correctly.

"I am leaving the School of Aspen," Haru repeated. "I have thought long and hard about this decision, Yoshi-san, and it was not made easily or trivially." Haru unsheathed his sword, the Sword of Outcomes, and stared at it for a moment. "I have watched you and others move on to receive a higher order of swords, but I feel I will forever remain at this level."

"Haru-san, there is no timetable on when to achieve these swords, they will come to you in due time. You must trust me." Yoshi pleaded with his friend. While he had seen many other students make the same decision, he could not accept it from one that had grown so close to him. Yoshi never paid any mind to the fact that he was ascending the level of swords while Haru remained behind. He thought of Haru as his equal, a fellow samurai, and most importantly, a friend. He was now presented with the possibility of losing that special relationship.

"I have achieved much at this school, learned much, and grown into a man," Haru explained. "The lessons I have learned will serve me well. But I realized that my goal in coming to this school, my outcome, was to be a samurai. I have clearly obtained the level of swordsmanship and education to be deemed as such and will carry my sword with great pride. I know I will serve my masters well. I have reached the level I need to be."

"But there is still so much more to learn," Yoshi responded with more than a hint of despair.

"For you perhaps, but not for me. It was the time working on the shrine that made it clear. Being in the prolonged presence of that spirit made me reflect on my own life and my own path. I thought about the deep passion you possess for everything you do and how I admire it. I admire it but cannot emulate it. For me, the School of Aspen has already given me all I need." Haru calmly sheathed the sword and returned to his bowl of rice.

Yoshi was left reeling. That evening and throughout the next day, Yoshi avoided his departing friend. He could not understand why Haru would not want to continue the path toward obtaining knowledge and wisdom. Yoshi thought of all the lessons he had not yet learned and how he yearned to someday receive them. His emotions varied from fits of anger at Haru for his desertion to sadness for losing a good friend. He also called into question his own values and decisions. *I am a greater warrior and student than Haru, perhaps I should consider myself a samurai. Why shouldn't I leave to seek out my destiny?*

He asked this to Benzaiten upon visiting the shrine. He knew Haru was leaving on this day, and he had not the heart to watch him walk through the front gates for the last time. "Do you have the heart to live with yourself if you do not say goodbye?" He was amazed at the clarity of the voice coming from the statue. He thought the god had manifested herself before him to provide wisdom. The rustling of leaves behind told him otherwise.

It was Kira. "I know you well enough that you would ache for eternity if you passed on this moment." She walked up and knelt beside him at the foot of the shrine. He knew she was right, but his head was still dizzy with the questions posed by Haru's departure.

"He believes he has all he needs to be a samurai. The school will acknowledge that he is a samurai. But how can he feel that way? I have reached such great heights, learned so much, and yet..." Yoshi cut off his thought, but Kira picked it right up.

"Why don't you join him? You are not being boastful to say you have achieved much more than he has. You are a great samurai, Yoshi-san. I know you have a destiny you wish to seek, why not seek it now?" She did not look at him as she spoke. While sincere in her suggestion, Yoshi sensed she feared his agreement.

"Would you like me to go?" whispered Yoshi in response. He also feared her response but slowly built up the courage to look toward her. As he awaited her response, he found himself mesmerized. The sunlight broke through the cloudy sky and found its way to Kira's face, giving her an alabaster glow that melted his heart. She was right, he had confessed to her many times of his desire to be a great samurai and seek revenge on the killer of his father. Not a day went by he did not think of that journey, but when he met her, an alternative destiny invaded his consciousness from time to time. A destiny of settling down with her, raising a large family, and growing crops as a simple man of the land.

"I would not want you to stay if it was not what was right for you," Kira finally answered. Turning to him, she sighed and smiled. "So much of what we have learned here, of what we have taught each other, has been that we each have our own unique path and way. I would sooner die than have you stay and deny your destiny because of some loyalty to me." A tear slid down Kira's cheek while she fought hard not to have another one follow.

Yoshi placed his hand on hers and held it tenderly. "I am not ready to leave." He knew for some time that a decision would have to be made, but not today. He also knew she was right about how to make that choice, but he could not admit it to her. Decisions are driven by one's values, what feels right to the individual. He had behaved and acted in manners that ran against who he was, and every time he did, he felt the pain. It was as if his emotions and feelings were a detection system alerting him that he was going off his path. He valued above all else the pursuit of knowledge and providing that knowledge to others. So much was still left for him to discover and learn, that leaving the school would leave him empty. Leaving Kira, especially at this moment, would open a void in him he feared could never be filled.

Together they rose from the shrine and descended to the campus. As they reached the main courtyard, they spotted Haru being escorted by two senior senpai. As was the custom when a student left the school, there was a ceremony in front of the main temple. In the ceremony, the student relinquished his Sword of Illumination, and in turn, he or she was handed a new sword. This sword was to be worn as proof that the recipient was a trained samurai from the School of Aspen. Even from their distant vantage point, Yoshi could tell his friend possessed an air of confidence and contentment. It seemed his somber gait of days earlier had been inflated to lift him off the ground.

As Kira and Yoshi watched the procession, Yoshi

suddenly thought of something he wanted to do. Excusing himself from Kira, he raced back to his quarters. Rummaging through his father's chest of scrolls, he searched for a specific one. Yoshi had all these scrolls memorized by now and could easily rewrite them. Tucked in the bottom corner of the chest was the scroll he was seeking. It told of the great duel Miyamoto Musashi fought with Sasaki Kojirō on Ganryu Island.

As the great samurai Musashi rowed out to an island to meet his adversary, he carved a sword out of one of the wooden oars in his boat. Upon reaching the shoreline and watching his foe approach, he sprung to action. His hand-carved sword was of greater length than the weapon wielded by Kojirō. Musashi's advantage caught his opponent completely off guard which allowed him to dispatch Kojirō in short order. Haru always shared how much he loved the ingenuity Musashi exhibited and that it was his favorite tale.

Yoshi knew the ceremony was not a long one and Haru would be departing soon. He raced back across the campus and to the temple, but the group had already dispersed. He ran over to the interior gate to find the servants shutting it. Hollering out for them to open it again, the servants hastily obliged more from fear of the crazy-sounding samurai than out of a desire to help. As the gate cracked open, Yoshi slipped through and raced down the stone steps. Below he could see the procession of Haru and the senpai nearing the outer gate.

Once he got within earshot, he yelled for them to wait. The stunned group stopped in their tracks and a smiling Haru ran up to greet his friend.

"Haru-san. Forgive me, but I have been suffering from a bout of severe selfishness. I have been worried about losing a great friend and not rejoicing as that friend finds his destiny. Haru-san, you are a great samurai and a great friend. Please take this as an eternal token of our camaraderie." Yoshi bowed deeply and presented his father's scroll to Haru.

Haru was clearly moved by the display and the gift. He seemed to want to respectfully decline the generous offer but somehow knew it would be to no avail. "Yoshi-san, you have a destiny that will take you to greatness," Haru whispered to him. "I will pray to the gods each day that our journeys will merge once again." With that, Haru accepted the scroll and bowed deeply in return.

As the gates closed shut, Yoshi felt a chapter of his life also closed shut. Haru was a friend and confidant who had shared Yoshi's experiences of being a student. With him gone, he felt that aspect of his life was over. He was no longer a young student learning the ways of a samurai. He had passed that stage. While he would never stop being a student of life, he was clearly more than just a student. In many ways, he was a samurai.

"It's pie in the sky." Tom took the blanket on loan from the old man and brought it up to his neck to fight off the evening chill. "People don't have an infinite number of choices. Sometimes you just have to opt for the lesser of two evils."

Tom thought about his own predicament. He was living in constant fear of losing his job and his ability to support his family. He was also afraid that this very same job was causing him to lose his family. If it was not physically keeping him away, he was mentally distracted during the time he was with them. *What choices did I have?* he argued to himself. "Take me for example," he finally opened up to the old man. "I hate my job. I hate what it is doing to me and my relationship with my family. What should I do? Quit? I can't find anything that will pay as much. So I choose to stick it out. The lesser of two evils." Tom had been reluctant to share any specifics about his own life with the stranger up until this point. But the late hour, the kindness of this complete stranger, and the utter hopelessness he was experiencing conspired to open him up.

"You actually ended up making a different choice, didn't you?" the old man offered.

"What do you mean?" a puzzled Tom asked.

"You are here."

The words stung Tom to his core. He wanted to object but could not muster the energy to put up a hopeless fight. The old man was right, and he knew it. When pushed to his limits and forced to decide, he chose neither to stick it out nor make a change. He just fled. "The truth is I made no choice," he finally whispered.

Tom felt defeated and the old man seemed to read it on his face. "Ah, but that is a choice in itself. When you are faced with a problem, how many times do you opt to do nothing and hope it resolves on its own? I find it works sometimes. The point that young Yoshi realized was his decisions do not have to be confined by circumstance."

"But they are confined," Tom countered. "The idea that you can just choose anything seems ridiculous. Sometimes you have to make a choice. Right or left. Yes or no. Win or lose." Tom was adamant on this point. His mind was framed to look at the world in a binary fashion. The world was either *zero or one*. In his world of finance, the numbers were a constant and could not be argued. They could be altered, massaged, or just simply falsified, but they were factual entities and would be proved out in the end. His decision to flee was viewed by him as a *zero* option. The problem he was attempting to overcome was coming up with the *one* option.

"I stand corrected, your decisions are confined," the old man conceded.

Tom was mildly taken aback by the old man's admission, although his victory felt hollow. He was hoping to be corrected and that the storyteller would offer an answer to this dilemma.

"You are confined in your choice by who you are. Decisions made that are incongruent to your identity will always lead you astray, and ultimately return you back to the same fork in the road."

"Or the same side of the road," mused Tom. He recognized the meaning in the old man's reply. His decision to just leave everything behind caused him great pain and strife because it ran counter to who he was. He sighed and stoked through another branch on the campfire. He knew returning was the right thing to do, but it pained him to have to face the same dilemmas all over again. "How does one make decisions that are right?" he asked.

"Not by being right, but by doing the right thing," answered the old man.

Both Yoshi and Tom were about to recognize the difference.

CHAPTER 17

Sword of Decisions:
Part II

Yoshi heard the echoing cries of battle before he saw the smoke breaking above the southern tree line. Without seeing the combatants, he knew it involved the rōnin gang that had been terrorizing the countryside, and who had killed his father. Tossing his bushel of recently harvested apples to the ground, Yoshi raced to the barn that sat beside his family home. Hung up in perfectly arranged order along the back wall was a full suit of samurai armor, illuminated by a beam of sunlight coming in through the roof. Yoshi hastily lifted each piece off its hooks and gathered them in his arm. In his zeal to rush out, he smashed into the rice paper door, ripping it from its attachments and sending it flying away.

Sliding off his shoes, Yoshi entered the family home. "Come, I need your help to prepare," he hollered. Through the thin paper veil of the door leading to the bedroom, he saw the matriarch of the family compose herself and slowly slide the door open. Greeting Yoshi was a woman ashen-faced with concern and dread. Fighting her fear, she let slip out the bright smile that won over the young samurai's heart at the School of Aspen.

"From the sound, the battle seems very close," Kira finally said. She took the pieces of armor from Yoshi and laid them out on the ground.

Without saying a word, Yoshi asked for assistance in suiting up by throwing off his garments. Like they had done hundreds of times prior, Kira meticulously, but quickly, secured each piece of iron and mesh around her husband's body. Once all the pieces were firmly tightened, she handed him his helmet and a single medallion, the same his mother shared with his father on the day of his death. Yoshi bowed slightly and she quickly departed, returning in a flash. In her arms was a long object wrapped in a white cloth. Gently taking the object, Yoshi unwrapped the cloth revealing a katana still encased in its sheath. Sliding it out of the grip of its cover, the sword's blade gave off a magnificent reflection. Engraved along the blade were the words: *The School of Aspen.*

Yoshi calmly sheathed the sword and slid it into his waistband. He was so focused on getting himself prepared physically and mentally for battle, he had not said a word to Kira. Looking at her now, words failed to reach his mouth. She remained smiling at him but with eyes glistening from tears. Yoshi sensed the energy she was exerting to prevent those tears from flowing could ignite the sun. He placed his hand on her ivory cheek. "I will be back," he said in the hope of calming her fears.

Yoshi turned to exit the front door and confront his fate on the field of battle. "Don't go!" Although Kira said it in a whisper, it sounded to Yoshi like the bellow of a thousand horns in unison. "Stay with me. Stay with your family."

When the moment had faced his own father, Yoshi's mother never asked him to stay. Yoshi had never asked his father to stay. While both yearned to speak those words when the time came, Kira was the one with the nerve to say them. "I have to," was the only response Yoshi could blurt out.

"But you don't have to. If you have learned anything, it

is that you have choices. You can be everything you want to be and still not have to fight. Stay with me. Learn with me. Love with me. Is that not all you have sought?"

The sound of the fighting grew louder and louder as Kira spoke. Yoshi turned to the open doorway and saw the battle had breached the farm fences and was inching closer. "I made a vow to avenge my father and that is what I must do."

"And you made a vow to love me and care for me. Does that have merit to you too?"

Turning away from Kira once again, he could see the fighting was now near the house's doorsteps. The site was ghastlier than he had ever witnessed. Men gruesomely stabbed each other. Limbs flew off torsos. The blood-curdling screams of a samurai's last breath rang unabated through the air. Yoshi's heart raced and his grip on the sword tightened. At any second, he felt like the muscles in his legs would explode, sending him rocketing into the fray.

"Stay here...with me," despite the roar of battle outside, he heard Kira's soothing voice as if it was coming from within his own chest. "Stay with..."

The morning bell awoke Yoshi, shooting him up from his lightly padded mat. He looked at the doorway of his room half expecting to have the battle rip through it. Nothing but the gongs of the morning bell greeted him. It took another couple of moments for him to realize he was still a student at the School of Aspen.

Although weighing heavily on his mind, Yoshi refrained from sharing his dream with Kira or Daichi. In stark and extremely vivid details, his dream forced him to face a decision he knew he would have to make someday. He sought to bury that thought into some deep region of his consciousness in a fool's hope that it would somehow disappear. While avoidance was not the way a samurai tackles issues, Yoshi could not help himself. Just like the scar from an old wound, the issue was always there, rising to the surface. He figured the dream was his dilemma bursting out of the area he had hidden it, telling him, *It must be addressed.*

A couple of days later, Kira cajoled him to take some time off from his studies to walk with her to the shrine. She had not seen it in its newly completed state and was anxious to take in the results of her labor. She did most of the talking on the hike up to the shrine as she related her excitement about the advancements she was making in her studies and the success of her musical group. While most of the musicians were female students, she boasted about a small but eager group of males who have joined them. It was a not too subtle hint for Yoshi. He smiled at Kira's hidden suggestion but chose not to respond. He was busy enough without adding endeavors to his full plate. *Besides,* he thought, *if my lack of musical skills made my own mother give up teaching me, why should I put that burden on poor Kira?*

She now wore the Sword of Values on her side, a sign of her recent promotion and advancement at the school. Just as excited as she was about her musical group, she was equally elated at her rise up the ranks. "I shall soon join you," she teased with an infectious smile of hers.

His smile and silence must have spoken volumes because Kira's smile faded and concern washed over her face. Yoshi did not want to worry her or bring her pain, but he was not ready to share what was on his mind. Not yet. He could almost see a question forming on her lips, but she said nothing and kept pace beside him.

The duo broke into the clearing and stopped to gaze upon the shrine. Covered in a glaze of frost, Benzaiten's shrine sparkled in the mid-afternoon sun. Kira remained still as she took in the beautiful site. While small compared to many other shrines of the day, it looked as magnificent as any of the greatest shrines commissioned by the Emperor. Filled with pride and reverence, they slowly walked up to the shrine and knelt in prayer. After several minutes in deep reflection, Yoshi stood up, bowed to the shrine, and walked away.

"Stay here... with me."

A chill ran up his spine; Kira's words echoing in his mind. They sounded exactly like those she spoke in his dream, beckoning him away from going to battle. He spun to her, his face white, unable to contain his despair, his fear. On the rational side of his brain, Yoshi knew Kira had only meant for him to stay with her a little longer before heading back to campus; but he couldn't stop the image of her from his dream, the sound of her voice. It all came bubbling to the surface, paralyzing him. He needed to tell her, but he had no idea how to begin.

Kira read his mind and whispered, "Talk to me, Yoshi-san."

"I had a dream the other night," Yoshi began. He described all the events from the dream in as much detail as he could recall. He depicted that rush of energy and excitement he felt as he prepared for the great battle that awaited him. He also described the angst and confusion he felt as she asked him to stay, to forget his vengeance in favor of her love. Even as he stood in the chilly winter afternoon, he felt the warmth of blood rushing throughout his body as his heartbeat raced. "I fear the dream is a portent of reality," he concluded. "Someday, I will have to make that choice and I dread it with all my being."

Kira stood silently as Yoshi spoke. To Yoshi, she seemed to be taking it all in and processing it in her own manner to develop a response. But none came. She looked all around at the area of the shrine and then lifted her face skyward, as if an answer could be found in the clouds. From the sky came her response in the form of one, then two, then hundreds of tiny snowflakes. Just like Daichi, Kira loved the snow but for a different reason. She had once told Yoshi that she loved the feel of snowflakes falling against her skin. He remembered her making him walk with her whenever the sky showered them. She could never explain it, but Yoshi could see it always brought her pure joy. Closing her eyes now and smiling, she absorbed each flake as they hit her ivory face.

"I wish to be with you forever Yoshi-san," Kira finally spoke. "And therefore, I always shall be. My love for you remains when you are with me and away from me. Wherever our destinies take us, whatever paths each of us choose, my love will follow you."

"As will mine." Yoshi swallowed hard. Battling to keep control of his emotions, he grabbed hold of her hand, more to steady himself than to hold her.

"Because of that, you never have to make that choice. We will always be together." Gripping his hand tightly, she leaned her head back and let the snow cascade over her face then returned her gaze to Yoshi. "And if you ever need a reminder of my love, remember the snow. Whenever a flake brushes your face, consider it a kiss from me." Kira pulled herself close to Yoshi and ever so gently placed her lips on his cheek, leaving it there for an extended moment, a moment Yoshi wished would never end. When she finally pulled away, Yoshi closed his eyes and faced skyward. As each flake landed on his smiling face, Kira's love melted over him.

"She showed me the greatest example of living in the world of *and* instead of *or*." Yoshi was going on like a wound-up little boy as he helped Daichi carry firewood to his cabin. During their expedition, Yoshi told his old master all about his dreams and fears of losing his love. He had never been so open about his emotions for Kira to anyone else. With each confession of his amorous feelings, he felt his heart beat a little faster and a little lighter. It was as if the revelations were unlocking a band around his heart.

Taking it all in with a wondrous smile was Daichi. After all the times Yoshi came to him sullen, confused, or frustrated, it must be an extraordinary sight for the old monk to see Yoshi so jubilant. A little reward to the old monk for his dedicated tutelage. "I am happy for the both of you, and also proud. You both have made a great leap in understanding the key to a samurai's decisions. Keep that in mind when you make choices."

The two crossed through the main courtyard on their way to Daichi's cabin. As they made the turn around the main temple, Yoshi spied in the distance the young student he aided, Takeshi. He had been looking for the opportunity to introduce Daichi to his own little potential protégé and this seemed like the perfect opportunity. "Let me introduce you to the young man I made such a difference with," said Yoshi. Just as he was about to call out the young student's name, he saw him begin to sprint in his direction. Yoshi glowed at the obvious sign of affection and respect. "The wisdom I imparted must have been more influential than I thought," he whispered to Daichi as Takeshi came closer.

It was only when the young man was a few feet away that Yoshi realized the young man had a different destination in mind. Turning his head around, his stomach nearly came out of his mouth at the sight of the intended target.

Yoshi felt the firm hand of Daichi grasp his shoulder to pull him away, but Yoshi felt compelled to continue watching as Takeshi sprinted up and bowed deeply before Togo. Taking a satchel from his new idol's hands, the young student marched a few paces behind the strutting student as they headed back across the campus.

Continuing their trek to Daichi's cabin, Yoshi did not utter a word. The air had left his lungs leaving speech out of the question. Spinning in his mind were dozens of questions, all one form of the greater query, *Why would he follow Togo?* Shock turned to anger when the duo entered the cabin and Yoshi disgustedly dropped the firewood on the floor.

"I should never have helped him." Venom spewed from each syllable of the sentence as Yoshi finally found the air to speak. "He does not deserve a scrap of my breath, of my knowledge, of my time. How dare he run into the putrid arms of that, that demon? If I had known, I'd have taught him a lesson with my bokken rather than with words." Yoshi paced back and forth as he continued with his diatribe. All the while, the old monk calmly listened, occasionally nodded in agreement, and made some tea for the two of them.

During a pause in the tirade, Daichi interrupted. "Care for some tea?"

A bit cold and with a throat sore from his rough dissertation, he stopped his rant and politely thanked the old monk for the offer. He took a small sip, expecting the usual flavorful taste of Daichi's special brew. He never expected what ended up hitting his taste buds. Almost as a reflex motion, his lips pursed, and he nearly spit the liquid out of his mouth. His fear of showing disrespect toward the old monk forced him to think better of it and bitterly swallow the horrible-tasting tea.

Studying his young friend's reaction, the old monk took a long sip of the tea without any reaction. "How do like the tea?"

Yoshi thought about lying and saying it was its typical delicious flavor, but he knew the old monk would be able to read any falsehoods. "To be perfectly honest, I think you did something different because it tastes, well, it tastes awful. Although, I do thank you for the offer and your hospitality." Yoshi's last sentence was a desperate attempt to avoid any sign of disrespect.

"And yet you decided to take me up on the offer of tea?"

"I was thirsty and expected your usual great blend of tea. This caught me off guard," Yoshi fumbled with the cup as he explained himself.

"Maybe you will never take me up on the offer of tea

again." The monk, without any sign of emotion, took another sip of the tea.

"Well, no. I would be happy to accept an offer of tea. I just hope the taste will be... a little more to my liking I suppose." Yoshi was a bit frustrated with the way this conversation was going. All he wanted to do was let out some steam about his feelings of betrayal and enjoy some tea. Now, he found himself in a senseless argument.

"I suppose if you had to do it over again, you would respectfully decline the tea," the monk egged on.

"Yes, but that is not really possible, is it? One can't go back in time and change what was done. This is silly." As the last word escaped his lips, he realized he was right. It was silly. It was silly for the old monk to suggest he would have turned down the tea. Yoshi had no way of knowing the tea would taste putrid. Knowing what he knew at the time, he would accept the tea. The idea of going back in time to redress his decision was just as foolish since it is impossible.

He also realized it was silly to question his decision to help the young Takeshi. He felt compelled to help the young student because that is who he is. His values always directed him toward the direction of sharing, helping, and providing knowledge. Denying that help to the young student would be denying who Yoshi was. "I helped Takeshi-san not because it was right, but because it was the right thing for me to do based on who I say I am and my values. It is not necessarily about the results."

"It is more than just the results, it is having an attachment to those results," the old monk finally answered. "Your expectation was that your actions would be received in accordance to how you wished them to be. You will live a life of constant disappointment if you constantly hold such expectations."

Yoshi's brow furled in puzzlement. "So, I should not care about the results of my decisions?"

"You should care about what you can control. Your decisions you can control. How others receive or interpret your decisions you cannot control. You do decisions based upon what satisfies your values and the path of life you wish to create. Attachments add an undue burden to your decisions—fear of denial, fear of rejection, fear of loss. They cloud what is most important."

"And that is living up to one's own values." Yoshi was beginning to understand with greater clarity. During his time at the School of Aspen, he had worked diligently on creating a life of balance. He has worked on his identity, mission and purpose, roles, outcomes, and values. All of these elements were necessary for his decisions.

"Do the best decision you can based on your values, and let it go." The old monk took another long sip of the tea. Holding the liquid in his mouth for a second, Daichi suddenly spit it back out into his cup. "My goodness, this is rancid tea."

It was unseasonably warm three days later as Yoshi walked toward the school's farm. It had been a hard day of lessons for Yoshi and his mind was still reeling from the deep philosophical debate in class that morning. He was also still coming to grips with letting go of the attachments to his decisions. "Do the best decision you can based on your values, and let it go," he heard the old monk say over and over in his mind's voice.

He knew he needed some *get out of his mind* time so when he reached the farm, he saddled up one of the horses and rode around the school grounds, eventually making his way to the main gate. After a brief explanation to the gatekeeper that he was going on a quick ride and would be back shortly, the gates opened and Yoshi let the steed fly, barreling down the hillside and into the forest.

With the air rushing across his face and blowing back his jet-black hair, times like this brought him back to the simpler times of his youth. As a boy, he loved letting loose his horse to lead him on an uncharted journey. The journey always ended up with the two, the horse and the boy, discovering new trails and eventually new ways back home. Today, it let the older version of Yoshi think about his life and his escape from it.

He thought of the engraving on the Sword of Decisions, *What decision that I do at this moment will create my life's path.* He fretted about what decision the Sword spoke of and what the consequences could be to his life's path. He felt the weight and responsibility of such a decision. Recalling Daichi's words, *"Make the best decision you can, and let it go"* put him at ease and caused him to relax his grip on the reins.

Without commands or pulls from Yoshi, his horse made turns and cuts through the forest, entering and exiting dales, swinging to his left and the right. "You have it right old boy," Yoshi shouted. The horse was serving as the perfect model. The horse did its decisions and stuck with it, never looking or circling back. It had ridden these hills and woods for years and trusted its own instincts, just as Yoshi now trusted his horse.

Suddenly, he pulled up on the horse to come to a stop. A revelation came to mind, and he just had to have the moment to himself. He leapt off the horse and circled around him, deep in thought. *Trust, that is the key. I place trust in others, in Daichi, in Kira, even in this beast, but do I place trust in myself?* The question was rhetorical, for if he was honest with himself, he knew the answer was no. The person he should have the most faith in, he failed to trust.

He looked the horse straight in the eyes, and oddly the horse returned his gaze. It was as if the horse understood what his rider was saying and agreed. Slowly, the horse stepped toward Yoshi and turned before him. The stance was a clear suggestion that it was time for Yoshi to mount the horse and take the lead.

He hopped on the horse and gained his bearings. He could judge from the position of the sun and the location of the great mountains to the west, which way was the direction back to the school. They were a bit farther out than he thought they would be. "The old boy still has some power in his legs," Yoshi said as he patted his stead along the side of the neck.

As he leaned back to begin his return trip, he caught something out of the side of his sight. Something looked odd laying in the mix of dirt and snow to his right. Cocking his head, he stared to get a better idea of it. While it looked slightly like a dead leaf, the texture was thicker and seemed larger than any leaf. He dismounted and walked over to satisfy his curiosity. As he walked closer, he gradually recognized it as a parchment, muddy and torn up a bit. He bent down to examine it. Taking it into his hands, a wave of dizziness and nausea befell him as he unfurled it. He now recognized the parchment, for only a few weeks earlier he had given it to his closest friend at the School of Aspen.

Damp and slightly torn, Yoshi turned it over and found a red stain on the back that had no other explanation but blood. He imagined Haru's face as he saw him for the last time, but slowly that visage turned to one of his friend's face in panic and then anguish. Something terrible happened and his mind spun with possibilities. He quickly jumped back on the horse and circled around the area looking for any more clues. Yoshi could tell from the way the branches were bent and broken that one or several people rushed out to the north. He directed his steed in that direction to follow the trail. To his dismay the trail he thought he had discovered ended abruptly. He looked frantically for any other clues or signs of a path but discovered none. In his frustration, he began shouting out for Haru, in a normal voice at first then increasingly louder. He reached a point when he could hear his cries echoing through the forest.

After one last yell, he heard something that was not his own voice bouncing back. The sound was distinctly different, and he rushed off in that direction, praying to the gods that it was somehow Haru. Following the ever-growing sound, Yoshi broke through the trees and pulled up on top of a hill overlooking a wide valley. Suddenly breaking through the line of trees, far in the distance was the source of the cries. It was a band of about a dozen men on horseback. Instantly, he recognized them as rōnin, assuming they were the ones who attacked the fur traders. He also concluded they must have something to do with Haru. The marauders caught sight of the lone man on horseback and directed their raging horses in his direction. Yoshi's blood boiled as he thought of the plight of his friend and his father. His first impulse was to meet them head-on and unleash the full fury of his anger. But the cooler side of Yoshi's psyche reminded him that, despite his great skill with the sword, one against twelve were odds even the great Mushashi would consider folly.

Turning back his horse, Yoshi gained his bearings and raced off in the direction of the school. Sensing the impending danger, the horse pumped his legs with every ounce of energy he could muster, heeding his rider's commands swiftly and without hesitation. Yoshi was asking much of the old horse to outpace the younger and faster foes. He knew there might come a point when the rōnin would reach him and he would have to engage them in battle. His mind raced with the options he could employ in such an event.

Those options looked like they would be used sooner than he had feared. The raucous sounds of his pursuers were closing on him fast and he knew he was still hundreds of yards away from the gates of the school. As he nearly crossed a wide clearing in the woods, Yoshi stole a look behind him. His heart nearly sank into his stomach when he spied one, then two, then the rest of the rōnin, entering the clearing from the other side. The split-second turn of his head prevented him from seeing the dead tree trunk lying in his path. Just as Yoshi swung his head back around, his horse leaped into the air to clear the trunk. Unprepared for the sudden move, Yoshi flew backwards, losing his grip on the reins. As soon as he sensed he would fly off the horse, he rolled his body to brace for the impending fall. Catching the ground with his shoulder, he rolled into a soft patch of snow. Stung but not injured, Yoshi did not allow himself a moment to clear his head. He immediately regained his footing and raced after his horse who he saw slowing down up ahead.

In one leap, he landed on the horse's back. Just as his legs kicked the horse into actions, an object shot past his right cheek. He felt the graze of its feather as the arrow stuck firmly in the tree just ahead. They were drawing very near, and he knew he would have to fight, but not here. He raced ahead looking for an area with a lot of brush and areas to camouflage. He knew the only method of fighting he had a chance to survive was with an attack and retreat tactic. Turning the horse to the left then the right to avoid the archer behind him from getting a clean shot, Yoshi's heart pounded through his clothes as he desperately searched for a suitable area.

Up ahead he thought he saw a clearing, which would not have interested him except for the fact he saw the outline of a man on horseback there. He thought he recognized it to be someone from the School of Aspen but was not confident whether it was genuine recognition or wishful thinking. Unfortunately, time did not allow any further analysis. Two against twelve was not great odds, but still better. He changed course and headed straight for the man on horseback.

Reaching the clearing, he was elated to find his instinct was correct. The clothing instantly revealed the figure to be a student at the school. The sudden noise caused by Yoshi crashing through the trees startled the student. He immediately unsheathed his sword and rushed to meet

Yoshi. Yoshi immediately hollered to allay any threats. "I am Yoshi, a student at the School of Aspen. We must prepare for battle." Even after they made eye contact with each other, it took the two startled students several seconds to recognize each other. Yoshi's elation came crashing down as he realized the identity of his would be ally.

"What nonsense are you talking about Yoshi-san," indignantly muttered Togo, his sword still ready for battle. The confusion and shock on his face cleared as he heard the thunder behind Yoshi followed by the sight of its source. As Yoshi circled beside Togo, the rōnin came pouring out of the clearing. Togo was stunned frozen at the sight, but the already agitated Yoshi took charge. Leaping off his horse, he commanded Togo to do the same. "Togo-san, you boast about being the best swordsman at the School of Aspen. If there was ever a time to show me your superiority, this would be it." Yoshi unsheathed his sword and prepared for the onslaught.

Yoshi's command woke Togo out of his trance. Regaining his composure, Togo took out his wakizashi sword, raised it above his head, and yelled at the on comers, "I am the great Togo of the house of Hansui. Come enjoy your last moment on earth if you wish." Yoshi knew Togo was a prideful and confident man, but this display of bravado caught him by surprise.

It seemed to have the same effect on the rōnin, because just as suddenly as they had burst into the clearing, they pulled back on their horses and came to a halt. The group held their ground sizing up the two young samurai before them. Yoshi was struck by the look of confusion in their eyes, but he did not understand why they would feel such a way. They clearly had superior numbers and greater experience. *How can they be afraid of just two students?* he thought to himself.

Neither of the two sides made a step forward for what Yoshi felt was an eternity. The only sound he could hear was his own labored breathing and pumping heart. His grip tightened on his sword as he studied his opponents and the surrounding area in order to formulate strategies. He looked at Togo and realized that if he was going to do battle, there was no other student at the school he would rather be standing beside. If he allowed his mind to wander, he would have laughed at fate for her sense of humor in drawing them side by side. But what he was about to embark on was hardly a laughing matter.

A lone samurai from the band rode his horse ahead of the group. Yoshi tensed up but was amazed at the calmness Togo displayed. Just when Yoshi was sure the attack was imminent, the most unexpected event happened. The apparent leader shouted out a command and the group of twelve turned and trotted quietly back out into the woods.

The young duo stood in silence until they heard the last of the rōnin fade away in the distance. Sheathing his sword, Togo bombastically slapped Yoshi on the back. "They were wise not to tangle with two soon-to-be graduates of the great School of Aspen."

"I believe they did harm to Haru," was the only response the still shocked Yoshi could muster. "I discovered signs... of a struggle." Yoshi could not bring himself to discuss it in any greater detail, still struck by the sudden turn of events. The shock was quickly overtaken with dread for the fate of his friend.

Mounting his horse, Togo studied Yoshi then the sky. "We do not have much daylight left. You've had a full day and probably an empty stomach. You can fight them another day." Yoshi listened to the suggestion and mounted his tired horse. The two rode back to the school in silence with Yoshi constantly looking and listening for any sign of trouble. His mind was overwhelmed with thoughts of Haru's well-being. As the sun began its descent behind the mountains, Yoshi and Togo saw the great iron gates of the School of Aspen. With the school so close, a new thought invaded Yoshi's mind. It was spurned by an off-the-cuff remark Togo had uttered earlier but it left a deep impression on Yoshi.

"...*two soon-to-be graduates of the great School of Aspen.*" At that moment he never felt so ready to leave the school and so compelled to stay.

CHAPTER 18

Sword of Decisions:
Part III

The campus was abuzz as news circulated about Togo and Yoshi's encounter with the rōnin and the unknown fate of the former student Haru. The reaction was a mixture of anger and indignation. "How dare these hoodlums attack one of us? Do they not know the great samurai that are housed here? We should go out and rid the countryside of them!" These were the common sentiments of the students and even senior senpai throughout the school.

For several days, the topic dominated the conversation across campus. In between classes, during meals, and during Yoshi's evening study group, students could not stop railing against the criminals. Yoshi's blood continued to boil as he listened to the discussions but refrained from joining. Walking back to their quarters one evening, Kira prodded Yoshi to speak about his emotions. He gave her the standard response that he was nervous, but he is calm now. "I just wish we could gather up a group of our finest warriors and track them down. We need to protect the area from these people," he lamented. Both Kira and Yoshi knew there was another reason Yoshi had for going after the rōnin. He would not admit it aloud but a part of him screamed out for revenge. Revenge not just for Haru, but revenge for his father. He saw this group as representative of the group that had slain his father and he itched at the opportunity to seek redemption.

An edict from the school's elders doused water over

Yoshi's flame. At the steps of the main temple, a senior monk read the statement issued by the elders. It reminded the students what their purpose was as attendees of the School of Aspen. "Steps shall be taken to remedy this situation," the monk read. "Students should not concern themselves with these matters but rather on the matters of learning, developing, and growing into the samurai they wish to be. A true samurai would never allow distractions to derail him from his destiny and path." The edict had its intended effect. During the course of the next few days, the angry conversations dissipated, and the student body and campus activities returned to a sense of normalcy.

Stealing away a few moments from his afternoon assignments, Yoshi trekked up to the old shrine. Despite the rest of the campus calming down, he still possessed the sting of rage in his stomach. This afternoon he thought some time with the goddess Benzaiten could soothe him over. When he reached the old shrine, he was taken aback to see someone else was already seeking her counsel. He considered leaving the visitor alone to his prayers but was stopped from departing by the stranger's voice.

"Please do not leave on account of me," said the old man. Yoshi instantly recognized the voice of Daichi. He was not in the mood for conversation but thought it was rude to leave him, so he walked over to the shrine and knelt beside the old monk. Expecting the monk to engage him in conversation, Yoshi was surprised when several moments went by without a word spoken. Eventually, Yoshi got around to the purpose of his visit and began meditating. Just as the air on the hilltop was cooling his skin, he hoped the goddess would douse the flame that raged inside him.

Why can't I let my anger go? he asked the mute statue. *What is stopping me from gathering up a few others and going after those murderers myself? I have the skill and ability to defeat them. I have the chance to exact my revenge. I am a samurai!* His thoughts rang so loud in his head that he stole a glance over to Daichi to see if he could hear them. The monk remained silent with his head bowed.

As he looked upon the mediating monk, Yoshi's internal debate eased, and he realized the answer to his questions. He could not leave because he had not finished with the School of Aspen. He knew there was more knowledge it had to offer. Who he was dictated that he needed to remain. His lust for revenge still held strong in him, but his temperament and logic kept it at bay. *This would not create the path for who I say I am,* Yoshi concluded.

Yoshi turned his gaze back to the stone-faced goddess before him. This revelation provided the serenity he sought. It also felt as if he stumbled on a valuable lesson.

The stress induced by his desire for revenge clouded his better judgment. By stepping back and taking the time to really study his decision, he made a choice based on logic and soundness. He concluded rashness and anxiety are detriments to decisions.

Yoshi also thought back to the Sword of Values engraving:

What values do I desire in order for me to fulfill the destiny of who I have chosen to be?

At the time, he considered the order of his values to be set in stone, but during his time at the School of Aspen, he discovered his values could evolve. The hierarchy of his values changed. Initially, the highest value was to get revenge for his father. Today, as he sat in front of the shrine, he smiled at the recognition that his highest value is to be a samurai that is in service of others and not in service of his own self-interest.

He suddenly heard the old monk beside him stir and rise up. "It is time for me to go, Yoshi-san."

Yoshi looked up to judge the position of the sun. "By the looks of it, I also have to get back to campus. Perhaps we can meet up again tomorrow and have a more vocal conversation." Yoshi was now eager to share his emotions and the discovery he had made on decisions.

"You do not understand," Daichi replied stone-faced. "It is time for me to leave the school. My path is leading me on a new journey."

The young samurai broke out into laughter that gradually lessened as he realized his mentor was not making a joke. Looking into his eyes, he searched for any semblance of levity but found none. His mind screamed for a reason. "Why?" was the only word he could muster.

"I have done all I need to do here. During my time here, I have learned much and grown as a man." He paused to look upon the shrine. "I have also grown as a carpenter." A smile finally broke out on the monk's face, slightly easing Yoshi's despair. "There is more knowledge I seek, more challenges to endure, more souls to encounter. Who I am requires I seek this path, just as who you are will determine your path."

Yoshi wanted to scream out for him to stay, to argue there are many more lessons he needed and counsel to receive. His heart wanted to grab the old monk and shake the decision out of him. If that did not work, he would prohibit, by sword point if necessary, the monk from leaving him. If this had occurred even just a few months earlier, Yoshi might have made such a display. But he had grown and matured greatly over that time. *"Each person has their own way and no man should judge another's path,"* he scolded himself as he recalled a lesson from one of his father's scrolls. Holding back his flood of emotions, Yoshi asked the monk when he would be leaving.

"Tonight. My possessions are few and what I cannot carry on one horse's back will be left for the school to do with as they wish. As for that odd contraption I ride, I would leave it to you, but the infirmary here has enough to do." That brought a chuckle and an acknowledging nod from Yoshi. He had not yet managed to get all the wheels aligned and with his old master gone, fretted whether he ever would.

The realization of the moment overtook them both. Swallowing hard, Yoshi broke the pause. "Daichi-san, you have been a mentor, confidant, tormentor, and teacher. But more than any of those, you have been a friend. I will cherish the time we have spent and the knowledge you have imparted for all the days of my life. Because of you, I am a samurai." He bowed deeply before the old monk.

Straightening his back, Daichi returned the bow with an even deeper one. When the two rose up, Yoshi thought he detected a welling of his master's eyes. He had always marveled about how well Daichi held his emotions in check, but he thought he saw the first signs of raw emotion from him. He had never felt more connected to Daichi than at that moment.

When the two of them reached the main campus, Daichi turned toward his cabin and Yoshi for the farm. Each gave a silent acknowledgment to the other and went their separate ways. Yoshi knew this was the last time they would see each other. The monk had a way of living his life without much fanfare and he assumed his departure from the School of Aspen would be consistent with this approach.

A wave of melancholy swept over him as he paused in his tracks and turned to see his mentor one last time. To his pleasant surprise, Daichi had done the same. The pupil and teacher locked eyes once more and bowed deeply to each other in silence. Before they left each other for the last time, the old monk shouted one more bit of advice. "Yoshi-san, remember, a Sword of Illumination is not a singular weapon, but rather a group of weapons that must be used in totality to be truly effective."

The next morning, Yoshi took an alternate route to his lessons by swinging by Daichi's cabin. Although he knew the odds were slim at best, he hoped he would have one more chat with his old master. Indeed, to his chagrin but not his surprise, Daichi's cabin was abandoned. All traces that he once lived there were gone. As he expected, the old monk must have slipped out in the night, although he was not sure if it was by preference or because he wanted to elude the marauding rōnin.

Just as he was about to leave, an object caught Yoshi's attention. In his haste to see if Daichi was still there, he almost missed the small book lying inside the cabin. Covered in a tattered leather binding, it was obviously left behind for him to find. Yoshi picked it up and etched on its cover read, *The Book of Wisdom*. His heart raced at the magnificent gift his mentor had left him. While he would no longer be able to seek his advice, the old monk had provided him a great source to aid him in his times of confusion. Yoshi quickly flipped open the book to read the first pearl of wisdom it had to offer. He rapidly flipped past the first blank pages of the book to get to the text; however, the flipping never ceased. To his dismay, the entire book was composed of blank pages.

He sighed in frustration and then smiled. His mentor had one last practical joke up his sleeve. He laughed at Daichi's chicanery and his own gullibility. *Like all the answers could be contained in one book*, he laughed to himself.

Circling back to the hall for his morning lecture, Yoshi spied a gathering of students and senpai near the great temple. Having just thought of the monk and the rōnin, a sick feeling crept into the pit of his stomach. The unthinkable took over his thoughts as he raced over to the crowd. Navigating through the crowd, Yoshi squirmed his way to the center of the attention.

Kneeling in the dirt with hands bound behind their backs were four beaten down warriors. Their heads bowed low, Yoshi could see their faces were spotted with mud and blood. He also recognized who they were from their armament. "Bet you did not think you would see them again?" Yoshi turned to see Togo standing beside him. The other students were slapping him on the back and congratulating him. "I thought about asking you to join me, but I would never want you to do something you felt was uncomfortable," smiled the great student.

Yoshi was both relieved at the capture and stunned with

how it occurred. He learned through others that Togo and a party of three others slipped out of the school last night and returned with the criminals towed behind their horses. They claimed to have gravely injured at least three others in their battle. "Following the code of justice, I thought it best we bring these heathens back to face their fate for the entire world to see," Yoshi overheard Togo telling a group later in the day. Togo had never looked prouder as he preened across campus. He had obviously been telling the story a myriad of times and his yarn grew more impressive with each recitation.

Yoshi took it all in without any animosity or jealousy, a fact that rather surprised him. He saw Togo in a different light. He still held the same assessment that he did things out of his own personal gain. Yoshi did not believe Togo's action stemmed from a desire to seek justice. Togo's change in appearance to Yoshi had nothing to do with Togo, but rather with Yoshi. Yoshi understood, clearer than ever before, that individuals act according to a personal and unique sense of self. Togo's decision to disobey the elders and hunt down the rōnin spoke to who he was. "Are you not at least a bit upset that you were not the one who captured the rōnin?" asked Kira as the two walked from the evening study group.

"Honestly I am not," replied Yoshi. "If I really wanted to do it, if that is who I was, then I would have chosen the same actions as Togo."

Kira stopped in her tracks and took in Yoshi. He stopped and was puzzled by her quizzical examination of him. "What is it? Is there something on my face?" Yoshi wiped over his face to clear away something that he could not.

"Something about you, I can't put my finger on it, but you look... older." Kira's confused look slowly morphed into a smile. "I fell in love with a young, impetuous boy full of wonder and curiosity. Tonight, I stand before the man I love, a man full of confidence and wisdom." Avoiding the taboo of a public display of affection, she snuck a grasp of Yoshi's hand and squeezed tight. The warmth and affection behind it encompassed Yoshi's entire being, enveloping him as if she hugged him with her whole body.

There were many sentiments he wanted to convey. Gratitude. Adoration. Commitment. The only words that escaped his mouth bundled it all into one. "I love you."

Holding Kira's hand, Yoshi stood before her on solid footing, without the least bit of wavering. At that moment, every aspect of his life had a congruency. She saw in him what he could never see but only feel. A man strong in his identity and purpose, confident in the roles he had to play, understanding of the outcomes he sought, possessing the values to guide his path, and finally, with the confidence and self-awareness that his choices are not things that occur by happenstance, but are conscious decisions driven by who he is. He stood there, balanced.

"Yoshi-san, please come with me." The voice startled the two of them and they quickly disjoined hands. Yoshi turned to see the familiar face of the senior senpai who had been his escort to the previous sword ceremonies.

Kira and Yoshi understood what this moment meant. No one at the School of Aspen held a sword beyond the Sword of Decisions. Some of the students who held them returned to stay at the school and others just disappeared without a whisper of fanfare. It was assumed they either left on their own accord or were asked to leave. Yoshi wanted to ease the uncertainty of the moment. "Kira-san, I shall see you soon." They bowed very formally to each other and the senpai escorted Yoshi to the temple in the mountain. Walking away, Yoshi casually stole a glance back to see Kira still watching him. He quickly turned back, fearing his desire to rush to her could overtake him.

"She is a lovely woman, Yoshi-san. You are fortunate to be in her acquaintance." Yoshi thought he detected a smile from the senpai. He obviously knew of their relationship. He wondered as they climbed the final steps to the temple what else he knew about Yoshi.

Through the same path they had taken five previous times, the senpai led Yoshi to the chamber where he received the swords; however, this time when the door was opened, the chamber was already fully lit with torches. Inside was a collection of twenty robed men and women of various ages. In prior ceremonies, the elders' faces were obscured by hoods, but tonight all faces were unconcealed and greeted Yoshi with smiles and warmth. The door closed behind him and he turned to see his senpai escort donning a robe similar to the others and joining the group.

To Yoshi's right was another figure. He was not wearing the ceremonial robe and had the same sword as Yoshi tucked in his waist. It was Togo. Both acknowledged each other with a slight bow. Togo did not have the same air of pride he possessed earlier in the day. In fact, Yoshi was surprised to see his fellow student was worried.

The assembled group in front of Yoshi and Togo bowed in respect to the two accomplished students, who returned the sign. Yoshi began to kneel before them as he had on the previous occasions but was informed to stop. The elder who had spoken at the very first sword ceremony stepped forward. "Yoshi-san. Togo-san. You have been summoned here today not as students but as samurai. You have both exhibited a mastery of the six Swords of Illumination offered at the School of Aspen. The acquisition of its lessons has made you the complete samurai that we seek to create here. Tonight, we take the Sword of Decisions from you and present you with a new sword." An elder stepped in front of Yoshi and Togo to retrieve the Sword of Decisions from them. Another elder stepped forward, bowed, and offered a brand-new sword to each. Yoshi immediately read its single word engraving, *Knowledge*.

"Each of you, in your own way, has mastered the knowledge we have imparted to you. Tonight, we ask you one question. We ask this not as a test, but a sincere request for you to share with us your insight on what you have learned. We stand before you not as judges, but as peers. We ask you... what is the secret of the Swords of Illumination?"

Before Yoshi even had time to repeat the question in his head, Togo spoke his answer. He recited as if he knew it was coming and had remembered the right response. "Knowledge is power. It enables its possessor to wield it like this sword, with cunning and craft to serve his masters and impose his will."

The group of elders politely murmured in agreement as the leader spoke. "Togo-san, thank you for sharing your insight. Your sense of purpose and direction has always impressed us." The group bowed to Togo.

Yoshi thought Togo's response to be impressive. It was obviously received well by the elders and perhaps was the answer they were hoping to receive. A part of him told him to just repeat Togo's answer in differing phrasing. He would have done this, except for one little thing, he knew the answer was incomplete.

The group turned their collective eyes to the student who had yet to respond. Pausing for a moment, Yoshi felt Daichi's book against his breast. Its empty pages blazed bright in his mind's eye. What he once thought was a joke, he now saw as the truth. The pages were blank for a reason, and he understood why.

"Knowledge is power," he said. The group nodded in agreement. "And the lesson of the Swords of Illumination is that the application of knowledge is the real power. The timing of that application is wisdom." Yoshi realized the blank pages in the book meant that for each reader the wisdom they possessed was determined by their own application of the knowledge they acquired. Wisdom cannot be taught just as one's values cannot be implanted into another. Yoshi continued, "Being wise means applying what you know in a way that maintains the balance of your life, that remains true to who you are, and that serves the world around you."

The group remained silent. There was no rumbling of agreement and the leaders refrained from saying a word. Yoshi thought they may not have agreed with what he said, but he did not fear it. He had never felt more confident about anything in his life. The leader finally broke into a smile that was mirrored by the rest in attendance. In unison, the group bowed deeply to Yoshi, who proudly returned the respect.

"Tonight has two purposes," the leader continued. "One

is to acknowledge your success in completing the training to become samurai. The second is to give you the opportunity to apply what you have learned to the most important decision you have faced since you entered our gates."

Behind the group of elders, a large wooden door was revealed as drapes were pulled to the side. The door creaked as it opened, and a little light poured into it revealing it was some kind of wide cave. "This cave leads through the mountain and to the other side of the range. Through it, you can depart the School of Aspen and set out on your destiny with the tools and knowledge you have been provided. This is one path you may choose. Your other option is to turn around and return to the School of Aspen as a teacher and counselor. We offer you the chance to share the knowledge you have acquired to train other students in the way of the samurai. We ask now that you make the choice that befits you."

Togo stepped forward first. "You have given me the great gift of knowledge as represented by this sword." Togo held the new sword up before him. "With it, I shall pursue my destiny and represent myself in the manner befitting a great samurai from the School of Aspen. I humbly offer my very heartfelt gratitude for everything you have given me. All that I accomplish from this point on, I owe to this school."

Yoshi was impressed by the humility and thankfulness expressed by Togo. He thought the significance of this great moment had moved him deeply. As he thought about his own decision, he was taken aback by what Togo did next.

The new samurai graduate turned to his erstwhile rival and spoke. "Yoshi-san. You are a great warrior. While we have had our differences and our conflicts, I respect you as a samurai and as a man. I have heard the tales of how your father was slain and I have often noted in your eyes the fire of revenge that burns inside you. I ask you to join me down the path and together we can seek the retribution that is rightfully yours. Our two swords combined can never be defeated."

Yoshi's shock at Togo's offer was shared by the entire gathering, who obviously had not foreseen this occurrence. All were stunned silent by the unexpected request. His mind reeled with the option offered him. Despite Togo's apparent character flaws, he would be an invaluable ally in Yoshi's search for revenge. Since that terrible afternoon at the Hamasuka farm, he had awaited the day he was fully prepared to undertake the mission to avenge his father. He had poured every ounce of effort he could muster over these years to gain the mental and physical skills necessary to become a samurai worthy of his father's name, and worthy of vanquishing his father's murderers.

Is this what it feels like when the dream is fulfilled? he asked himself. He wanted desperately to slip to his knees both to collect his thoughts and to maintain the balance he thought he was losing. He closed his eyes and returned to his debate. *What is stopping me from going out there?* It was not fear. He was extremely confident in his abilities. He did not even fear death. As the great Musashi professed and his own father illustrated, a samurai must have a resolute acceptance of death. *Are you not a samurai?* he asked rhetorically. The question triggered something else in his mind. It took him back to his first days at the School of Aspen, when questions of identity and purpose riddled his mind. *"I seek to enrich my soul through the obtaining of knowledge and wisdom. In turn, I shall share this enlightenment through my actions and words in order to serve the world around me."* He asked himself, *How does this fit into my role as avenger?* The answer was poignant and a revelation. It did not. The one person keeping him from seeking out his revenge was the one person he could never elude, himself.

Are you not a samurai?! he screamed at himself countering this argument. *Be a samurai and take up your sword. Spill the blood of your father's slayer.*

"Yoshi-san, a Sword of Illumination is not a singular weapon, but rather a group of weapons that must be used in totality to be truly effective." Daichi's last words of advice invaded the argument; *"...be used in totality,"* continued to ring in his head.

The Sword of Identity defined who he was, not just to himself, but to the world. *"I am samurai."*

His identity was further defined by the Sword of Mission and Purpose. *"I seek to enrich my soul through the obtaining of knowledge and wisdom. In turn, I shall share this enlightenment through my actions and words to serve the world around me."* The statement never mentions revenge. It is a mission not of selfishness, but of servitude.

The Sword of Roles taught him that while who and what he was remained constant, his actions and behaviors could change to best fit the situation he faced. At this moment, Yoshi felt he was still the student and needed to study Togo's offer as a student.

The Sword of Outcomes showed him that he need not live in the world of *or*, but he can exist in the world of *and*. Togo's offer seemed on the surface to be an either/or option. Fulfill his destiny or not. However, there were other options—options that allowed him to fulfill every desire. Revenge can take many forms. One would be to kill his father's murders. Another would be to live a life that would make his father proud, thus giving his father an everlasting life. Yoshi realized his true outcome was never to just exact revenge, but rather to make his father's vision of Yoshi come true. To live out his destiny. That would honor his father. That would be the form of his revenge.

The Sword of Values taught him to trust his internal compass, the guide that will always point him toward his *true north*. Yoshi closed his eyes and allowed his mind and heart to work as one. What direction did his value set beg for him to drive? The answer was clear. It all stemmed back to his identity and mission statement—*"I seek to enrich my soul through the obtaining of knowledge and wisdom. In turn, I shall share this enlightenment through my actions and words to serve the world around me."* His *true north* was not in the same direction Togo was heading.

And then it hit him. The Sword of Decisions was about applying all those other swords and making it his model to guide his decisions. When he walked into the School of Aspen, he valued revenge above all else. Using all the swords in concert was the mechanism to change one's priorities in thoughts, words, and deeds for life. The moment at hand was his opportunity to show the elders, and himself, that he truly understood and could apply not just the Sword of Decisions, but all the Swords they had shared with him.

He opened his eyes and locked them with the senior elder. The expression of realization that emanated out of Yoshi's eyes elicited a smile from the elder. *Now you understand,* was the unspoken message Yoshi got from the elder.

It suddenly came to him like the moment he fell in the hole and figured out the location of the Sword of Identity. Like the moment at the koi pond when he discovered his sense of self. Like the many moments of revelation he experienced at the School of Aspen. Like the moment he knew he loved Kira. The Swords of Illumination had to be used as one—one weapon in achieving what the school really taught its students; how to lead a life of balance and destiny.

"Togo-san," Yoshi finally broke the silence. "I am honored and moved by your offer. The journey and destiny I had foreseen when I first entered the gates of the School of Aspen differs from the one I seek now. The day may come when I face my father's killers; I will face them down and mete them the justice they deserve. However, the samurai I have become chooses life. Life that allows me to grow and serve others in whatever way I can. A life that emulates my father's life rather than his death."

Yoshi expected him to be embarrassed or angry, but in another surprise of the evening, Togo responded with a wry smile and deep bow. He then turned to the gathering of elders and bowed deeply to them. Without a word, Togo took the lit torch hanging along the cave's entrance and within seconds he was enveloped by its darkness.

"Yoshi-san, we understand that was a difficult decision for you to make, but we are glad you will remain with us here at the School of Aspen." The assembled elders began to work their way out of the chamber when Yoshi's words abruptly stopped them.

While he was happy to please the elders, he knew staying would not keep with his own sense of balance. Balance for Yoshi meant to be something more than a samurai, it meant to *be samurai*. It was more than just semantics. When his father spoke of samurai, he never used terms like warrior or fighter. He always used it in ways to describe servitude. Being samurai meant being in service of others. His masters. His loved ones. The world at large. To be truly samurai, Yoshi knew he needed to obtain as much knowledge as he could gather and dedicate himself to that never-ending journey.

With a deep breath, he closed his eyes recalling his father's final words to him, *"My final advice to you is to always seek. Seek knowledge. Seek guidance. Seek friendships. Seek love. Never stop the search."* Opening his eyes, he addressed the elders, "Elders of the School of Aspen, I beg your indulgence." Yoshi held out his newly received sword. "I cannot accept this sword." The elders had enough surprises for one evening and did not appear especially ready to face another one. "I recognize the achievement that obtaining this sword symbolizes and I am humbled by your awarding of it. I am equally honored to have the chance to stay here at the School of Aspen. I have many reasons to settle down here for some time."

Kira's face immediately filled his vision. Her face had the same snow-kissed glow that melted his heart. *"My love for you remains whether you are with me or away from me. Wherever our destinies take us, whatever paths each of us choose, my love will follow you."* She knew he had to make this choice and understood.

"What is it you are requesting?" the elder asked.

"This sword and the offer to stay here is an end of a journey that I believe I am still a long way from completing. The Swords of Illumination have shown me a new way of being and allowed me to recognize who I am and how to lead a life that fits into that identity. These swords have shown what it takes to live a life of balance, but I am not too proud to acknowledge I still need to know how to implement these lessons to make them a natural part of my existence. If I want to really be a samurai, I need to be samurai. In order to accomplish this honor of serving others, I realize there is more to learn. I can only help others up to the level I have helped myself. Deep in my soul, I know there is more knowledge out there to mold me into the man I want to be, the man I need to be."

Bowing before the elders with his new sword stretched out, Yoshi made one final request. "I ask you to take this symbol of graduation for I have not ended my acquisition of knowledge. Allow me to leave the safe confines of this school and seek out that which will make me whole."

The sword was lifted from Yoshi's hands as he heard the group chatter. Instead of the tone being somber and indignant, it was joyous and excited. "You were right, he is the one" was the only comment Yoshi could make out clearly. He stood upright to see the group smiling back and approaching him with congratulatory pats on his shoulders. There was a youthful spirit in the chamber as even the oldest of the elders looked young. Yoshi was plied with compliments from all the elders.

The senpai who had been his constant escort provided some clarification. "Only a select few students have achieved mastery of the six swords and received the Sword of Knowledge. Fewer still have recognized it as a false sword. Knowledge is an infinite quantity, and no person can claim ownership of it."

The lead elder interrupted the senpai by placing his hand on his shoulder and gently moving him aside. When he moved, Yoshi noticed a new door slowly open from the opposite side of the chamber. This door also led into a cave-like entrance, but unlike the one Togo departed through, this one was already illuminated with torches along its walls. "You have made a bold choice Yoshi-san. Through that cave lays a path toward what you seek. Just as with any great journey it is not without hardships, difficulties, and, yes, even peril. This cave will lead to the other side of the mountain from which this temple is carved. It will set you on the path you crave."

Yoshi looked at the elders with questioning eyes. There was so much more he wanted to know, but he could tell from their eyes that those answers would be up to him to find. He turned to the senpai and made one final request. "The young samurai I was with tonight, Kira, would you please give her this and tell her I request she hold it until we meet again." Yoshi removed the chain from around his neck. Hanging from the bottom was the medallion that was his mother's final gift to his father.

"Of course," replied the senpai as he took it from Yoshi's hands and stepped away. "All your other belongings we will return to your family home." Yoshi turned to the group in the chamber. A wave of emotion crashed upon him. The moment forced him to recall the stages of life he had experienced up to this point and all he had endured. At this moment, he was the impatient boy always asking his father to share more stories. He was the heartbroken child who witnessed his father's death. He was the wide-eyed teen staring at the Sword of Identity. He was the scared boy seeking to find his way to a strange new school. And now, he was the man about to embark on a new journey armed with the knowledge and experiences of what the School of Aspen had provided him.

Of all the emotions he felt, there was one that was overwhelming—gratitude. "Thank you for this honor," Yoshi said to the group. He bowed and turned into the cave, walking without a hint of hesitation, down its path.

The flickering flames of the torches along the walls gave the cave an animated appearance. While it was a tunnel burrowed by the hand of man, Yoshi had the sense that he was in a living object with the walls heaving in and out with each intake of breath. The cave was lined with cracks and crevices. They leaked out water that slid along the rock and gave the tunnel a luminescent glow. The crackling of pebbles beneath Yoshi's steps reverberated and echoed throughout the cave. Initially, he thought the voices accompanying him on his trek emanated from his own mind, but soon he believed the cavern was speaking to him.

Its words started off soothing but also challenging. The cave asked a series of random questions that confused him. It asked Yoshi about the path he follows, what governs his life, what is he thinking, and what is he saying. The inquisition grew louder and more jumbled as he continued his path. Soon the words merged into one ear piercing sound. Yoshi attempted to escape it by running as fast as he could through the tunnel. A light up ahead told him the end of the cave was near. As he raced for the exit, the sounds dissipated until all he could hear was his own labored breathing.

Slowing down, Yoshi walked to edge of the cave. Near the exit he spied a shiny object encased in the wall. It was not until he was upon the object that he recognized what it was. Above the object was an engraving that read: *For those who seek the path of total illumination.* Below it was a brand-new Sword of Illumination. Taking it from its perch, Yoshi read the engraving on the metal blade:

Sword of Beliefs

He felt the same exhilaration he felt the day he opened the bottom of his father's chest and found the first Sword of Illumination. As much ground as he had covered since that day, he realized that this new sword symbolized that there was still much more yet to learn. To be the samurai he wanted to be, he needed the tools and knowledge that the Swords of Illumination possessed. Just as that day many dawns ago, he felt an overwhelming eagerness to start that journey.

Sliding the sword in his waist, Yoshi stepped out of the cave and into a great valley. He had traveled through the mountain and arrived at its far eastern edge. To the north was a wide plain and to the south lay a vast forest. He scanned the landscape to judge his best course to begin his journey. As he looked out, he was startled to find the solution, not to where he will travel, but rather how he will travel.

Laying up against the side of the mountain to his right was Daichi's odd vehicle. "Thank you, old friend," he said laughing out loud. Mounting the vehicle, he peddled it across the valley. It was a bumpy ride, but a far less bumpy ride than the first time he rode. While the spokes were still not all aligned, Yoshi felt confident the journey ahead would resolve that. As he headed for the vast plain to the north, his thoughts drifted back to the School of Aspen and, in particular, to one of its students.

"And if you ever need a reminder of my love, remember the snow."

And just then, the snow began to fall.

CHAPTER 19

Right Turn

The sun was ascending out of its resting place in the east as the final words of the old man's tale lingered in the dawn air. Tom sat watching the last embers of the campfire slowly burn to exhaustion. He should have been exhausted too. He had not a moment of sleep since he rose from his bed twenty-four hours earlier. The toll these twenty-four hours had taken on his psyche was enormous. Stress and hopelessness made him snap and flee his family and his life. He nearly ended his life either by accident or on purpose. He was stranded and lost with a broken-down car. Finally, he spent the evening taking painful stock of every aspect of his life as a stranger told him a fantastic tale.

All these events combined were enough reason to leave Tom completely drained; and yet, he found himself filled with vigor and energy. He found in the tale of Yoshi the samurai similarities to his own life and struggles. As the old man regaled him with the fantastic tale, Tom felt compelled to examine his own life with a more critical eye. It had left him feeling unhappy, embarrassed, and pained. It also left him hopeful.

"It's about being balanced, isn't it? The real lesson of the Swords of Illumination is about being balanced," Tom offered after a long pause. "At the end of his time at the school, Yoshi found a sense of equilibrium, how to live a life in line with who he really was. And so, he got on his proverbial bike and rode off."

The old man smiled in acknowledgment of Tom's

insight. Tom finally understood the bigger lesson of Yoshi's journey. On the surface, it was a story about a man ready to be a samurai and take on the world. But Tom could see that all the knowledge and lessons learned at the School of Aspen were designed to create a life of balance. Tom wasn't sure if he made these realizations because the old man helped to enlighten him or because the pain in his heart opened him up to a new level of understanding.

"Yoshi's tale is also one of application. You are right to see that the lessons of these first six swords were designed to illuminate how to lead a life of balance. In the end, though, the school only provides tools. The sharpest blade will carve nothing without first being placed into the wood. Not unlike many universities and schools today, the School of Aspen had many students enter and leave its gates, all provided with an education. Of those students, only those few who actually applied that education profited fully from its benefits."

Tom shot up and started pacing like a man possessed. "That's what I have to do. I have to start doing instead of talking. Acting instead of thinking. For too long, I've allowed outside circumstances to form who I am. It has gotten to the point that I don't know that person. I've allowed this stranger inside to take me down a path that has led to God knows where." Tom stopped to study his surroundings. "I've got to get back. Back home. Back to me." He was in a frenzied mood. He opened his cell phone and held it skyward in vain to get a signal.

"Do you have any idea how far it is to the nearest town? Forget it, let's just start walking and we'll find something." He kicked dirt over the lingering flames to extinguish them as he gathered up the items from the makeshift campsite.

Bemused by the display, the old man joined in the breaking down of camp and followed the excited Tom back up to the roadside. As they reached the top of the hill, Tom made a beeline to his car. "What the heck, I'll give it one last try, and then we'll head up the road." Fumbling with his keys, he finally got the right one in the ignition.

Before turning it, he closed his eyes. He heard the sound of his own heart racing at seemingly a million beats per second. He was giddy at the anticipation of heading back and starting his life with a new-found focus to create balance. He was going to learn to enjoy his family. He was going to create a job experience he can enjoy and profit from. He was going to spend more time working on his own physical and mental well-being. He was going to be the man he vowed to be at his father's funeral.

Then Tom suddenly opened his eyes. A wave of nausea overtook him. He feared that at any second the few contents of his stomach were going to come out. The tasks he had running through his head overwhelmed him. The life he led had taken him down so far into a well of despair; he knew it would be a long climb out. There was so much to do, and he had no idea where to start.

The old man wandered over to the open driver's side door. Tom looked up at him with eyes wide thinking, *What do I do now?*

The old man placed a reassuring hand on Tom's shoulder. "It is a large pill to swallow, isn't it?" the old man stated more than asked.

Tom slowly nodded his head in resignation, but then he recalled something from Yoshi's tale. "I am focusing on everything I have to do rather than what I want to be."

"And who are you?" the old man asked.

Tom paused for a moment. He knew the answer to the question was critical to everything that will follow. He wanted to take a long time to respond in the appropriate manner, but suddenly the answer sprung from the wellspring of his subconscious. He did not have to contrive an answer; he already knew what it was. The answer was there all along.

"I am Tom Henderson. I seek a life that constantly invigorates my soul and allows me to fully enjoy the time I spend with those I love."

"Then that is what you have to be. That is your state of balance." The two engaged in a long stare that evolved into a smile. Tom broke the glance and turned back to the ignition. With a deep sigh, he turned the key. Without a second of hesitation, the engine turned and purred perfectly. Tom thought he should have been stunned, but given all the revelations of the evening, he was not.

He turned back to the old stranger who was grinning from ear to ear. "Hop in and I'll give you a ride to wherever you are heading."

"Thank you for the kind offer, but I will be heading in one direction while I believe you will want to head back the other way."

"I'm sure it will not be that far out of my way. It's the least I can do," Tom pressed. "You have done so much for me." Once he heard the words, he thought they did not sufficiently express all that this stranger had done to help him. This man had come out of nowhere at Tom's most dire moment. He provided nourishment and warmth and a sense of security. And through his story, he gave Tom the greatest gift of all... hope.

"Honestly, I am fine. Your gratitude and the smile in your eyes are thanks enough. I wish you all the best Tom Henderson." The old man took a step back and bowed deeply to Tom.

He found it a deeply moving moment capping an evening of equally moving experiences. Tom stepped out of his car and returned the stranger's bow. He straightened up and then offered his own sign of gratitude and respect; he extended his hand. The old stranger clasped his hand and Tom hoped he felt the power of warmth and appreciation it transmitted.

"Thank you, my friend." Tom released the hand and returned to the driver's seat of his car. Shutting the door, he pulled out onto the road and made a U-turn back in the direction he came. He had no idea how long or how far he was away from home, but he felt relieved that he was heading to where he needed to be.

As he drove away, he stole a look in his rearview mirror to catch one last glance of the old stranger. Blinking his eyes to make sure he was seeing what he was seeing, Tom burst into hearty laughter at the vision he saw.

Moving away in the opposite direction was the old man... on a bicycle.

The Beginning.

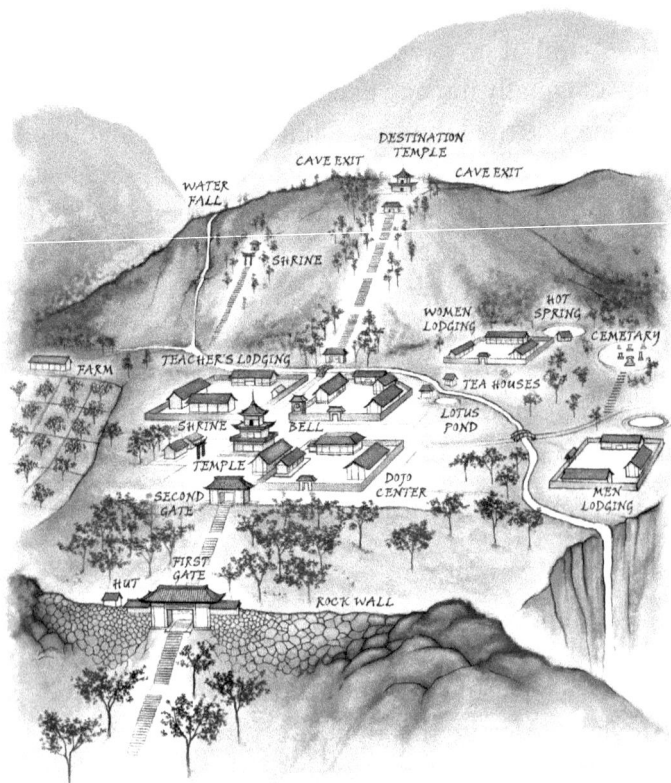

SCHOOL OF ASPEN

PERIOD 1645-1700

DESTINATION
TEMPLE
CAVE EXIT
CAVE EXIT
WATER
FALL
SHRINE
WOMEN
LODGING
HOT
SPRING
CEMETARY
FARM
TEACHER'S LODGING
TEA HOUSES
SHRINE
BELL
LOTUS
POND
TEMPLE
DOJO
CENTER
SECOND
GATE
MEN
LODGING
FIRST
GATE
HUT
ROCK WALL

Epilogue

Congratulations on reading the adventures of the *Swords of Illumination*.

My earnest desire is that the words from this tale provoked thoughts within you on how you may create your own destiny and self-identity. Remember though, these words and your thoughts are only the first part of the equation. Ultimately, it requires actions and deeds in this physical plane for you to truly live the life you desire. As Yoshi did, create your identity by connecting with the higher consciousness master inside of you and use the mystical language of the "I AM." Once you have your identity, connect all your actions to that identity in order to experience who you say you are.

If this book resonates with you and you believe as we do that these concepts shared within it will change the quality of people's lives, we invite you to share your experience and this book with others. This simple act of sharing could have a tremendous impact on the people around you and potentially the world at large.

In addition, we are excited to share that *Swords of Illumination-Book 2* is coming soon and will continue the journey of the remaining *Swords of Illumination*.

The proceeds of this and future books will directly impact our ability to create in this physical plane a school dedicated to sharing and teaching these strategies and others. This academy will also have a particular focus on offering these skills and concepts to our youth. Can you imagine where you would be if you were taught these insights when you were in your youth?

Swords of Illumination may stir in you one of two compelling paths.

If you desire to be like Yoshi and to learn how to incorporate the lessons of the Swords in your own life and you are willing to invest in yourself, we invite you to contact Samurai Success and speak with one of our world class coaches. We would be honored and excited to be in service of your success. You can reach us at info@samuraisuccess. com or visit our website samuraisuccess.com.

If you found yourself intrigued by the Daichi character and would like to experience the exciting opportunity to serve others as they change the quality of their lives, then we offer a path to truly become Samurai as one of our outstanding Samurai Coaches. If you are interested in learning more about this opportunity and our extensive training program, please contact us at careers@samuraisuccess.com or visit our website samuraisuccess.com.

Most importantly, remember, "Destiny is a byproduct of your self-created identity." Be congruent in words, thoughts, and deeds to the person who you say you are, and your destiny will be a rich and fulfilling experience in this world.

Now we invite you to take those first steps by applying the information you learned from this book so that you can live the life that fulfills your unique identity and destiny.

About the Author - David C. Olcott

D avid C. Olcott is founder, president and CEO of Samurai Success, Inc., an international executive, organizational and personal coaching firm headquartered in Denver, CO.

Throughout his more than 35 years of professional coaching experience, David has worked with numerous individuals, organizations and companies throughout the United States and Hong Kong.

His coaching focuses on developing strategies and structures that provide for sustainable growth and productivity. Even during the direst of economic times such as in the aftermath of 9/11 and in the 2008 financial and 2020 COVID crisis, Samurai Success clientele have enjoyed record growth by following his proven methods of success.

His clients praise his uncanny ability to make complex ideas understandable and to propel them to consistently achieve seemingly out of reach goals.

David is also a nationally known motivational speaker and lecturer. His dynamic and positive approach energizes audiences to move from being a worrier to blossoming into a warrior. During many of his presentations, he has motivated people without any martial arts training to join him on stage and smash boards with their bare hands.

Prior to founding Samurai Success, David was a #1 national trainer for Anthony Robbins and was the business manager to the #1 selling real estate agent in the world. David has also enjoyed a distinguished career in the world of public service.

He served as the chief of staff for a member of the Florida State Senate and served as the campaign manager and legislative aide to, at that time, the youngest woman ever elected to the Florida House of Representatives.

David is master certified in Neuro-Linguistic Programming (NLP) and has earned a Bachelor of Science in Finance from Florida International University. He has trained in the martial arts for more than 15 years and holds a second-degree black belt in Aikido. David is also an accomplished motorcycle racer who has competed against top-level racers throughout Colorado.

David is married to Dr. Lorena Lavarne and they have one son, Josh. They spend their time at their homes in Colorado and Oregon.

Samurai *Success*

www.ingramcontent.com/pod-product-compliance
Lightning Source LLC
Chambersburg PA
CBHW072134090426
42739CB00013B/3186